Consuming Families

This book explores contemporary families as sites of consumption, examining the changing consuming contexts of family life, where new forms of family are altering how family life is practised and produced. It addresses key social issues—childhood obesity, alcohol, social networking—that put pressure on families as the social, economic and regulatory environments of consumption change.

Jo Lindsay is Associate Professor in Sociology at Monash University.

JaneMaree Maher is Associate Professor and the Director of the Centre for Women's Studies and Gender Research at Monash University.

Routledge Advances in Sociology

For a complete list of titles in this series, please visit www.routledge.com

79 **Cultural Capital, Identity, and Social Mobility**
The Life Course of Working-Class University Graduates
Mick Matthys

80 **Speaking for Animals**
Animal Autobiographical Writing
Edited by Margo DeMello

81 **Healthy Aging in Sociocultural Context**
Edited by Andrew E. Scharlach and Kazumi Hoshino

82 **Touring Poverty**
Bianca Freire-Medeiros

83 **Life Course Perspectives on Military Service**
Edited by Janet M. Wilmoth and Andrew S. London

84 **Innovation in Socio-Cultural Context**
Edited by Frane Adam and Hans Westlund

85 **Youth, Arts and Education**
Reassembling Subjectivity through Affect
Anna Hickey-Moody

86 **The Capitalist Personality**
Face-to-Face Sociality and Economic Change in the Post-Communist World
Christopher S. Swader

87 **The Culture of Enterprise in Neoliberalism**
Specters of Entrepreneurship
Tomas Marttila

88 **Islamophobia in the West**
Measuring and Explaining Individual Attitudes
Marc Helbling

89 **The Challenges of Being a Rural Gay Man**
Coping with Stigma
Deborah Bray Preston and Anthony R. D'Augelli

90 **Global Justice Activism and Policy Reform in Europe**
Understanding When Change Happens
Edited by Peter Utting, Mario Pianta and Anne Ellersiek

91 **Sociology of the Visual Sphere**
Edited by Regev Nathansohn and Dennis Zuev

92 **Solidarity in Individualized Societies**
Recognition, Justice and Good Judgement
Søren Juul

93 **Heritage in the Digital Era**
Cinematic Tourism and the Activist Cause
Rodanthi Tzanelli

94 **Generation, Discourse, and Social Change**
Karen R. Foster

95 **Sustainable Practices**
Social Theory and Climate Change
Elizabeth Shove and Nicola Spurling

96 **The Transformative Capacity of New Technologies**
A Theory of Sociotechnical Change
Ulrich Dolata

97 **Consuming Families**
Buying, Making, Producing Family Life in the 21st Century
Jo Lindsay and JaneMaree Maher

Consuming Families

Buying, Making, Producing Family Life in the 21st Century

Jo Lindsay and JaneMaree Maher

Routledge
Taylor & Francis Group
LONDON AND NEW YORK

First published 2013
by Routledge
711 Third Avenue, New York, NY 10017

Simultaneously published in the UK
by Routledge
2 Park Square, Milton Park, Abingdon, Oxfordshire OX14 4RN

Routledge is an imprint of the Taylor and Francis Group, an informa business

First issued in paperback 2015

Library of Congress Cataloging-in-Publication Data

Lindsay, Jo.
Consuming families : buying, making, producing family life in the 21st century / by Jo Lindsay and JaneMaree Maher.
p. cm.— (Routledge advances in sociology ; 97)
Includes bibliographical references and index.
1. Families—Economic aspects. 2. Consumption (Economics)—Social aspects. I. Maher, JaneMaree. II. Title.
HQ519.L56 2013
339.4'7—dc23
2012040040

ISBN 978-0-415-89921-5 (hbk)
ISBN 978-1-138-95241-6 (pbk)
ISBN 978-0-203-55523-1 (ebk)

Typeset in Sabon
by IBT Global.

To Paul in recognition of the negotiation we do together every day and to Isobel and Hugo for making life so much bigger, and better

To Alice, Lily and Chloe Alexander—with gratitude for a sensational education

Contents

Preface

In the years of researching families and planning and writing this book, the everyday lives of families, both lived and observed, provided the inspiration for central ideas that underpin *Consuming Families.* Wonderful research work by Allison Pugh (2009), David Buckingham and Sara Bragg (2004; 2011), Sonia Livingstone and colleagues (2007; 2009; 2012) and Gill Valentine and colleagues (2010; 2012) showed us new ways to see and understand the consumption work families were doing. Equally as important were day-to-day experiences with others' families and with our own. Each day offered instances of families trying hard to negotiate the joys and challenges of life and of consumption. Most days offered contests and compromises. Decisions made are often full of doubt and unease. In *Consuming Families*, our aspiration has been to recognize family strategies of love and care, as expressed in family consuming practices, as driven by preferences, priorities, resources, tensions and hopes. Family strategies necessarily have uncertain outcomes. But mostly families are full of endeavor and hope as they try them. In the contemporary panics about family failure, this book is an effort to see and honour family work and care in everyday consumption.

Acknowledgments

For an important month in the writing of this book, JaneMaree was a Visiting Fellow at the Centre for Research on Families and Relationship at the University of Edinburgh. Her sincere thanks to all at the Centre for the Fellowship and the wonderful opportunity it offered to think about families and relationships in such an inspiring and generative environment.

JaneMaree's colleagues in the Centre for Women's Studies and Gender Research, especially Amy Dobson, have been great sources of information and reflection. Fiona Brookes' wonderful PhD work on the 'belonging' of girls has been an inspiration in the process of writing this book.

JaneMaree would like to acknowledge that family as always has played an important role in sustaining life and work. Love and thanks to Margaret for meals, Anthony and Rachel for space and to Tim for that and much more.

Jo would like to acknowledge the wonderful opportunity she had to try out and talk over ideas in her time as visiting scholar in the school of Geography, Politics and Sociology at the University of Newcastle UK and then at the Morgan Centre for the Study of Relationships and Personal Life at the University of Manchester in early 2012.

Sincere thanks also to Jo's colleagues in the School of Political and Social Inquiry, students in her Families, Relationships and Intimate Life unit, her family Paul, Isobel, Hugo, Russell, June, Darren and Jesse and friends Kim, Jeremy, Jenny, Wayne, Rob and Sylvia. Thanks all for your patience and support as time wore on and the excuse of 'just trying to finish this book' grew thin.

The studies on which we draw have been funded through a range of agencies and schemes. We are grateful to all for the research opportunities they provided.

The *Childhood Obesity* study is an ARC funded Discovery project *Childhood obesity: mothers, children and liberal public health* (2010–2011). The research team was lead by Associate Professor Suzanne Fraser. Other team members included Associate Professor JaneMaree Maher, Professor Jan Wright (University of Wollongong), Professor Alan Peterson, and Dr Claire Tanner. Dr Kate Seaar worked on the project during the development phase and provided great insights into the area. This project investigated current public discussions of and approaches to childhood obesity as they impact on mothers and childcare workers caring for children.

The *Family Time* Study was conducted with Anne Bardoel and jointly funded by the School of Political and Social Inquiry and ACREW at Monash University.

The *Consuming Families* study was initially funded by the School of Political and Social Inquiry at Monash University. The research team included Professor John Coveney at Flinders University, who also provided funding to support the research.

The *Alcohol Consumption Contexts* study was funded by VicHealth and Jo Lindsay is grateful to Malcolm McCall, Hannah Walker and Amanda Lanarus for splendid research assistance.

The *Drinking Biographies* study was conducted by Associate Professor Jo Lindsay, Dr Jenny Advocat and Associate Professors Lyn Harrison, Peter Kelly and Chris Hickey and funded by Drinkwise and the Australian Government Department of Health and Ageing.

The *University Drinking* study was funded by an ARC Linkage Grant with Industry Partners, University Colleges Australia, the Victorian Health Department and New South Wales Health Department. The project team included Associate Professors Toni Schofield, Jo Lindsay and Julie Hepworth, Professor John Germov and Drs Fiona Giles, Rose Leontini and Tara McGee with assistance from Rebecca Brown, Cathrin Bernhardt and Audra Glavas.

Parts of Chapter 2 were previously published in Maher, J., Lindsay, J. and Bardoel, A. (2010b) 'Freeing Time: The 'Family Time Economies' of Nurses', *Sociology* 44(2): 269–287.

Parts of Chapter 4 were previously published in Maher, J,, Fraser, S. and Wright, J. (2010c). 'Framing the Mother: Childhood Obesity, Maternal Responsibility and Care', *Journal of Gender Studies* 19: 233–247 and in Maher, J., Fraser, S. and Lindsay, J. (2010a) 'Between Provisioning and Consuming?: Children, Mothers and 'Childhood Obesity', *Health Sociology Review* 19(3): 304–316.

Our thanks to colleagues and publishers for permission to make use of this work in this book.

1 Introduction
Family Life and Consumption in the 21st Century

Consumption is the key social issue of our time: socially, environmentally and economically. Our consuming practices, our interactions with goods and markets, our overuse of the environment are all troubling components of contemporary Western life. Yet a focus only on the ills of contemporary consuming practices obscures the sustaining necessities of consumption. Consumption is as crucial for human survival as it is for the survival of market economies (Humphrey 2009). While there may be some choices about what we consume, consumption itself is not a choice. Identities, relationships, belonging, and personal and health outcomes are achieved through consumption. Families too are created through and sustained by consumption. In *Consuming Families: Buying, Making, Producing Family Life in the 21st Century*, family consuming practices are our central focus. We are interested in the role of consumption in family life, in the prevalence of negative assumptions about consumption in families, and in the dominance of stories of family failures in consumption control, especially in relationship to children. We explore contentious issues of childhood obesity, alcohol, media use, and sex and sexualisation, but we argue for a more careful and a more generous account of family consumption. Consumption is most often understood in terms of individual desires and satisfactions. Yet much consumption is done for others (Morgan 1999). And even individual consumption decisions may be seen as part of an individual's desire to connect or belong (Featherstone 2010; Pugh 2009). Consumption within families, and by individuals for families, constitutes care, connection and belonging.

We recognise the troubling nature of many contemporary consumption issues. Excess consumption is seen as dangerous to our communities, our health, to the environment and even to the very markets that drive consumption practices (Humphrey 2009). There are widespread fears about increased narcissism, selfishness, changes to intimacies and a lessening of social responsibility (Bauman 2007). There are fears that our materialism is leading to the loss of social and community connection. How do such fears intersect with contemporary ideas about family and family life? The relationship between family and consumption is at once everyday, and contentious and contradictory. Consuming is a necessary part of family life and family relationships; the shelter, nourishment, and caregiving so commonly linked to family life all require consuming practices (Folbre and Nelson 2000; Humphrey 2009). Without consumption, the comfort and care of family cannot be achieved. But increasingly the reach of the market into the spaces of home previously framed as private has been understood to create particular threats to family life, and for vulnerable family members. Fears about the loss of individual social connection and the rise of greed are reflected in fears about reduced commitment between family members and reduced expectations of care, love and affection. At the same time though, obligations for families to ensure good consumption for children in terms of healthy diets, protection from risky consuming especially in regard to alcohol and sex, and corrupting media have intensified. As government supports and care provision shrinks, family obligations to provide moral and educational support and material goods are intensifying. So while some forms of consumption in families are bad, other forms of consumption are clearly part of good contemporary parenting and care.

Consuming Families is concerned with this complex and contradictory relationship between contemporary practices of consumption and the making and shaping of family life. Families have always been key sites for consumption. But in recent decades, contests over childhood obesity, the sexualisation of children, the media practices of children and teenagers, and young people's use of alcohol and other drugs have dominated media and public policy discussions of Western family life. Issues of responsibility, parental control and whether children and young people are too active in a consumer world have become central in social policy debates, and in educational, media and health realms. Family consumption, especially consumption by vulnerable or dependent family members, has become a critical site of social contest, regulation and debate. This spotlight means that for families, the daily struggles about good and appropriate consumption are newly visible and ever more complicated. Consumption choices and consumption practices are often deeply contentious for, and within, families.

For us, this sense of fear about families and family consumption needs to be more carefully and deeply explored. Families are changing. Narrow definitions and meanings of family have been challenged and contested; there is increasing recognition that family forms are diverse and dynamic. Changing patterns of partnership, parenthood, friendship and sociality mean that the traditional (or perhaps more properly modern) conceptions of the family as biologically linked parents and dependent children can no longer be sustained at the centre of debates about families and family life. In most developed countries, this nuclear family form is no longer dominant and new forms of family are increasingly recognised in social convention and by state institutions (Lindsay and Dempsey 2009; Stacey 1998). Even when such recognition is partial or inadequate, new family practices make new family forms (Silva and Smart 1999), which are then included in social life.

These changes have driven insistent calls to recognise other relationships that do the work of family (Budgeon and Roseneil 2004; Lindsay and Dempsey 2009; Roseneil and Budgeon 2004; Stacey 1998; Valentine 2006). Roseneil and Budgeon (2004) argue that the term 'family' limits social analysis and understanding; for them the term cannot encompass social thinking about the complexities of love, relationship and support in the 21st century. The call to recognise relationships beyond the family and 'new' families is vitally important. Yet the notion of 'family' continues to have strong resonance in everyday life as perhaps the main site of intimate connection, authenticity and belonging (Ribbens McCarthy 2012). The concept of family particularly echoes in enduring nature of care obligations of parents for children.

In *Consuming Families*, we are primarily focused on interactions between parents and children and the role of consumption in the discharge of caring obligations. This focus is not because we consider that this family form is the dominant or pre-eminent form or because we take for granted the heterosexual couple with children in defining family. The parent/child families we discuss include single parent and post divorce families, and lesbian and gay families though to date there is little specific information on different family consumption practices. We recognise, too, there are many other family types that do not include parents and children. But the consumption issues of interest to us concern interactions between parents and children and how consumption practices and desires are shaping contemporary family lives. The regulation of intake has become central in how we understand parental roles and obligations in the West. The parent-child family is where children's assumed vulnerability is to be protected and where parents are tasked with managing the consumption of media, food, alcohol and sexualised images and products. The consumption of these products in particular, is seen as threatening to children, and to childhood. The protection of children requires competent parental consumption and control, and the training of children as responsible and restrained consumers. The cultural focus on parent-child families as sites for facilitating and regulating consumption, and the dominance of stories of failure and conflict in family life, as children apparently grow fatter, watch more unsuitable television, and develop ungovernable appetites for consumer goods, is our central interest here.

Discussions of families must always recognise the fluid and dynamic nature of family formation, the intricate relationships that exist within families and the situation of the family in terms of the state. Important processes of social change are occurring in gender relations, in modes of parenting and in the social divisions between adults and children, and creating changes in family structure and in roles within family life. New forms of family and new ways of doing gender in family life have emerged. Yet there are predictable continuities too. In heterosexual families mothers continue to do the bulk of consuming work and child care; mothers are primarily cited as responsible for improper or overconsumption. Of course men have family lives and are involved in everyday consumption and family care but in many families they play a secondary role in these activities (Buckingham 2011). Families are negotiating these patterns of gendered continuity and rapid social change concurrently in their everyday practices.

Relationships between the family and the state are constantly evolving too. Industrialisation, the development of public health and hygiene infrastructures, and the rise of mass education in Western nations all impacted on how the family was located in relation to other social institutions (Ahlander and Bahr 1995; Jagger and Wright 1999; Lasch 1995). Contests arose over the role of the family as a socialising agent, and the perceived encroachment of state agencies into family lives. But the role of families in securing the well-being of nations was clear: healthy families meant strong nations. A 'direct association between the health of the nation and the health of its families' (Jagger and Wright 1999, 23) was created by the British State in the 19th century and in other Western nations too (Reiger 1985; Gillies 2011). Families were thus seen to have a central role in developing and delivering citizens.

In more recent decades, the role of the state has been complicated by the emphasis on individual responsibility in social discourses. Choices, rather than structural constraints, are identified as critical in how well people, and families, do (Gillies 2011; Pugh 2009). Health, education, diet, caregiving and a range of other elements are more often framed as the responsibility of individuals and by implication, families, than as the responsibility of states. This particular mobilisation of individual responsibility has coincided with significant changes in how states define their responsibilities to their citizens. States in developed nations have been withdrawing from active roles of care and support, creating instead paradigms where individuals 'choose' to interact with state supports and agencies for needed services. Discourses of mutual obligation are created around the provision of services; again reinforcing the responsibility individuals have to make competent consumption choices about their own well-being. In Australia, for example, new conditions have been created for welfare payments in some indigenous communities where children's school attendance is required for benefits to be paid. Work projects to receive income support are commonplace in developed economies and welfare regimes often enshrine tasks and obligations for those who need assistance. As states withdraw from support for care, the provision of education and other forms of social support, there is a 'renewed emphasis on families as a source of support' (Jagger and Wright 1999, 25). The withdrawal of social support structures means those individuals most closely concerned with the well-being and maintenance of children move to ameliorate the gaps in state provision. Families work to ensure that the lessening of state support does not negatively affect these most vulnerable citizens. Jagger and Wright have described this movement in the UK as 'setting the family "to work" in the 1980s and 1990s' (1999, 28, see also Edwards et al 2012; Gillies 2011; Peel 2003). In this landscape of individual responsibility and choice, families, like individuals, can seemingly choose how they make their way; children's well-being can be secured by 'good' parental choices

So, the rise of 'individual responsibility' does not diminish the role of families but instead intensifies it. Families are still key social institutions (McKie et al 2005) and family life is always 'a public concern' (Gillies 2011, 2). 'Families are positioned to provide for the satisfaction of [both] material and emotional needs' (Silva 2010, 55); they are vital cogs in states securing the care and sustenance of citizens. In contrast to the emphasis on family choice as the key element of successful family care and provisioning, we accept the terms and conditions of achieving such satisfaction of needs are necessarily embedded in wider social and political structures and opportunities. This further recognition of how parental choices are constrained is rarely acknowledged in public discourses about 'poor' consumption in families. The moral obligations of parents are clearly articulated and usually accepted (Ribbens McCarthy et al 2003), but analyses of how resources and opportunities enable and define child-rearing projects (Brannen and Nilsen 2005; Gillies 2005; Vincent and Ball 2007) are less common. Inequalities in childhoods as they are shaped by parental access to resources for care are not comprehensively accounted for (Gillies 2005; Lareau 2003; Peel 2003; Pugh 2009; Vincent and Ball 2007).

In *Consuming Families*, the active role of families in mediating and modelling good consumption practices is a central interest. But, for us, this role must always be understood in relation to the social and economic conditions particular families face. In exploring how different families, and different family members, negotiate and enact consumption, we seek to illuminate both the agentic and structural elements of family practices. In the repetitions of everyday life, families respond to, contest and mediate existing social opportunities and obstacles. Social and economic conditions constrain families; within these existing constraints, families define priorities and make accommodations that reflect their own values and aspirations (Pugh 2009; Tubbs et al 2005). In this sense, each family is drawing on 'common cultures' (Thomson et al 2011) of good parenting, but is governed by the material and cultural resources available in constituting its own family life. For us, this sense of agency and constraint in families centres consumption in family life. Family consuming practices create and sustain family lives in contemporary societies. It is the daily practices of consumption—planning, purchasing, preparing, and using—that express and achieve family life, identity, belonging and care. This positioning of consuming practices at the centre of family life is captured in the phrase 'consuming families'. In their daily practices, families consume time, goods, social conditions and discourses as they do family. In the course of everyday living then, they are consuming families by definition. The term 'consuming families' was used by Jan Phillips (2008) to describe the consuming practices within families and by family members that create family life. She argues grocery shopping, cooking, eating and a multiplicity of other practices, make family life, 'as adults and children together constitute themselves as "consuming families" ' (Phillips 2008, 93). While contemporary stories of family change have often been concerned with the ways in which market forces are winnowing out the affect and connection of family life (Hochschild 2003), Phillips' term reminds us that consumption sits constructively at the centre of family life (and always has). It invites us to understand the creative and constitutive aspects of consumption in family life. This is our project in *Consuming Families*: to consider how and what families are consuming everyday and to see how families are both made and tested by their consuming practices. Our decision to focus on contentious issues, the places where family consuming practices are cited as problematic: media, food, sexualisation, alcohol, reflects our interest in the widespread contemporary willingness to see the family in decline (arguably not a new or true story—see Jagger and Wright 1999; Smart 2007; Stacey 1998). It also reflects our desire to contest the current focus on the negative rather than creative aspects of family consumption (Buckingham 2011; Martens et al 2004). Our use of the term 'consuming' positions family activities, family 'doing' (Morgan 2011a) as central but also acknowledges the intensity of consuming pressures in contemporary family life. Families are consumed as well as consuming. We acknowledge these tensions while seeking to move beyond blame and individualised responsibility. We aim to illuminate the resilience and creativity in family consumption practices, as they are shaped by social and economic conditions, by family and individual preferences, and most importantly by interdependency, commitment and love.

Each of the chapters in this volume addresses a contentious social issue at the nexus of consumption and the making of family life in the 21st century. We examine the intersection of family time and children's consumption, family food practices in the shadow of the panic over childhood obesity, teen drinking in the context of public anxieties about youth binge drinking, consumption of sexual commodities in the shadow of the panic about the sexualisation of girls and how new media inflects contemporary family life in the context of fear about destructive media influences on young people. We now outline our approach to the concepts of family and consumption and our central argument about the 'embeddedness' of contemporary consumption practices in family life. Consumption practices in families are primarily 'relational' (Buckingham 2011) and are used to sustain and create family life. Families use consumption to care for each other, to connect with each and to belong within their wider communities and social contexts. Gender and intergenerational relationships are shaped by different ideals and habits of consumption. We highlight the deep contradictions of consumption particularly in affluent Western societies and the tensions these contradictions create for families. We consider the role of the market in simultaneously creating problems in family life and then seemingly offering solutions to families seeking to manage work, care and intimacy in a rapidly changing social landscape. We argue that the everyday (food, cleanliness, the routine 'embodied practices of intimacy', Gabb 2008, 81), the productive and pleasurable (treats, holidays, parties) and the contentious (children's independence in consumption, the prescriptions of state and society, changing family forms and traditions) are all aspects of family consuming. They all need to be understood as making family in the 21st century.

RECOGNISING THE CONSUMING FAMILY

When we talk about consuming families, a series of conceptual and social disjunctions are mobilised. Pre-industrial families were understood as productive units where sustenance, care and economic production intermingled. Family members were all involved together in the maintenance of family life. The development of industrial capitalism and related urbanisation, changing patterns of production, and new gendered divisions of care related to new forms of employment, repositioned families. Formerly sites of production, families now were primarily sites of consumption in Western societies and economies, although many have challenged the explanatory power of such sweeping accounts (Ahlander and Bahr 1995; Smart 2007; Zelizer 2005). These changes in family lives engendered a sense of family life as distinct from the economic and public spheres. Family life, so it goes, should be free from the taint of commerce. The rules of exchange, commodity and competition that govern markets should not govern family life, where commitments, ethics of care and selflessness should apply (Taylor 2004; Zelizer 2005). Part of the contemporary unease about consumption in family life then is rooted in our sense that the family should be a haven from the market that threatens the relationality, interdependence and intimacy invoked by the concept of family.

But the distinction of family life and the market is idealised and inaccurate: both historically and in contemporary societies (Zelizer 2005). Consumption should be more fully understood as a necessary part of human existence and experience (Humphrey 2009) rather than as antithetical to human well-being. Families have to engage with markets to achieve and deliver care. Janelle Taylor (2004) has observed motherhood, despite its iconic status *as* care and love, cannot be freed from 'the taint of consumption' (2004: 3; see also Cook 1995; The VOICE Group 2010; Thomson et al 2011). Such an observation is equally applicable to the intimacies of everyday family life; markets are necessary for families to source the economic resources to consume and to acquire goods. Families must consume in order to survive, so markets are inevitably part of family life. In fact, as Viviana Zelizer has observed, the assumed distinction of economic and intimate relationships consistently contradicts everyday experience.

> First, the mingling of economic transactions and intimate relations regularly perplexes participants and observers, and it does not perplex them because it happens rarely. On the contrary people are constantly mixing their intimate relations with economic transactions. (Zelizer 2005, 11)

In Zelizer's view, analyses of household intimacy must account for the role of economic relationships and exchanges. Household dependencies and relationships are also economic obligations; these are always intermingled. Purchases of goods and services, and all other familial interactions with markets such as family work-care patterns are necessarily part of family life. Daily consumption decisions about what to buy, eat or give are life events routinely experienced 'everyday'—in the sense Morgan identifies (2011a: 6)—but their everyday quality doesn't diminish their importance. These everyday decisions create the moral and ethical economies of family life (Hall 2011; Morgan 2011a). They reflect and reinforce relationships, belonging and identity. Consumption in all its aspects is central in family life.

But changing family forms and obligations mean that family consuming practices and decisions are increasingly complicated and potentially contentious.

> The character of everyday family life is gradually changing: people used to be able to rely upon well-functioning rules and models, but now an ever greater number of decisions are having to be taken. More and more things must be negotiated, planned, personally brought about. And not least in importance is the way in which questions of resource distribution, of fairness between members of the family, have come to the fore. Which burdens should be allocated to whom? Who should bear which costs? Which claims have priority? Whose wishes have to wait? (Beck-Gernsheim 2002a, 92)

This sense of negotiation and compromise in family consumption, and the importance of accounting for the engagement of different family members underpin our approach in this volume. We understand family life and family relationships as created through everyday negotiations of consumption. For us consumption is a complex, and often contested, enactment of care. Goods are provided but in post scarcity societies they must also be limited for competent care to be achieved. Extant panics about food and alcohol excess are intensifying the tensions experienced in families about 'good' consumption decisions and proper practices. Materialism and intimacy are seen as inherently in conflict. Children's appetites, piqued by clever marketing and media, are increasingly difficult to restrain. The colour, noise and worry generated in public discourses about consumption draws attention away from the creative and constitutive forms of consumption in family life.

Recent academic work in the sociologies of care, family and childhood has worked to relocate consumption as part of rather than inimical to family life. Scholars have sought to recast and reinterpret the intermingling of resource and market influences in family care and relationships. Daniel Cook (1995) considered the ways the baby clothing industry mobilised mothers' roles as consumers. He pointed to the creation of 'an ideology of maternal consumption' (1995, 515) where purchased goods reflected women's 'rational' and committed decisions to their children's well-being. Although the market is instrumental in shaping the form of the need and the specific types of goods required, mothers' material provisioning for their children also demonstrated their commitment to the sustenance and nurture of their children. Allison Pugh (2009) explored how family decisions about goods and gifts reflected parents' social and emotional aspirations for their children. For the children, in turn, goods located them as 'cared for' (Pugh 2009, 64). Pugh emphasises the 'vibrancy' of these consumer exchanges as part of family practice and as constituting family life. Her attention to children's needs for belonging and how this longing is addressed within families is an insightful contribution to the field. Thomson and colleagues (2011) illuminated the role of goods in how mothers make the transition to motherhood. Although such consuming transitions are not always comfortable, mothers and families cross the 'commodity frontier' (Thomson et al 2011, 18) in order to ensure well-being and care for their children. Buying prams and baby grosuits allows the market into family life, but is a crucial aspect of readying oneself for the obligations of parenthood. Consumption practices and decisions thus play a critical role in how families, and different family members, do family. Both symbolically and materially, consumption practices, patterns and disjunctions are important in constituting family life.

In turn, Zelizer (2005) asserts that markets are shaped by family life. She criticises recent accounts that diminish the economic importance of household relationships and intimacies.

> Authorities, critics and professional economic analysts often hold to an illusion: since the decline of family farms and domestic crafts, they say, households have lost their economic function. Households once did important economic work, but now they only consume. (Zelizer 2005, 215)

Zelizer asserts this view of family is mistaken: economic and familial interconnections are everywhere. 'Living together produces shared economic problems, opportunities, rights and obligations for everyone who takes part' (Zelizer 2005, 213; see also Folbre and Nelson 2000); family practices shape markets. She uses the routine and everyday work of food provision as an example of such interconnectedness. Food production and consumption in the family context occurs in existing economic conditions and enacts and produces familial relationships.

> Feeding the family provides an obvious yet often forgotten intersection of caring and economic activity. As Marjorie DeVault (1991) has shown, the largely invisible, unpaid labour of planning, shopping, and preparing meals involves constant, often contested, negotiations of family relationships. (Zelizer 2005, 163)

The development of new forms of convenience food and online shopping for example shows the intermingling of family needs and market forces. As mothers' time dispositions change, markets respond and reinforce new possibilities. Family schedules and needs and market trends operate in multi-directional flows.

Silva and Smart (1999) extend this interrelationship of market and family beyond goods and practices. They argue for the need to consider the 'interplay between sections of the labour market, or welfare, and changing forms of intimacy' (1999, 6). Families actively position themselves in society in relation to extant social ideologies and have both agency and presence in the market (Uttal 2009). The consuming family then is both in and of the market. Such an assessment needs to be understood not as a condemnation of contemporary family life, an assessment that subtends many of the consumption panics we explore in *Consuming Families*. It is rather urging greater recognition of the requirement for family life to be mediated and produced in and through relationships with markets, in and through consuming practices. While social and market forces are often assumed to act on families, families also act on, and with, the resources offered outside the family context (Cook 2009a; Silva 2010). Family is full of 'intersections of intimacy and economic activity' (Zelizer 2005, 214) and best understood through frameworks that encompass family practices, market activities, and family intimacies.

One of the difficulties of accepting consumption as a familial practice, as part of the relationality of family rather than antithetical to it, is the individualising cast of consumption. Consumption is most often seen as fuelled by individual appetites and desires, directed to individual satisfactions. Sociologists often emphasise the competitive nature of consumption and the way that individuals use it to position themselves in status and class systems (Bauman 2007; Bourdieu 1986; Lury 1996; Patterson 2006). Yet we ask how does consumption, understood as the province of individuals, intersect with the relationality and interdependence of family life? We focus on the relational aspects of consumption. In all relationships there is a tension between collective and individual desires and decisions. We explore this tension in families as it expressed in the difficult consumption issues around which each chapter is organised—goods, media, food, alcohol and sex. We locate this tension, and the resulting conflicts between parents and children, between families and social norms, as an integral part of family life.

CONSUMPTION, FAMILY IDENTITIES AND INDIVIDUAL BIOGRAPHIES

> The dominant public discourses in the western world, particularly in its emphasis on markets and the consumer, supports and celebrates individualisation and individual choice. Autonomy and independence are held up as desirable goals for human beings which thereby makes it difficult to address the ways in which people are dependent upon one another. The interaction and interconnectedness of individuals are what constitutes the social fabric of all social institutions, what constitutes society. (Brannen and Nilsen 2005, 426)

Brannen and Nilsen (2005) offer an important way to think about individuation and interconnection together, which is helpful for our analysis of consuming families. Assumptions about the meaning and impact of individual consumption are complicated and sometimes contradictory. Miller and Rose (1997) identify deep divisions in relation to consuming subjectivities in contemporary life. On one hand, individuals can express power and pleasure in their consuming choices. These choices allow them to 'enact sociality in a creative and innovative manner' (1997, 1). The contrasting view is that such choices draw individuals into compromising relationships with market forces. Such choices are never free from taint or constraint: 'the pleasures, powers and meanings produced' cannot be understood as 'individual achievements' (Miller and Rose 1997, 1). They are rather expressions of something false and diminished. These contradictory approaches to individual consumption are vitally important in the sphere of family life. They produce and drive the complexities of collective family consumption, of individual consumption within family groups, of converging and diverging tastes, preferences and aspirations. The uneasy interactions of individual and collective desires, of promised satisfactions and inevitable disappointments, fuel the sense of threat in all consuming practices especially as they translate into family life.

For it is not only the consuming practices of families per se that are characterised as threatening to family life in contemporary Western societies. It is also the potential for individual consumption choices to draw resources away from the family. The rise of consumption in family life may reduce expectations of care and obligation in ways that threaten the well-being and coherence of contemporary families. Individuals may follow their own course at the expense of collective obligations. Children's appetites may overwhelm parents, damaging family life and children's own development. The 'autonomy and independence' produced through consumption have the potential to undo the relational connections of family life in a range of different ways.

We argue that these assumptions about individual consuming practices as damaging to family life need to be more carefully scrutinised. The debate about the individualisation and the family is often presented as an either/or dichotomy. According to the individualisation thesis, the contemporary family involves more freedom, democracy, choice and instability (Beck-Gernsheim 2002b). Thus, family relationships are looser and seemingly less committed than they were in the past. People's ability to choose for themselves raise fears family obligations may recede. Critics of the dominance of the individualisation thesis, however, point to the strong commitment of people to their families and to their family relationships (Ribbens McCarthy 2012; Smart 2007; Wilson et al 2012). For us, a fuller view of the role of consumption in creating family life is needed to understand the tensions between individual and family consuming practices.

Family life is clearly changing in response to more complicated individual biographies. The identity of a 'family' can no longer be assumed, but must be actively defined by its members (Beck-Gernsheim 2002b; Silva and Smart 1999; Stacey 1998). Janet Finch says:

> The emphasis on families as constituted by 'practices, identities and relationships' means that the fluidity of family life is not defined by shifting membership so much as by the continually evolving character of the relationships—how individuals talk to each other, act towards each other and the assumptions on which their relationships are conducted. Thus the question 'Who is my family?' is really a question about relationships—'Which of my relationships has the character of a "family" relationship?' (2007, 69)

This requirement to articulate and define family gives greater weight to how the individuals define their own family groups and how they belong to such groups. While the term 'family' often previously assumed a normative identity and shared choices for all members (Gabb 2008; Morgan 2011a), there is now is greater recognition of the co-existence of the shared *and* the individual interests of family members. If 'contemporary family arrangements are diverse, fluid, and unresolved' (Stacey 1998, 17), different family members are necessarily more active in creating and specifying their own forms of belonging and connection. Consuming practices within families are key sites where these intersecting familial and individual biographies can be reflected and contested. Rather than seeing consumption in the family as threatening, we argue there is a need to see family consumption practices and decisions; as a group, as individual members and in conflicts over consumption, as a vital element in the constitution of family life and the practices of care. A family's decision about a holiday or a new television offers an opportunity to articulate an important aspect of family identity and priorities. An adolescent's decision to work part-time to buy clothing or goods not provided at home reflects both family priorities and individual distinction within the family group. Conflicts over food or technologies, areas of interest to us here, are important sites where family members relate to each other and families articulate themselves through their consuming practices.

In our exploration of family consuming, we don't seek to adjudicate on the extent to which consuming choices, are 'threatening' families. We are instead interested in the ways in which consuming practices (and consumption conflicts) operate as sites where familial care, belonging and distinction are expressed and negotiated. Thomson and colleagues (2011) have observed that narrating social change is active work, and we argue consuming practices are one way families engage with intersecting individual and collective desires and experiences. While individual biographies may be seen to fuel consumption that draws resources away from family life, and as a result, diminish family connection and interdependence, the need to create an individual biography also presses individuals to specify their sense of belonging and connection in the family. Individual and family consuming practices and conflicts demonstrate the intricacies of connection and individuation. How families, and individuals within families, talk about and struggle with consumption offers important insights into the constitution of contemporary families and relationships within them.

The choices family groups make, about goods, holidays, food, media, articulate and define family identity and family life; they distinguish 'my family' from other families. Different families make distinctive consuming choices (Bourdieu 1986). Individual members within families also use consumption in order to signal both their belonging and their difference within the family context. 'I am a vegan though my family eats meat'. The tracing of family and individual consuming practices shows how individual biographies and family connections intersect and intertwine in everyday life. In this fluid and dynamic family landscape, where 'families [are] agents of self-reflexivity . . . not just a passive bedrock for wider structures' (Silva and Smart 1999, 2), the notion of child consumers raises particular questions. Children's assumed vulnerability and suggestibility mean that their desires and choices must be subjected to parental care and protection yet as we discuss below children are active consumers themselves (Buckingham 2011; Pugh 2009). This emphasis on individual family members making different consuming choices is a central concern for us in regard to children's consumption.

PRODUCING COMPETENT CHILD CONSUMERS

The autonomy and individuation of children has been a particular site of tension in consumption debates, with a sense of children's power and agency within families emerging in conjunction with more sophisticated global marketing practices that address children as consumers (Marshall 2010). The drawing of children into more direct relationships with markets has created fears for children and about childhood (Kline 1995; Schor 2004). At the same time, discussion and negotiation have become preferred models of contemporary parenting (Lareau 2003). So, while negative interpretations of 'children's consumer culture . . . dominate' (Martens et al 2004, 161) and questions about vulnerable child consumers and proper parental control abound, parents are now expected to assist children to become competent and discerning consumers (Cook 2008a, 2008b; Ekström 2010). Children are 'consumers-in-training' (Kline 2010a, 255), even as they are characterised as profoundly vulnerable citizens. These tensions over children's consuming are central in *Consuming Families*. How are families called to mediate children's consumption of food, media, sex and alcohol? How do families adjudicate in their daily practices between the need to control children's consumption and the requirement to create competent child consumers? (Cook 2008a, 2008b). And importantly, how do children in families challenge, draw from and educate parents through their consumption practices?

In debates about consumption there is high anxiety about children growing up too fast or as Buckingham (2011) terms it 'kids getting older younger'. Children are presented as media experts playing in dangerous cyber worlds their parents know nothing about. Fears abound that they are willing participants in a sexualised culture, that teens binge drink well before they are legally allowed to and that children and young people grow fat on junk food. At the same time, new forms of economic dependency are emerging where young people rely financially on their parents for a longer time (Newman 2011). In Western democracies not only childhood but also young adulthood has become 'scholarised' (Zelizer 2005); most young people are required to focus on their secondary and tertiary education and supplementary part-time work. Adult children remain at home dependent on their parents for much longer and the baby boomer transitions to adulthood of full-time stable work, marriage, home-ownership and child bearing are increasingly difficult to achieve and delayed (Furlong and Cartmel 2007; Heinz 2009; White and Wyn 2008). Children's and young people's consumption is thus contradictorily located in contemporary family life in the West. Independent consumption and dependent consuming are all part of how families support and raise children. Interactions and negotiations will be multi-layered and dynamic. 'Families help in the constitution of personal autonomy' (Silva and Smart 1999, 6), while simultaneously exercising control through the intimacies of everyday life (Gabb 2008). As Ekström (2010) argues, family influences and consumer socialization in families are best understood as reciprocal rather than unidirectional processes.

The provision of material sustenance, and the associated use of goods and services, is crucial for children to grow (Maher et al 2010a). The negotiation of the market to achieve adequate provision for children is a core obligation within families. But part of that obligation is to support children to become independent, to choose confidently and wisely for themselves. Children's active engagement in the consuming practices of family life cannot be understated. Children have significant capacity to influence families in terms of food (Curtis at al 2010; Marshall and O'Donohoe 2010), media use and acceptable social performances of adolescence and emerging adulthood. Daniel Cook (2008a) challenges the persistent dichotomy between the 'empowered child' and the vulnerable child in consumption debates, urging nuanced recognition of children's capacities as social actors. Like adults, child consumers in the family will be both agentic and constrained by social conditions. They will be influenced by external market pressures and by more local family constraints. Part of our aim in *Consuming Families* is to seek out a more nuanced account of the strategies, and struggles, of parents as they support their children's development as consumers. How do different families define age-appropriate consumption, especially in the difficult areas of alcohol, media and sex? How do parents weigh consuming independence against parental control? Are there better ways to understand parental 'failures' to regulate consumption tightly enough?

In debates about appropriate parental control of consumption, concerns about children's vulnerability are intimately linked to concerns about how care is provided in contemporary social contexts. In the following section, we outline our thinking about the intersection between consumption and care, recognising as Silva (2010) urges, that consumption and care are bound together and bound into family identities and the daily practices and provision of care.

CARE IN CONSUMING FAMILIES

The relationship between care and consumption is contentious. Markets are necessarily involved in how people gain resources to provide care (Folbre and Nelson 2000; Zelizer 2005), but care itself is often seen as necessarily distinct from marketplace and its drivers. Proper care is driven by love and altruism, not profit and individual desires. The intermeshing of the market and care is therefore complicated: some elements of care can be readily seen and measured, others are not easily identified and challenge conventional market frameworks. Caring labour necessarily centres people's motives and intent and dispositions (Folbre 1995; Tronto 2003). Care is created too through the commitment of 'feeling, acting, thought and time' (Hochschild 1995, 333). 'Care is a result of many small subtle acts [both] conscious [and] not' (1995, 333). But some of these acts are necessarily market-based. Purchasing goods, seeking out services, working for money to buy needed family resources; these are all caring acts. In our analyses, tasks, market resources, family obligations and love are threaded together to constitute care. This interweaving of care and market seems most helpful to us in understanding the role of consumption in family lives.

While care cannot be reduced to time, all definitions of care do encompass activities that are temporally bound. 'Caring takes place through time and occupies time' (Bowlby et al 2010, 53). The intersection of time and care has fuelled a key 'family' issue of the late 20th and early 21st centuries, a widespread worry about whether we have enough time now to care for our families. Women's new educational opportunities, the needs of a 24/7 global market place (Presser 2003), and the fact that male breadwinner wages no longer suffice, mean that mothers have maintained workplace attachment even as they do the primary care for children. New forms of family offered freedom to women but also meant women could no longer rely on lifetime support through marriage. They must now commit hours outside the home to paid labour as well as hours inside to care. This shift in maternal employment allows the market to penetrate more obviously into family life, as external workplace schedules increasingly define and determine family time.

These connections between women's employment, family time and contemporary family consuming practices are intricate. While women's wages are increasingly seen as necessary to family life (McDowell 2007), the family lives that are sustained by dual incomes in particular are seen as potentially tainted by excessive materialism and exchanges of goods for care. And while the 'intersections of intimacy and economic activity' (Zelizer 2005, 214) are both commonplace and necessary, assumptions about the contaminating effects of the market make it harder to accept economic contribution as a form of intimate care. Although 'caringscapes' (McKie et al 2002) inevitably include paid work as well as unpaid family labour, and we argue cumulative acts of care across the spheres of work and home should be included in definitions of care (Maher 2009), economic care often raises fears of the emptying out of family love and intimacy. Money and the attached consumption pressures and possibilities, it is feared, take precedence over 'real' forms of love and care.

These fears about market contamination of family life through consumption are interlinked with the creation of some new family care obligations driven by the centrality of consumption and the elevation of individual choice. As we observed earlier, good outcomes for individuals and families are now linked to 'good' consumption choices. The care obligations of parents necessarily include the effective regulation of consumption within the family home. The feeding of children in the West, for example, has moved beyond questions of sustenance and survival to more complex requirements that parents provide and manage the healthy diets for children that avoid excess consumption. These diet prescriptions are tied to longer term developmental goals of securing the best outcomes for children, then tied in turn to national goals of healthy and productive contributors to healthy societies. Parents are increasingly held responsible for good consumption decisions, as part of good care for children.

Immediately the consuming tensions become clear. Exhortations to parents to feed children with a view to their longer-term health and well-being do focus on care. But they address 'better' child outcomes to be achieved by consumption and cultivation (see Lareau 2003; Vincent and Ball 2007). Such exhortations are in effect an inscription of the marketised elements of consumption (securing competitive advantage, rational decisions about best practice, investing wisely) right at the heart of good parental care. This inevitable but difficult nexus is one of our key interests in *Consuming Families*. In our explorations of difficult consumption issues, we rely on a broad and encompassing definition of family care as including economic work and consumption as including emotion and creating intimacies: a 'generous' account of family work as Marjorie DeVault (1991) describes it. We consider families and individuals in families are necessarily consumers, and that consumption makes families as well pressuring them. We aim to draw in consuming possibilities as well as consuming challenges. We look at the efforts parents make to achieve good consumption outcomes, as much as we do at the successful achievement of such outcomes. If '[w]hat makes work in the family context distinctive is a sense of stewardship accompanied by solemn obligations, intense loyalties, and moral imperatives' (Ahlander and Bahr 1995, 64), family consumption practices, decisions and testing conflicts over *how much of what is best* reflect that sense of commitment and obligation. As Silva and Smart have argued, although family forms are changing and definitions of family are changing, 'a basic core remains, which refers to the sharing of resources, caring, responsibilities and obligations' (1999, 7). Understanding how families discharge these responsibilities through their everyday consumption is our primary objective in *Consuming Families*.

CONSUMPTION CONFLICTS AS CREATING FAMILIES

In many of the issues we explore in this volume, fears of bad consuming practices in family life are overwhelming. The sense that parents are failing children, giving in too readily to childish demands, being distracted themselves from their caring responsibilities by materialism, that families are taking on and in too much, is prevalent in Western societies. But our interest in these contentious consumption issues where troubling notions of excess dominate is fuelled by our sense that the 'dangers of consumption' discourse often drowns out the creativity and connectedness in family consumption. Stephen Kline has commented on bleak prognostications about:

> the problem of managing consumer socialization in the risk society. Its dystopian vista is one on which shopping has become tedious, and where children are spoilt, disruptive and demanding. Indeed family life [has] degenerated into a constant struggle over health and social control. (Kline 2010a, xiii)

This sense of daily struggle and degeneration in family life dominate the issues that we explore here. Media, food, alcohol and sex, are all aspects of children's and young people's consumption that have created panics in Western societies in the last several decades. The place of the family in these hot button discussions is complicated and sometimes contradictory. Families are sometimes seen as protectors against the forces of consumption that threaten children's well-being and in many ways, childhood itself. Good family meals, heightened family awareness, increased parental monitoring, parental involvement in education and children's social activities are all routinely cited as offering protection for children and assisting them. In more sophisticated accounts of the consuming transitions of childhood, parental practices and oversight are linked to children's likelihood of developing capacities to make good choices for themselves. On the other hand, parents are as often seen as the problem in families, ceding to excessive consumption demands that that threaten children's well-being and long term development.

It seems almost impossible for families to get their consumption right. Very often these discussions of parental failure often draw on classed assumptions about those best placed or more willing to regulate consuming practices correctly. For example, in discussions about healthy eating, working class parents are often cited as less attentive to the concerns of health and diet and more pragmatically focused on cost and daily sustenance (Gillies 2011; Lareau 2003). Sometimes, in the face of these 'failures' of the family, states and regulatory institutions are called on to assist families with policing the boundaries of family life and the borders of childhood. Governments work on managing fast food advertising, curbing the availability of sexually explicit material to minors, or building in safeguards around net access for children. But parents are on the ground and doing the daily work of regulation. They are compromising and compromised. They are likely to be their own harshest critics. The contrast between the 'family ideal we live by' and 'the families we live with' (Gabb 2008, 15) is a painful gap in family life for parents and children as family consuming decisions are critically evaluated, especially in relationship to the well-being of children.

> Family lives under changing circumstances are the focus of public scrutiny and debate in contemporary Western societies, with the needs of children accorded a status of public accountability. (Ribbens McCarthy et al 2000, 785)

We acknowledge that some parents in families may not take enough care of their children. But most research suggests that families do take their responsibilities, for children's health, care and good consumption very seriously (Ribbens McCarthy et al 2000; Pugh 2009). Consumption decisions are difficult and conflicts do emerge. Mistakes and arguments are part of family life. Unease about consumption produces and defines family identities and connections too. Our investigation of these difficult issues locates such conflicts and tensions as part of family relationality and care, rather than as a necessary reflection of failure. We are inspired by the sense of families are making their way through these contentious consuming landscapes with care and attention to the well-being of children and to their relationships to each other.

In their recent project working with children and families, Allison James and Penny Curtis (2010) found children saw food practices as central to family life but clearly recognized the intensity of consuming pressures. Ruptures, breaks and discontinuities shaped family food interactions. Morgan (1999) reminds us that family life is both reproduced and undermined everyday. As we noted at the outset of this volume, Jan Phillips (2008) used the term 'consuming families' in her account of the rich and complex enactment of family life that occurred in a shared visit with her son to the grocery store. She argued negotiation, mediation, expression of individual preferences and the experience of conflicts were part of family consumption. Her idea of collaborative consuming practices in families is particularly valuable in capturing the multi-directional, intergenerational and creative uses of consumption in creating family life. 'Adults and children anticipate, collaborate, and not infrequently problematize family relations and meanings through consumption practices' (Phillips 2008, 99).

Including contests and conflicts as part of good familial consumption is important. 'Individuals [consume] as members or on behalf of households' (Morgan 1999, 27), as well as consuming as individuals. Family belonging, individual differentiation and changing family practices will be expressed and informed by consumption contests within family groups (see for example Curtis et al 2009) and between family members. Children's transitions to independent consumption will be informed by such contests. It is the tensions and connections created though family consumption, the negotiation of individual and collective, the private and the market, of love and resourcing that is our key focus in *Consuming Families*.

In *Consuming Families*, we draw on a range of research projects that we have completed over the past decade. These projects have investigated a diverse range of social issues, including young people and sex, alcohol consumption, family work-life balance and accounts of motherhood. Increasingly our exploration of relationships and familial connections has focused on the centrality of consumption as constitutive of family lives and relationships. We have come to see the consumption of time, of resources, and of ideologies and ideals as integral in the making of family life in the 21st century. In this volume, in part inspired by Carol Smart's (2007) imaginative and 'evocative' (2007, 185) refiguration of her existing project data in *Personal Life*, we have integrated our earlier findings into new frameworks of consumption and family life. The rich and constantly evolving literature on changing family lives and experiences and the new approaches to consumption have informed our desire to bring together different and troubling consumption issues as they define and inform family lives and relationship in contemporary Western societies. In our appendices, we provide details of all the projects on which we draw and that underpin our topics of interest. We have tried in this book to allow participants to speak for themselves about their family lives and to reveal the complications and challenges of consumption in family life. Much research into family consumption focuses on family failures and deficiencies. We aim to draw out the care, attention and love embedded in family consuming that is threaded though accounts of consumption worry and strife.

In Chapter 2, "Consuming Goods and Ideals in Family Life" we explore the consumption of time and goods in families in contemporary industrialised countries. Families are increasingly enmeshed in markets as communication technologies, blurred work and home boundaries and new social networking practices remake home life. There are new pressures on family time as women move into paid employment; the time and material goods needed to create secure family lives are often understood to be in tension. If social and material capital and 'good choices' are now seen as central to successful family life, what do such requirements mean for families experiencing disadvantage? We consider how the consumption of goods and other consumables, particularly family holidays, are enmeshed with entrenched concerns about the loss of family time. Although materialism and the exchange of goods often signify threats to family care in intimacy, in a rapidly changing global context, in our analysis, goods are best understood as material provisioning and as symbols of family intimacy and care as well.

In Chapter 3, "Text Me: The 'mediation' of Everyday Family Life", we explore the meanings and practices of new media in the home. These media options intersect with widespread fears about the purported dangers of the streets for young people and increased expectations of parental supervision in children's movements from home to school, even though the rise in maternal employment has made such supervision more difficult. In this chapter, we look at how different families manage and engage with new media platforms. We discuss Internet communities, new social dynamics of social networking sites such as Facebook and the implications of the technological mediation of youth lifestyles for existing family relationships. Children's media-created absences from family life are lamented. The availability of internet and mobile phones, and the take-up of these technologies, offer young people a way to live rich social lives and create their own social environments apart from adults. They have expertise in these online social contexts and technologies that parents may struggle to emulate. Yet parents provide the material resources for such consumption, and in debates about cyber-safety, they are required to monitor children's use of and security in these new environments. Conversely communication technologies may engender new forms of familial communication and intimacy; this is particularly the case for transnational families whose connection across geographical and social borders has been transformed. We recognise new media environments as both enabling and challenging for families and family relationships.

In Chapter 4, "The 'Big' Issues of Childhood: Family Responsibility for Children's Weight", we look at family food practices and widespread panic in developed nations about childhood obesity as a sign of excess. Food is a critical element of care; food consumption is central to family life. But in the domain of food, notions of excess and overconsumption have become a cause for public concern in affluent Western nations particularly. Poorly managed food consumption is now commonly understood to put the health of individual children, and nations, at risk. Avoiding childhood obesity, cited as one of the 'critical' public health issues of the 21st century, is now central in successful parenting and 'family meals' are increasingly located as protective social resources for children. We offer a critical analysis of the ways mothers in particular are made responsible for children's diet and health and how this plays out in differently resourced families. We explore the importance of food as sustenance and in the creation of family life in the everyday and argue for more creative and generous thinking about family food consumption practices.

In Chapter 5, "Youth Drinking and Family Alcohol Cultures", we explore young people's initiation into consuming of the 'adult' substance of alcohol. The creation of competent child consumers is seen as a central responsibility and obligation in this consumption sphere. Parents and adolescent children face entwined and individual challenges in regard to contentious products such as alcohol. Drinking, and learning to drink responsibly, are important markers of the move to adulthood; parents manage and produce family drinking cultures in relationship to youth activities and market drivers. Alcohol consumption is a cause of pleasure and problems for young people and parents alike. In this chapter, we explore the shifting relationship between the state and the alcohol market and discuss the implications of the domestication and feminisation of drinking. Public concern about alcohol is firmly focused on young people drinking in the nighttime economy yet most drinking occurs as part of everyday family life at home and often in the presence of children.

In Chapter 6 "Seeing It and Doing It: Sex in Families", we explore the consumption issue that arguably provokes the most public concern and debate. In the 21st century, young people inhabit a world that is more open about sex and family lives are changed as a result. Parents are expected to 'talk' to children about sex and support key public health messages about safe sex and healthy sex lives. Yet there is widespread community outrage over the 'sexualisation' of children and young people negotiating 'raunch' culture. We consider how shifting sexual norms (in relation to young women's new sexual assertiveness, same-sex desire and sexual information) change how young people and their families negotiate the transition to sexual maturity. We look at sex as a consumer commodity that now mediates both short and long term relationships for young people and at complicated social expectations about openness and regulation of sex. We explore how families are drawn into wider social debates about how and when sex is ok.

In Chapter 7, "Conclusion: A New Purchase on Family Life", we draw together our central arguments about the embeddedness and creativity of consumption in contemporary families. Although we recognise the intensity and difficulty of the consuming pressures families face, and the potential for conflict and failure, we argue consumption needs to be more generously understood as a framework for creating new forms of family life and connection and maintaining care and love. Both individual and collective aspirations for family life and belonging are expressed and achieved through consumption. Family consuming practices are integral for family intimacy and family care. In families relationships drive, inform and shape consumption, indeed we have come to see that consumption in families is profoundly relational. Families are being changed and challenged by contemporary consumption, and most particularly by the difficult issues of media, sex food, and alcohol. But consumption is central in the practices of family and relational consumption within families expresses and reflects their commitment and care, especially for children.

CONSUMING AS MAKING FAMILY LIVES AND FAMILY LOVE

The impossible and yet totally necessary intersections of consumption control and creative consumption in family life take place in the West in the shadow of increasingly loud and blaming social and public health discourses. Success in consumption is achieved when an individual consumer identifies available consumption options and makes good decisions about how and what to consume. By implication, successful parenting involves making 'good' consuming decisions for children and refusing access to 'bad' consumables. These are impossible aspirations in most families once children begin to consume independently and particularly for families facing economic and social hardship. The outcomes of individual and family consumption decisions are emphasised, and frequently derided, at the cost of a fuller and more accurate account of the ways in which familial resources and opportunities constrain and determine consumption choices (Gillies 2005, 2007; Lareau 2003; Pugh 2009; Vincent and Ball 2007). Family obligations to manage consumption effectively are profoundly impacted by states' withdrawal from their roles and responsibilities in relation to the care and well-being of citizens. Families are increasingly under scrutiny (Gillies 2011; Edwards et al 2012) but many families struggle to access needed resources to achieve good outcomes for their children. Some families are targeted for allowing or enabling bad consumption. In *Consuming Families*, we seek to draw out the other important aspects of the family consuming story: the love, nurture, care and responsibility in everyday family life.

Jacqui Gabb (2008) has suggested that although the family has attracted so much attention, there is still work that needs to be done, particularly to capture the 'silenced voices' of parenting and love as they are expressed in everyday experiences in family lives. Allison Pugh (2009) too argues for more attention to the love and aspiration of parents in the difficult consuming choices that they make. The call to look more carefully at familial love and care is not new. Judith Stacey's *Brave New Families* was first published in 1990. In the Preface of the 1998 edition, Stacey challenges those critics who assumed she was simply valourising new family forms. Stacey argues her analysis clearly recognises the stresses in new family forms and the economic and social pressures created, especially for women and children, by these new social structures. Yet in the following quote, Stacey talks to some of resilience and creativity that underpins our exploration of contemporary family consumption.

> [O]ut of the ashes and residue of the modern family, [women and men] have drawn on a diverse, often incongruous array of cultural, political, economic, and ideological resources, fashioning these resources into new gender and kinship strategies to cope with postindustrial challenges, burdens and opportunities. (Stacey 1998, 16)

Stacey's recognition of the work that women and men are doing to create sustaining and nurturing family lives is an insight that we feel has significant value in thinking about family consumption. Efforts from parents are evident in every aspect of family consumption. They are present in the ways in which children receive the benefit of these efforts and return obligation, regard and love, the way children move towards independence and distinction from parents, which is always also a reflection of parental care and familial success. The threads and complexities of personal relationships (Smart 2007) are expressed in the daily consumption practices of families and in how seriously and carefully family members approach consumption. Each family member attends to external forces regarding consumption decisions while responding to familial priorities and hopes.

> [A]s social actors seeking to exercise agency in the negotiation of our relationships, we try to meet the conflicting demands and expectations placed on us by ourselves and all pertinent social structures (family, work, cultural background, etc.). (The Voice Group 2010, 377)

These conflicting demands and expectations are particularly important in the contentious consumption we track in this book. We begin from the premise that consumption like other family practices, is relational and part of 'the essential labour of life' (Ahlander and Bahr 1995, 55). In each of the chapters, we consider how parents and children negotiate their consumption as families and as individuals within families to create and make family life. We look at the opportunities and tensions generated in contemporary consumption contexts, and explore how parents and children discharge their consumption roles and responsibilities with their own families. We search out how love, care and connection, mediated by contemporary consumption contexts, are expressed and experienced in family life.

2 Consuming Goods and Ideals in Family Life

Claire, in our *Family Time* study, lamented the impact that consumer objects, and time spent at work to acquire them, were having on her family life.

> We rarely get a family holiday . . . We've got some nice things; we just don't have any time. (Claire, female nurse part time; Bill, male partner full time; two children)

Claire's comment talks directly to the fears of materialism that saturate discussions of family life in contemporary Western societies. In her dual breadwinner family, money and time are in tension; the tradeoffs she and Bill make don't feel quite right. They are able to acquire material goods because of their working patterns but they feel time pressured. Their decisions about the consumption of goods and the disposition of time are troubling to her. In *Consuming Families*, we are focused on contentious consumption issues in family life. As Claire has identified, the intersection of new patterns of employment and fears of materialism is one of these deeply troubling issues. There are fears that 'too much' work, 'too many' possessions and 'not enough' time together are ruining family lives and reducing family intimacies and connection. There are fears that parents are trading off goods for care and that children are being offered excess material sustenance and not enough love and time.

In this chapter, we explore here two forms of consumption where questions of control, balance and 'too much' are central: the consumption of family time and the consumption of goods and objects. In Western societies, there are widespread concerns about the loss and the speeding up of time, and consequent effects of time 'poverty' on family lives. Worry that time is being consumed by the market and consequently lost to the family abounds in discussions about workplaces and in national and international fora (Bianchi et al 2006; Hochschild 1997; OECD 2002; Pocock 2006). While the forces that consume family time are often identified as external, such pressures are most often managed inside the family where decisions about how to deploy the available family time have to be negotiated (Bianchi et al 2006; Maher at al 2010c).

In a connected public concern, there is widespread worry about the consumption of goods in family contexts, especially by children. Materialism and instant gratification are feared to be changing the nature of childhood (Schor 2004; Pugh 2009). Kim Humphrey suggests that work, consumption and the speeding up of time are 'deeply interconnected' (2009, 19) and operate together to fuel major concerns about patterns of excess consumerism. Allison Pugh (2009) observes that parent-child exchanges are now *saturated* with commercial pressures. Managing the demand for goods is now an inescapable part of family life. The ubiquity of children's consumption, by children and by parents for children, is often seen as one of the key intrusions of the market into the sphere of family life (see critical analyses by Buckingham 2011; Marshall 2010; Zelizer 2002), where other values, *not* competition, acquisition and accumulation, should prevail.

Both of these stories about contemporary consumption raise concerns about too much power residing in the market and in consumption, and not enough power in the family. They create fears that family love and care can no longer be protected from the reach of the market (Folbre and Nelson 2000; Hochschild 2003). These stories are profoundly interconnected because it is feared that goods are being substituted for lost time. 'Many parents attempt to substitute stuff for time. It does not work well with children. They don't mind getting the stuff, but they don't see it as a substitute for parental time' (Pocock and Clarke 2004, 51). Pocock and Clarke's (2004) observation from their work with Australian children suggests parents are trading material objects for the time they can no longer give. It raises the spectre that material desires are driving both parents and children away from each other and away from sustaining family intimacies and connections. For us, these two difficult consumption pressure points, family time and excess goods, need to be considered together. Time at work does in one sense take away from family time, but it is simultaneously necessary to sustain family life. Folbre and Nelson (2000) remind us that working for money allows people to discharge their obligations of love and care; it is not primarily a sign of either rampant materialism or individualism. Purchases in family life of goods, or even holidays or presents are a critical part of how families manage love, nurture and care in wealthy societies. There are intimate connections between time committed to work, time committed to home and the role of goods and other consumables in family life.

In this chapter, we explore these fears about family time consumption, as new structures of paid employment (especially related to women's care but also to the intensification of a 'long-hours' culture) put pressure on family life. When concerns about parental absence and the presence of 'too many' goods in the home come together, worries flourish about a 'consumer culture' that is both ubiquitous and inescapable as David Buckingham (2011) describes it. Children's consumption especially becomes an 'urgent social problem' (Buckingham 2011, 5). We draw on research we have conducted on family time and care for children to illuminate the link between contemporary patterns of employment and people's material aspirations. We aim to draw out a fuller and more complicated sense of what families are doing about time and goods.

Fears that children are being short-changed as parents work and that goods are being used to substitute for parental attention are common, but they may obscure what happens in families and how decisions about time and goods are being made. '[I]t is not sufficient to compare idealized conceptions of home and market, nor of love and money' (Folbre and Nelson 2000, 134). For as Zelizer (2005) has astutely observed, love and money do go together all the time, not least because money is necessary to secure well-being and survival in families, to express and sustain care and to signal intimacy. More nuanced accounts of the consumption of time and goods in family life as Humphrey urges, need to move beyond the simplistic fears that people are now 'placing commodities at the centre of life' (Humphrey 2010, 32) and disregarding other social, moral and familial obligations. Instead, we need to understand the role that dispositions of time and expenditure on goods play in families' lives.

Goods cannot do the work of care alone, but we argue 'goods' are part of the creation and sustenance of family intimacy and they are purchased relationally—either in negotiation with other family members or for other family members. Goods or 'stuff', as Daniel Miller (2010) says, while taken for granted, form part of 'an exterior environment that habituates and prompts us' (2010, 51). Stuff shapes and reflects our behaviour and identity even when we are not conscious of it (Miller 2010). Stuff in the home reflects and sustains family life and family relationships. Pugh's (2009) study of what and why parents buy for their children illuminated the depth of parental desire to give the 'best' to their children that they could. Similarly, the designation of 'quality time' (in special events or family holidays or less dramatically a Friday night family movie) does reflect a sense of 'time famine' (Gillis 2003, 159) but also signals how important families think spending time together is. DeVault said different elements of family work are 'braided together' (1999, 54) and we argue goods, care and time cannot readily be disentangled. How families negotiate temporal compromises, gifts, promises and treats are part of the work of family relationality; families make themselves in exchanges of time and goods.

Janet Finch's (2007) concept of display offers a valuable framework for thinking about the function of material goods or consumables such as holidays in relation to contemporary family time pressures. Finch argues that the dynamic forms of family emerging in Western societies mean that family inclusions and exclusions, 'who my family is', can no longer be assumed. They must be displayed in order that family belonging and family form are clearly communicated.

> Building on the analysis in which 'doing family things' is at the heart of the way in which people constitute 'my family', my central argument is that *families need to be* 'displayed' *as well as 'done'*. By 'displaying' I mean to emphasize the fundamentally social nature of family practices, where the meaning of one's actions has to be both conveyed to and understood by relevant others if those actions are to be effective as constituting 'family' practices. (Finch 2007, 66)

Display is therefore a necessary addition to 'doing' because it ensures the meaning of the family practices are clear, that the families and family meanings created by the practices can be recognised and understood by family members and in wider social contexts. This insight seems particularly useful in the context of widespread tensions about 'lost' family time and about materialism encroaching into family life. It allows us to consider how different family time practices and different approaches to material 'goods' (defined broadly here to include special events such as family holidays as well as material objects) are negotiated within families to signify and constitute family life.

We take Finch's analysis about the need for display, in the context of fluid and dynamic practices of family life, to consider how contemporary families 'do' time, gifts and holidays, what they might be taken to mean within families, and how family decisions about such practices relate to extant social constructs and patterns. As Finch has observed, there are different:

> . . . degrees of intensity in the need for display, depending on circumstances. By this I mean that there are certain circumstances where the need for display becomes more intense, at least for the moment. This may be because new individuals—new relationships—come into the picture. But equally it can result from circumstances changing. (Finch 2007, 72)

The 'changing circumstances' Finch is describing relate to the inclusion of new family members and the creation of new forms of family on contemporary societies. But it seems helpful to us to see the widespread fear that families are no longer committing enough time to each other, and therefore must show commitment through special events or goods as a 'changing circumstance' that might warrant particular forms of family display. As Thomson and colleagues (2011) observed social changes need to be actively narrated by participants and for contemporary families, material expressions of love are one way of narrating new forms of belonging and connection.

In this framework, even conflicts about time and goods are part of creating family intimacy and connection. Family lives are replete with conflicts about when, where, how and on what to spend time and money. With the development of more democratic, less authoritarian modes of parenting relationships between parents and children will necessarily involve such disputes and conflicts. There are a 'variety of forms of human connectedness' (Ribbens McCarthy et al 2012, 81) in family life that involve individual and collective objectives and aspirations. These individual and collective aspirations are sometimes in tension and such tensions allow families to articulate their sense of family to each other and beyond. Disputes over what types of purchases and over the proper management of time are sites where different family members express and achieve both belonging and distinction. They are an important part of how children try out and develop independence.

Fears about how families are managing the consumption of time and the 'spend-work' cycle are central in discussions of contemporary family life. After all as Arlie Hochschild observes, 'time is a symbol of commitment' at work (1997, 69), but is also crucial in good parenting (Pocock and Clarke 2004). Changes in family time patterns especially in terms of extended hours of paid work create fears about negative family impacts. In this first section, we look at the tensions created by working time in the context of family life. Paid working time is necessary to sustain families. But expansions of working time through the movement of mothers into the labour market and the extension of hours at work, in conjunction with worries about rising materialism, are feared to have tipped the balance.

ABOUT CONTEMPORARY FAMILY TIME: A STORY OF PRESSURE AND SCARCITY

Western societies have faced considerable change in the provision of all types of care in the last several decades, particularly in the organization of employment and of family life. Mothers' participation in employment is identified as the most significant aspect of the temporal reorganisation of family life in the last half-century (Bianchi 2000; Bianchi et al 2006; McDowell 2007, 2008; Pocock 2003). This change has put pressure on the time adult women have to allocate to family care (Bianchi, 2000; Jacobs and Gerson 2004; Pocock 2006). Fears have arisen about how children are now cared for within families. There have been on-going debates about whether children are missing out, and about whether increases in men's caring labour are enough to cover women's absences (Hook 2006). Finally, there have been sustained discussions about whether governments and employers are doing enough to support time-stressed families (Craig 2007, 2006a, 2006b; Craig and Bittman 2008; Lewis 2009) as labour market demands reach into family life and reduce time for family care (Pocock 2006, 2003; Strazdins et al 2004). Hochschild (2003) argues these changing temporalities create the potential for the 'thinning' out and diminishing of care in the family context. She has explicitly linked this loss to the reach of the market into family life, to the 'commodification' of intimacies and love.

In particular, worries about care arise as more mothers do paid work. Women continue to be held primarily responsible for the care of children despite other obligations such as employment (Hays 1996). So women's work time is closely linked to children's care time. Even though paid work sustains families and is part of good parenting and arguably good mothering (Folbre and Nelson 2000; McDowell 2007, 2008), the economic sustenance of families is often cast as allowing the market too much into family life (Bryson 2007; Hochschild 2003, 1995; Pocock 2006).

We are interested in exploring this fear and what it means in family life. The negotiation of family time is an important element of the relationship between parents and children; the use and consumption of time reflects family ideals and aspirations. Work/family negotiations are clearly family practices (Morgan 2011a) and offer insights into how different families understand and priortise time together and the work needed to sustain family life. In particular, discussions about holidays and 'free' time reflect contemporary worries about the needs of children in relation to care and time. And while children can't make decisions about time when they are young, they can, as Hochschild (1997) observes, insert themselves into family time patterns. Through their needs, through negotiation and sometimes through disruption, they are inevitably part of creating 'family time economies', the concept we have used to capture the ways families use and negotiate time (Maher at al 2008).

In our *Family Time* study, couple families with children did struggle with managing time for work and family and their sense of time as a precious resource was evident. But these families thought very carefully about how their time was consumed. They did see time as both commodity to be saved and used, but they simultaneously saw family time as something indefinable beyond commodification that needed to be freely available within family life and to children. Helen's comment reported below typified the attention these families devoted to working out sustainable family schedules: 'Time with your kids is precious . . . I don't want them to miss out' (Helen, full-time nurse; Brian, full-time nurse; two children).

FAMILIES EXPERIENCING TIME PRESSURE AND SEEKING FREE TIME

In our *Family Time* study, concerns about having 'enough' family time were evident among the twenty couple families with children to whom we spoke. Although these families had relatively good access to some forms of flexibility such as shifts (Lindsay et al 2009a; Maher at al 2010c), this access did not fully alleviate a sense of family time scarcity. The families felt their time together did need to be actively protected in order not to be consumed by work or other 'busy' activities. At the heart of these struggles was an aspiration for 'free time' that was not committed to scheduled activities. Time that was unorganized and spontaneous was valued as Julie's comment showed: 'It's all those little things that happen in families [that are important]' (Julie, nurse currently not working, John, full-time nurse; five children).

Three key themes emerged in this yearning for 'free time' in these families. The first was the reluctance to rely too heavily on formal childcare as it was linked too closely to adult work schedules.

> Give them a start in life where they're not rushed off to childcare at 7am. (Lucy, part-time work, Nils, full-time nurse, two children)

> I wouldn't like him to be at either before school or after school care because there is not a lot of home time. (Eliza, full-time nurse, James, full-time, flexible, one child)

> I think it's really unfair on them to have an hour of childcare in the morning followed by school and then childcare in the afternoon. (Grace, part-time nurse on night shifts, Drew, full-time professional, two children)

Pocock, in her research, found similar patterns where shift work was used to 'enable [parents] to "be there" for their children' (2003, 202, see also Garey 1995) and to minimize formal childcare. In our study, reservations about formal childcare focused on preserving unstructured time for the children. The desire not to 'rush' points to the taylorization and tight scheduling that suffused discussions of family life in these nursing families. This sense of taylorization underpins contemporary concerns about 'lost' family time (see Southerton 2006; 2003). For example Janey the young girl in Hochschild's (1997) Amerco study, dawdled in response to her mother's need for her to hurry up to meet the family's work schedule. Although Pocock and Clarke (2004) were talking to teenagers, their participants expressed desires for free time with their parents; just 'hanging' about was valued and these teenagers were quick to notice when parental work pressures and long hours spilled over into family life. Such acute observations about time reflect the incursion of the market into family life but show family resistance to the complete commodification of time. They illustrate the complexity of family time economies. The families we spoke to were busy at work and with children's activities (see Maher at al 2010c) but they also were consistently renegotiating work patterns to achieve schedules that didn't feel so rushed and pressured. While strategies varied for achieving work/care balance, there was consistent endeavor to ensure that there were periods of unstructured time in family life.

This was particularly evident in discussions of weekends (see also Bittman 2005) and holidays, where the desire to create 'free' family time was reaffirmed. Weekends were crucial in family life, especially as children got older. A number of the nurses had commenced weekend work when children were young as a strategy to maximize parental time for children (with fathers caring on the weekends). But when children's schedules became more rigid due to school, weekends were an opportunity to ensure at least one day together:

> We don't plan anything Sunday. (Sarah, part-time nurse on night shifts, Richard, full-time engineer, three children)

> I just wanted *not* to be organized for a day. (Miranda, part-time nurse, Sebastian, full-time professional three children)

Similar attention was devoted to family holidays, with holiday time seen as vital in sustaining family connections. The absence of family holidays created stress and was relatively rare; most families created time for breaks, often using casual status in nursing work (where absences for school holidays were unproblematic) to achieve them:

> We think holidays are very important . . . because you get time to have some perspective and to enjoy and have fun together. (Miranda, part-time nurse, Sebastian, full-time professional, three children)

> Holidays are important for us, that's something we look forward to all the time . . . just breaking up the routine. (Lucy, part-time work, Nils, full-time nurse, three children)

> Holidays—we try and take a few holidays every year because that's sort of the main time that we get family time. (Diana, full-time nurse, Alex full-time professional, two children)

For these families, holiday times are important family times. Yet, the meaning and purpose of family holidays is variable and complex. Pugh (2009) says children use family holidays to stake claims for belonging and recognition in their school context. A good family holiday was an important commodity for children in her study. For our participants, good family holidays were simultaneously commodities to be worked for and a commitment to family time together as the following discussions about the cost of holidays funded by extra time at work illustrate.

Lucy: Small trips, and then we went to Queensland to see my parents. And we're booked to go to New Zealand in February. So now we do extra jobs that have meant we've had a little bit of extra play money.

Nils: And cashing in on the cheap flight deals now with the new airlines starting, and Air New Zealand has a good deal where the ticket was $7.00 one way.

Interviewer: $7.00?

Nils: Yeah so we're going to Queenstown for a week. But the tax is still the same.
Interviewer: $100.00?
Nils: Yeah $200.00 per person one was I think, so we were up for $800.00 for the whole family . . . We thought it was good at the time; we haven't been yet so we'll see when we get back.
Lucy: Oh, it's half the cost of our airfares.
Nils: Yeah it was, that's true. So yeah holidays are important for us in a way, that's something that we look forward to all the time, going away. (Nils, full-time nurse, Lucy, part-time work, three children)

Interviewer: Do you have family holidays at those times?
Susie: No, not in school—not really in school holidays. We have our family holidays separate [to avoid crowds . . .] and it's cheaper. And we just don't see much big issue about that. It's mainly a crowd thing for me. You know, if you try to go somewhere during school holidays, everyone's there.
Craig: Yeah and hard to get flights and everything.
Interviewer: So how often do you take a family holiday?
Susie: Every year we'd have a family holiday of at least 2 weeks or generally 2 weeks and then the other school holidays, usually in September I go—take the children with other mothers—like, you know, we do a 3 or 4 mothers with—like, in September we had 4 mums and 11 kids and we went up to Echuca and stayed in cabins in the caravan park. (Susie, part-time nurse, Craig full-time work, two children)

These couple discussions show complex intersections of decisions about work, family costs and family time. Holidays (and the budgeting of time and money needed to achieve them) are at once instances of market forces in family and resistance to such forces. Families are actively seeking time away together to play and hang about, even when such time is gained through more work and the consequent pressures on family schedules. These negotiations about how to use and accumulate different types of family time reflect the complexity of time use in family life: it is both a commodity and an element beyond commodification.

The commoditization of time is generally recognized as a characteristic of contemporary lives:

> Into the twenty-first century, our relationship with time continues to be one of commodity-valuation: we speak of time-"saving" measures and of "spending" time wisely, as if time were a currency to be saved or spent. (Adema 2000, 118)

Families are clearly experiencing time stresses (Jacobs and Gerson 2004; Pocock 2006; Presser 2003). Jennifer Silva and Allison Pugh (2010) found parents are continually trading off time at work against other time commitments they think are important for their children. In her exploration of work/life at Amerco, Hochschild (1997) describes how parents bargain with children and how children bargain with parents about time. She gives the example of Vicky in conflict with her daughter about long days at summer camp. Vicky was offering more weekend time instead.

> Vicky was urging Janey to accept a promissory note against future parental payment. The bargain was this: If you're a good girl and "do your job" by being on your own from Monday through Friday, I promise to give you a great deal of attention on the weekend. (Hochschild 1997, 83)

Janey is unconvinced: she is unhappy about 'the time credit' (1997, 84) system now in place in her home. For contemporary families, such negotiations about time and a simultaneous yearning for free family time (Bittman 2005; Maher et al 2010c) are part of everyday experience. 'Although they hardly ever become real, ideas of family time are still vividly cherished' (Mestdag and Vandeweyer 2005, 305).

Folbre and Nelson (2000) suggest that goods and services being imported into the home may carry new and different meanings and values in contemporary timescapes. They suggest that within intimate care contexts, new decisions may be being made about which activities, or which types of time, need to be protected and which can be partly delivered though the market.

> There is good reason to believe that the personal and emotional content of home life is becoming more and more concentrated in a relatively small number of activities, such as sharing meals or telling bedtime stories, for which substitutes cannot be purchased. (Folbre and Nelson 2000, 129)

The fact that time is commoditized, and that working lives create time pressures for families should not obscure the braiding of different forms and meaning of time in family life. 'Time [is] a negotiated resource' (Morgan 2011a, 167); some time is necessarily used to accumulate resources through employment (Folbre and Nelson 2000). For the couples in our *Family Time* study, time given to work to accumulate for holidays should be understood both in terms of commoditized time and as part of the relational work of family life. Goods, holidays and time are all consumables and family decisions about goods, about holidays and time will reflect the role of the market in family life. But such decisions are also profoundly relational and demonstrate family consuming practices focused on connection and care. Holidays are best seen as both consumables and family time. In valuing holidays, families are interacting with the market (through work and the money spent on the holiday) but they are also preferencing free time together. These time commitments and associated expenditure are often aimed at producing 'memorable' times in family life (Tubbs et al 2005). It is this braided approach to consumption, time and care where interconnected family aspirations and pressures are being negotiated that we explore in the next section of this chapter. In her discussion of family time pressures, Hochschild links time and gifts in negotiations between parents and children.

> [W]hen children react against a speedup at home, parents have to deal with it. Children dawdle. They sulk. They ask for gifts. (Hochschild 1997, 51)

But we argue that the purchase of goods is not simply evidence of commodity culture or reflective of efforts to alleviate the effects of time scarcity in contemporary family lives. These purchases reflect the provision of material comfort and the building and maintenance of family relationships. Goods reflect and express love and care in families.

FEARS ABOUT EXCESS CONSUMPTION IN FAMILIES

If stories about family time are defined by a sense of scarcity, stories about the acquisition of goods are defined by fears of excess. Clive Hamilton and Richard Deniss in their polemic *Affluenza: When Too Much is Never Enough* (2005) neatly summarise the dilemmas facing modern consumers and the feared impacts of overconsumption. Such accounts are suffused with a 'sense of pessimism' (Jackson 1998) about contemporary consuming practices especially in families.

> As a rule, no matter how much money people have they feel they need more. Why else would people in rich countries such as Australia keep striving to become richer, often at the expense of their own happiness and that of their families? (Hamilton and Deniss 2005, 5)

Hamilton and Deniss (2005) talk about 'luxury fever', about excess, about people's lives overcome by goods. For Hamilton and Deniss, 'families' are being damaged by individual consumption desires and drives. But, as we have argued, consumption in families is both individual and collective: much consumption by individuals is directed to maintaining and sustaining family. Accounts of luxury fever talk to excess but ignore the embedded and routine nature of much everyday consumption where care and consumption are necessarily bound together (Silva 2010). The acquisition of goods is an important aspect of how parents ready themselves for parenthood and create themselves as caretakers for children (Cook 1995; Miller 2010; Thomson et al 2011).

Thomson and colleagues (2011) say goods are a crucial part of how mothers imagine themselves as mothers; they point to 'the work of commodities as preparatory, expressive and identity producing' (2011, 198; see also Taylor 2004). People's 'emotional connections are expressed and felt through ephemera' (Pugh 2009, iv). She urges a full and generous recognition of the reasons parents have for buying stuff for their children, even when it puts pressure on family budgets. Pugh's approach insists that we see the provision and exchange of goods in families as part of love and connection as well as a reflection of the market in family lives. Sharon Zukin and John Maguire (2004) argue that not enough work has been done on the meanings of goods in family lives and relationships (2004, 174). They suggest that we cannot currently adequately account for ' "cultural circuits", where products both reflect and transform consumers' behaviour' (2004, 178) or fully understand how individual and collective identities are shaped and expressed through consumption. We cannot readily understand how families use goods to make and sustain family.

In family lives, consumer desires are shaped by and expressive of family connections and by the place of individuals within family structures. There are many valuable examples of the embedding and transformation of goods in family life; many accounts recognise how family life is in turn changed by the presence of such goods. Valentine (2006) explored family IT use and found children's expertise created new and potentially more intimate and democratic family structures. While such technologies are often feared as alienating in family life (Silva 2010), Valentine found relationality was being created and enacted. Gifts too are routinely exchanged within parent-child family groups: they are a vital currency in the demonstration of love and connection (Komter and Vollebergh 1997). The gifts parents give to children are influenced by markets and brands but are also informed by parents' love and desire to give children what they want (Clarke and McAuley 2010; Halkoaho and Laaksonen 2009; Komter and Vollebergh 1997; Nieuwenhuys 2006). Children are active in negotiating their own gifts, as well as the gifts that will be given to others (Zelizer 2002). Gifts are expressions of family relationships and connections as well as market objects. In considering family consumption of goods then, we need to attend to what it is that families actually do with the goods they purchase (as well as the ones they don't), to understand what consuming practices mean and do in family lives. We need to acknowledge the negative potential of consumption of goods in family life but see the complex positive family work that is done by goods.

Pocock and Clarke (2004) directly explored the nexus between the goods families buy for children and how children understand the exchange that is taking place. Their study about the relationship between family dispositions of time and consumable goods found young people were astute observers of parental lives, family pressures and attempts to mediate time shortages by purchases. These young people knew parents suffered from guilt about work and about work spillover especially and were very aware of 'guilt-induced consumption' in their parents. They were relatively pragmatic about this guilt and quite happy to benefit through gifts, although Pocock and Clarke found they preferred time with parents.

> Most young people are not on the lookout for material compensation; they prefer more time. 'Contrition through spending' appears to work better for the market than for young people. It therefore seems sensible for parents to avoid compensatory spending, not least because earning more money to buy more stuff means sacrificing more time. The 'cure' becomes the disease. (Pocock and Clarke 2004, xii)

Arnold and Lang's (2006) account of garages crammed with unused consumer goods, from their study with 24 US families, addressed the same intersection of stuff and diminished family connection as Pocock and Clarke (2004). They talked to families about the goods they bought, about how they furnished different rooms and about how they used their homes in everyday life. They conducted measurements of how individual family members used the different spaces of their homes. Generally they found parents had little leisure time with children, so family outdoor spaces, although beautifully maintained, were little used for shared recreation time. Goods were overwhelming family life for these families.

> [M]any young dual-earner families seem to exacerbate their stress and frustration by buying more possessions than their homes can absorb, adding to their debt and routinely conscripting crowded garage spaces to function as chaotic storage rooms. Few of these middle-class families show signs of imminent relief from an energy-draining work-and-spend cycle. (Arnold and Lang 2006, 46)

Both of these studies stress the overwhelming nature of the work-spend cycle often emphasised in characterisations of contemporary family life. These negative findings about family goods and time were echoed by some of the couples in our *Family Time* study who expressed resistance to the 'excess' consumption of goods in family life. These couples were very clear that time at home (meaning lesser time at work) was more important to them than material goods. They accepted the necessity of lowering their material expectations in devising their family work/care strategy. Suzie and Craig were pleased they had bought a 'cheap house', had a 'small mortgage' and bought second hard goods.

Craig: The other thing is too is that if you have a look at people's lifestyle now, when we first got married we bought a cheap house. We had a very small mortgage. One that we could afford.

Suzie: We had a good deposit.

Craig: We had a good deposit, so therefore it didn't put us under financial [stress].
Suzie: We bought second hand furniture, yeah.
Craig: We didn't have the financial constraints. . . . Now what happens is now is that people that are the same age as us when we first bought our house, they want everything. Right? They want the car.
Suzie: New everything.
Craig: They want the big house with the pool and everything else. They're not, we've sort of built ourselves up to where we are. So we haven't put ourselves under that financial strain. Then what happens is that the family comes along, or even so they may have to put off having a family because of those financial constraints. Then the family comes along, she has maternity leave for 12 months and then for that 12 months they're pushing it uphill to be able to meet their obligations. (Susie, part-time nurse, Craig full-time work, two children)

Similarly Martha and Kevin expressed modest expectations about consumer goods; these expectations defined their family approach to work.

Kevin: Our expectations aren't big.
Martha: And I think the problem of the day is the young people today have a lot of
Kevin: Higher expectations.
Martha: Well, they're more needy.
Kevin: More needy.
Martha: They want new everything. They want to keep up with all the technology.
Kevin: Want to have the trips every year or every six months.
Martha: They've all got the latest technology and everything and like we just don't probably value that as much. And we're prepared to go without. Yeah, so I think that that's it . . . I mean if we want something we get it, but we don't.
Kevin: We plan for it. We don't just go out. We're not impulse buyers. We sort of go 'okay, well we need some'.
Martha: Yeah. Because we know people that have gone out to Harvey Norman [a furniture and electrical store] on Saturday and bought a new telly and a new couch.
Kevin: Spend ten thousand dollars on [it].
Martha: And we just, we just would never ever do that. (Martha, full-time nurse, Kevin, part-time tradesman, two children)

Diana and Alex feel that time with children is most important. They prioritize family time over what they perceive to be excess materialism.

Diana:	Your kids ultimately I think are important. Everybody says to me it's for such a short time really, I mean you can always go back and get your qualifications, you can never get the time back with your kids.
Interviewer:	Yeah.
Diana:	And they need you, so yeah.
Interviewer:	Okay.
Diana:	I think yeah, that's the biggest yeah. And money is not everything.
Alex:	No, you can have a bucket load of money and be unhappy.
Diana:	Yeah it's important
Alex:	Or like
Diana:	It's important but it's not going to bring you joy . . . (Diana, part-time nurse, Alex full-time electrician, two children)

Mary also talked about reducing time at work to make time at home, even though this strategy created financial pressures.

> I would say enjoy your kids, and if one of you can work part time, or not work at all, do. Even if you struggle financially, the time with your kids, you can never—my aunty who's had five kids, she said 'You can never ever have your time back with your kids. You can always earn money later on when they go to school'. She said 'And plus, those years are precious'. And I agree (Mary, part-time nurse, Matthew full-time boilermaker, two children)

Each of these families understands time at work, time at home and the acquisition of goods as interconnected. In these accounts, material goods are located in conflict with the more highly valued notion of time with children, or 'free' time at home. The wider social story of work/spend is part of how they think about work and time in their own families. But each family responds differently and actively to these external pressures in light of their own family aspirations and preferences. Mary's account of what her aunt said about 'precious' time acts as an important moment of family display: her family's turn away from money is intergenerational. The invocation of 'other' people, and other families, acts to distinguish and validate the decisions made by Martha and Kevin. Suzie and Craig were proud of their decisions about second-hand furniture, yet, as we saw earlier, made family holidays a priority in their family budgeting.

Several important observations emerge from how these families manage the ideals and practices of consumption in their lives. The first is that they are reflexively responding to consuming pressures, not simply accepting the need to acquire. Decisions about time and about material expectations are part of family conversations about priorities; they express and create family life and family relationships. Consumption, and particular consuming practices, are not simply externally imposed but rather negotiated in the context of each family's social and economic conditions, priorities, histories and preferences. Family decisions about what is important are quite different, reflecting the variability of families and their consuming relationships. And as Thomson and colleagues observe, we need to understand 'the work of commodities as preparatory, expressive and identity producing' (2011, 198).

Although Pocock and Clarke (2004) and Arnold and Lang (2006) identify the potential for goods to overwhelm other aspects of family life, a fear expressed by our participants too, there was nonetheless considerable evidence that consumption was both actively contained and creative, as the following comment by Laura shows. For Laura, giving older children money and time away from parents is part of family life—a necessary and positive step for children to take in developing independence. She makes it clear that couple time together without children is important too.

Laura: Now that they're older and safe, Greg needs to go down to Bunnings [hardware store] or something I'll say "oh, I might come for the ride". You know, just so you can spend a bit of time together, wandering around Bunnings looking at stuff together, because it's, you know, no problem at all leaving them now. Especially that short amount of time. It's more if I'm working, if he's working and I'm working and it's school holidays, you sort of go 'okay, well what can we do to break it up for you? Here's fifty dollars. Go shopping. Catch the bus. Take yourselves off to the city, spend the day there, out of each other's hair'. Or you know 'who wants to have a sleepover out and who wants to have someone in?' (Laura, part-time nurse, Greg, full-time nurse, two children)

Laura's comment reinforces the need to think carefully about how consumption, and money and time, are operating in family life. Laura emphasizes the changing needs of children, where the move through adolescence into adulthood is marked by new dispositions of family time and family goods. Children's transitions to differentiation and independence are an important aspect of family life. Valentine (1999) remarks that the period of parent-child dependence is brief: 'we spend a relatively short span of our total life time in this form of household' (1999, 494). Developing independent consumption practices (Martens et al 2004) and allowing older children to express different tastes or aspirations or accepting teenage dissatisfaction with family gifts (Nieuwenhuys 2006), doesn't necessarily reflect problems in family life created by consumption. Such moves can also be understood as necessary forward steps in family life and in children's development. They reflect family relationships, priorities, differences and care.

The complexity and diversity of family negotiation and display can clearly be seen in the choices made by different families in our *Family Time* study. Martha and Kevin talked about televisions and couches, *and holidays* as things that can be put off. For the other families we interviewed, family holidays were necessary; they were not primarily consumables, but significant commitments to family time together. Although Kevin and Martha see televisions as luxuries, many have observed that televisions can be important goods in the production of family togetherness too (Valentine 2006). Other research has emphasized this variation too. Carolyn Tubbs and colleagues (2005) found low-income mothers used treats to express love and celebration with their children. Allison Pugh's (2009) detailed work on how differently resourced parents shopped for their children revealed the complex balancing of limited money and the wish to provide children with desired Gameboys™ and expensive sneakers. Priorities, family objectives and parental aspirations and resources are expressed in diverse and complex ways in relation to the market. But all families in her work thought about their purchasing decisions and importantly thought about their children's well-being in their consumption considerations.

So did all the families in our study. We recognize the stresses families face in terms of consumption and the reach and pressure of the market. But family interactions around consumption cannot be reduced to responses to those pressures. Family decisions about goods and time are not simply imposed on families. They form a vital part of how families talk about themselves and to each other about what is important in family life. In the final section of this chapter, we use the example of mobile phones as goods that become part of family relationships. (We explore the role of mobile phones in mediating contemporary family life more fully in Chapter 3). Phones given as gifts to adolescents, we argue, are embedded in and enable other family practices and family connections. These intimate uses of consumables further illuminate our contention that conflicts about goods and time in family life need to be understood as part of the making of family as well as pressures on family intimacy and love.

LIVING TENSIONS: HOW FAMILIES MANAGE

Mobile phones offer a particularly rich site for thinking about family relationality and goods consumption because growth in use across the West has been phenomenal. Mobile phones are consumer goods and objects of distinction in consumer culture. Yet mobile phones enable an always 'on' and interconnected state that invokes fears that family connection and intimacy are being negatively affected by technological incursions and absences (Henderson et al 2002; Wacjman et al 2008; Yoon 2006). Children's demands for phones, and fears that phones draw children away from parents, are commonplace.

Henderson and colleagues (2002) in the UK explored the acquisition and use of mobile phones by different groups of teenagers across the country over a three-year period. They found mobile phones were very often given as gifts to young people, but these gifts were then embedded in family relationships and interactions in complicated ways. These mobiles were both consumables and instances of family relational practices: they required ongoing negotiations between parents and children.

> First, phones operated as *commodities* within a material economy. Second, phones provided a *medium* for an economy based on the generation and exchange of social capital. (Henderson et al 2002, 499)

Mobiles, especially desired brands or upgrades, were often given as gifts at Christmas time to young people, but payments plans and financing were renegotiated between parents and young people over time.

> Use expanded with 'pay-as-you-go' and parents frequently played a role by purchasing the phone as a (Christmas) present (see also Livingstone and Bovill 1999). By the end of the study, more young people were moving to contracts, and in some cases sharing 'family phones', with a trend towards parents paying for their line rental for either a Christmas or birthday present. In sharp contrast to the family landline bill, young people generally accepted personal responsibility for financing their calls. (Henderson et al 2002, 498)

These shifts in the use and meaning of the phones demonstrate the complexity of goods as they are used in family life. These goods are exchanged between parents and children and are simultaneously market objects and symbols of care and love. They reflect and facilitate relationship and connection. Negotiations of phone plans and appropriate contact between parents and children represent an important consumption transition, as teenagers are encouraged to become competent consumers. These interconnected processes reinforce the importance of not making assumptions about goods and how families use them. Though consumables such as mobile phones are often seen as at odds with family life, the practices such goods enable—for example in facilitating family scheduling and other 'routine time practices' (Silva 2010, 52)—are clearly constitutive of family life and connection too.

CONFLICT AND CONNECTION IN GIFTS AND TIME

Our objective in this chapter is not to suggest that family purchases are not troubling issues, both within families and between different families. Indeed, we recognise goods create significant worries for parents every day. There are powerful examples of the tensions parents experience as they think about how and what to buy for children. Pugh (2009) noted the unease of middle-class parents who *could* buy most of what their children desired but felt obliged to rein in the consuming appetites of children. Working class parents in her study were unable to buy all of what children wanted but tried to provide enough for their children to feel safe and valued. Pocock and Clarke (2004) found teenagers in their study were dissatisfied with goods in lieu parental time; they recognised their parents' guilty purchasing and were not convinced. The Voice Group (2010) in fact described all parental consumption (especially that of mothers) as infused with ongoing ambivalence as parents try to negotiate sustainable and appropriate consumption with children under considerable pressure. This ambivalence was reflected in our most recent studies too, as many of the families were worried about how they were spending time and money.

But such worries and concerns are not the only part of exchanges of goods in family life. Daniel Miller's (2004; 2008b; 2010) explorations of objects in family lives provide lovely examples of how goods make family life and relationship. His (2008a) rich account of the Clarke family and their highly decorated home (epitomized in the Christmas tree with hundreds of ornaments) shows objects as an integral part of the Clarke's family life. Photos, knick-knacks, all of the stuff in the house, have an attached constitutive familial meaning for family members. Commodification, and the penetration of the market, occurs in tandem with and is constrained by 'rich and complex social relationships' (Folbre and Nelson 2000, 134). It is this sense of the relationality and connection of consumption decisions that we have endeavoured to capture here.

Goods, and discussions about goods, and expenditure on family holidays, we argue, are about love and care as much as they are about trade-offs and market substitution. Gifts make children feel cared for: they act within families as signs of love and outside families as signs of parental regard and commitment, as Pugh (2009) also observed. Special family times, such as reserving a free day on the weekend or saving up for a family holiday, work to create memorable family times and build family interconnections. Tubbs and colleagues (2005) observed birthdays and treats in low income families and said 'these treats conveyed to children that they were deserving of special moments' (2005, 85). Even conflicts about what to buy, for whom and when, require family time and effort to negotiate. In the commitments of resources and time, families signal their commitments to each other. Their consuming practices are necessarily relational and constructive. Such practices are the materialisation of belonging, family identity and family meanings.

Such an interpretation of course needs to be located in relation to the broader social and economic contexts families are managing. Gillies' work (2007) with marginalised mothers demonstrates clearly that limits on resources means access to goods is always contingent and that the meaning of certain goods—for example the provision of more expensive branded goods in families facing financial difficulties—may operate as special acts of love and care rather than as responses to imposed consuming pressures. Roper and Shah (2007) found children talked about brands as having an effect on how they managed at school; better brands were linked to less teasing because they secured children's value in the eyes of peers. The different forms of surveillance and attention faced by working class parents may in fact require demonstration of 'good parenting' by the purchase of the 'right' or 'best' goods, however defined. 'Arguably, family competence is increasingly being judged through a display of the 'correct' practices' (Gillies 2011, 84) and good consumption is an important aspect of doing and displaying family properly. For low-income parents, already facing social scrutiny and surveillance, decisions about how and what to purchase may be even more complicated and potentially troubling as resource stresses play their part.

Miller (2008b) argues it is problematic to make assumptions about how 'things' matter to others. This is vitally important in how we recognise family decisions about goods. In everyday family life, objects, material culture and family events, such as meals out and holidays, will matter to the family as whole but will matter also in complex and distinct ways to individual family members. Diverse family consuming practices (of time, of goods or gifts) reflect and reinforce family priorities and sometimes reveal different hopes and aspirations. Goods, their meaning and their materiality in family life do work to create family life (Miller 2008a; 2008b). The families in our *Family Time* study did struggle with the use and disposition of time and goods, but their struggles emerged as a key part of how they defined and formed their family lives.

Whatever the social constraints parents face, the parenting of, and provisioning for, children inevitably involves gaps, conflicts and dissatisfaction. While family is often presented as the place for protection and the satisfaction of all needs, in fact family life can never fully satisfy and protect. While unhurried family time is an aspiration for most families, family schedules most often involve pressures, compromises and compressions for all members. Negotiations about family purchases, about gifts, or holidays conducted between family members, and between children and parents, are often contested and complicated.

In our view, these lived gaps underpin some of the consistently negative interpretations of contemporary consumption (Martens et al 2004; Buckingham 2011). We would argue gaps and disjunctions and dissatisfactions and conflict about time and purchased goods are central to the construction and experience of family life. Gaps are where adolescents distinguish themselves and work on both belonging and being independent. Even for younger children, taste and preference operate as ways to secure and insert self into family practices and identities. 'Children's consumption within households takes place in a context of incessant negotiation, sometimes cooperative, other times full of conflict' (Zelizer 2002, 389). Fears about dissatisfaction and conflicts should not blind us to the important role such negotiations play in the making of family life as collective and as simultaneously reflective of individual family members' hopes and aspirations. Alison Weir suggests 'we can recognize and affirm an ideal of home as a space of mutuality and conflict, of love and its risks and struggles, of caring and conflictual connections to others' (2008, 8) rather than assume that disputes and disagreements especially about time and goods are inimical to family life. This is the framework we adopt for thinking about goods and time in family life.

Nancy Folbre and Julie Nelson support 'a more open and balanced framework for addressing issues of love and money' (2000, 124). Polarized accounts that celebrate or lament the intermingling of markets and family life cannot produce rich understandings of how families use goods and negotiate time. We would argue that accounts of contemporary family time that lament lost time and the tainting effect of the exchange of goods, or events and holidays in family lives are perhaps drawing on idealized accounts of family life and of family time where conflict is not present and where external temporal pressures do not intrude.

In recognizing contemporary time pressures in families, we cannot assume the story is only one of depletion and diminishment. In studies of everyday life, different temporal spheres always intermingle, collide and reshape family time and decisions. Family schedules are complex and variable as our couples in the *Family Time* study showed. They reflect both external time pressures and the changing temporalities within families. Different family members will find and need family time in different ways. Folbre and Nelson (2000) astutely observe that the 'specifics of dependency are very different for a five-year-old, a 15-year-old, a healthy 65-year-old, and an ailing 90-year-old' (Folbre and Nelson 2000, 125). Teenagers may need to diminish their family time as they seek to distinguish and differentiate themselves as Wilk's (2010) account of how teenagers experience family meals makes clear: adolescents often find this family time dreadful. Chitakunye and Maclaran (2008) make a similar observation about 'quality time'.

> Although Sam finds a spot in her busy schedule to create quality time (time created by parents to interact with their children away from the demands of the labour market) over a meal, her children employ the speed-eating tactic to escape from this time frame. Why? First, they want to escape from parental control at meal times because, in their words, they "want to eat where they want, when they want and whatever they want to eat". Second, speed eating signifies a rebellion against traditionally inscribed family mealtime roles. Thirdly, speed eating is an expression of individuality because the children are making a choice as to whether or not they interact with parents at mealtimes. (2008, 221)

Katherine Newman's (2011) account of the phenomenon of 'accordion families' where adult children are unable to leave home due to inhospitable social and labour market conditions adds yet another layer to contemporary family temporalities.

Valentine describes 'the home as a site of multiple and sometimes contradictory consumption practices between adults and children, between siblings, and between adult partners' (1999, 502). In family lives, consumption practices are about both market and family pressures and aspirations: they are commercial and intimate concurrently. An account of the provision of certain types of goods in family life (such as brand toys in families under economic pressure) or decisions about time that emphasise only the ways in which the market is entering family life are too simple, as they don't address family negotiations, conflicts and contests about time and purchases. Seeing current family time practices or purchasing patterns as poor or inauthentic replacements for some better idealised family life doesn't allow us to see the complexity and intimacy of family exchanges. It obscures the love, care and attentiveness that go into family schedules, that underpin the purchase of goods for a material environment where children feel safe and protected and the special value of family celebrated in holidays and presents.

CONCLUSION

Sharon Zukin and John Maguire (2004) say Christmas gift giving is a complex process of resolving conflicts between the family and economy.

> Ethnographic and historical research suggests that Christmas gift giving is a complex process of resolving the conflicts between the family and economy. The gift transforms the abstract commodity into an expression of love and a means of producing and maintain kin relationships, which Christmas shopping—the process of wresting significant gifts from the impersonal world of the mall—affirms the family's collective identity against a backdrop of an anonymous market economy. (2004, 187)

This story of gift-giving as a way to express and in part resolve complex sometimes contradictory pressures for contemporary families captures many of our key points in this chapter. The purchasing of goods and the disposition of time are difficult for families; dissatisfaction and conflict often results, no matter what the outcomes. Very often, strategies are tried (part-time work, 'free' day, some presents and not others), then discarded and families go back to the drawing board. In contemporary consuming societies, final resolution of such conflicts is perhaps best seen as an aspiration rather than a living possibility for families. But there are, we argue, a number of ways to interpret the renegotiation of family strategies, family conflicts over time and goods, and the dissatisfaction in family life.

Buckingham (2011) offers a useful outline of conventional accounts of consumer culture where satisfaction in fact can never be achieved. In these conventional accounts, the drive to consume more to address needs that can never be fully met by consumption structures consumer engagement as an endless cycle of consumption, dissatisfaction and more consumption. In this story, families are trapped in work-spend cycles (Schor 2004; Pocock and Clarke 2004) while the important connections and relationships of family life are neglected. But Buckingham (2011) contests this limited explanation of consumption. Instead, he urges a more complicated view of consumption that might more fully encompass its relational and creative aspects. This seems an important call to us. Dissatisfaction in family consuming practices and outcomes is intimately linked to the repetitions and dissatisfactions of caring for children. The set of family activities that constitute caring are never done and they are never completely satisfying. Parental care and the repetition of routine practices of care are on-going but conflict, disagreement and the dissatisfaction of both parents and children are always part of family life. Consumption, as part of doing family life, will always be partially unsatisfying even as it is nurturing and sustaining.

An important part of our project in *Consuming Families* is to draw out the threads and hints in existing work that consumption is not only pressure and taint. In this chapter, we have argued that time pressures and the goods families buy are not simply evidence that markets are exercising too much influence in family life. Rather, they also illuminate the complex struggles over work, time, love and care that are necessarily part of family life. The relational work of negotiating, contesting, reorganising and accepting makes and connects families. Dissatisfaction, efforts to resolve conflicts and consuming compromises are constitutive of family life as well as threatening. In the following chapter on media in family life, we seek out the same possibilities of love and connection in media use that we have argued for in interpreting how families use time and goods. The intrusions of the market, and families' experiences of consuming pressures are very real. But family connections and intimacies are occurring alongside and intermingled with such pressures. As we consider the forms of consumption that are figured as threatening to children; media, food, alcohol and sex we aim to illuminate the persistence of care and nurture in the lives of consuming families in the 21st century.

3 Text Me

The "Mediation" of Everyday Family Life

Many of the fears about excess consumption in Western societies revolve around the role of the media. The media is a key conduit of information about both good and bad consuming practices (too much food, too much alcohol) and about proper family roles and egregious failures in the management of children's consumption. Advertising and branding create dreams and desires in ever-younger consumers. Disturbing images of teenagers drunk on the streets are broadcast into family homes. Such stories are reflective and creative of the consumption panics in which we are interested. The use of media itself is a focus of panic too. There are concerns that young people are addicted to Facebook, and mobile phones; they are made socially vulnerable and physically inactive in their attachment to media technologies. Families no longer communicate as screens act as the alienating wallpaper in family homes. The pressures created by media technologies in individual and family lives are real and undeniable. Young people and children are growing up in newly technologized social worlds and the effects of such changes are in part unknown. But throughout this book we argue that consumption in families is about care and connection as well as about the incursion of market forces into family life. We seek to centre how lived consuming experiences transform market goods and commodities into the threads braiding together contemporary family life. In this chapter we argue media technologies are consumed and domesticated in family lives. They are constitutive of family communication and connection as well as of the consuming pressures and the currents of individualisation subtending contemporary lives.

The last several decades have seen rapid developments in media platforms and communication technologies. The diversification of media allows for greater choice for individual media consumers; in family homes, computers, televisions, game consoles and i-platforms mean individual family members can be physically co-located but experiencing completely different media products. In particular, communication technologies have multiplied and individuals now have a range of choices about connection and communication. What does this media autonomy and diversity mean in contemporary family life? How do these technologies shape and influence family intimacies and care?

In this chapter, we explore a set of media platforms, charting the benefits and difficulties of media consumption in family life. We look at technologies such as televisions, mobile phones and other screens in the context of everyday family practices. We draw out how such technologies facilitate as well as challenge family care and connection. Communication technologies have become a critical avenue for 'doing' family—for scheduling family activities and maintaining contact and intimacy despite physical separation. Texts, emails and family Facebook friends allow for connection in pressured contemporary family schedules. Teenagers have access to new independent communication tools but their social lives and activities are also newly visible and available to their parents. Although younger children have access to the external world through communication technologies that their parents may not fully control, media platforms also connect them with grandparents and absent family members in newly intimate ways.

In the media consumption realm as in all others, parents seek to socialise their children into competent consumers. In everyday discussions about (and conflicts over) mobile phone and other media use, responsibility, appropriateness, surveillance and costs are negotiated. Issues of trust, maturity, independence and connection have always been central in family life but are now also negotiated through media consumption. We argue for greater recognition of the multi-directional nature of media consuming practices in family life, and greater recognition of the work families do in creating care and connection through media consumption. As Silverstone and Hirsch (1994) observe,

> Information and communication technologies, be they institutionalized in broadcasting as for example in the case of television, or in close proximity to the worlds of work or school, as in the case of the computer, have to be seen as constitutive of the domestic as well as themselves being domesticated. (1994, 5)

THE PANIC AND THE PRACTICALITIES

New media technologies are understood as transforming human connections and relationships. Young people are growing up in mediatised environments and the impacts of being 'wired' are multiple and complex. Yet fears about the negative impacts of media use, on children and young people in particular, dominate public debate. Children and teens are seen as particularly vulnerable to harm from the media—cyber bullying, exposure to violence and porn and sexting are prominent themes in current affairs reporting. Concerns about 'too much sex' in childhood, our theme in Chapter 6, are intimately connected to the proliferations of media platforms and their reach in contemporary Western societies (Dobson, 2011; Ringrose 2010). Fears about child vulnerability in public spaces and are also on the rise and have impacted on how children and young people move in public spaces; there are increased expectations of hands-on parental supervision (Scott et al 1998; Zelizer 1985). The new opportunities indoors and the constraints on movement outdoors combine to entrench media as a key social space for young people. Parental obligations to allow independence and encourage media literacy are in tension with exhortations to check out their children's FaceBook pages and scrutinise Internet search histories.

There is public anxiety too that the young are pursuing their online lives at the expense of family relationships. Alienation and narcissism are often feared as consequences of newly wired lives (Twenge and Campbell 2009). Family intimacies are seemingly threatened by access to the world and the fact that physical co-presence in the home no longer guarantees that families are talking to each other. In this context, new media platforms have complicated and sometimes diverging uses and complex meanings in family life. The Internet and mobile phones offer young people a way to negotiate freedom 'out' in public though still under the surveillance of their parents. They can create rich social lives and develop their own identities and social environments apart from adults while remaining in the domestic context. Thus, these media platforms keep children safe in the home at the same time as they expose them to potential threats parents cannot fully contain.

We argue that media use in families warrants closer and more nuanced consideration. Silva (2010) suggests much analysis about technologies in family life depicts the movement as one way: technologies invade family life. But she urges recognition of two-way flows and influences and more attention to how families integrate and domesticate technologies in their everyday practices. Despite the prevalence of the panic (Critcher 2008; Livingstone et al 2012; Lumby and Fine 2006), there is still limited information on how families are absorbing and engaging with new media platforms as part of family life. The diversity of family practices in relationship to media requires more careful attention: 'factors in the home shaping media consumption are little understood' (Kline 2010a, 164). It is frequently assumed that media use inhibits family intimacy and lets the outside world invade family space but in this chapter we look to the multidirectional nature of communication technologies—where media technologies allow individual expression but also embed intimate connection beyond physical presence. Our central focus is on the way media platforms are being domesticated within families. How are families rehearsing and reinforcing family life in newly mediated environments?

The mediation of everyday life through technologies has developed rapidly over the last 30 years and continues to change. The generational nature of media experience and exposure is evocatively reflected in adults' (and academic and policy makers) tendency to use the term 'new' to describe now established and ubiquitous technologies. In Western countries both children's and adults lives are now 'saturated' by media with high rates of TV, mobile phone and Internet use (Livingstone 2009), even though parental understanding of media platforms may be different to their children's use.

One of the important drivers of media use in family life, in the ready adoption and domestication of communication technologies, is the changing nature and structure of family life. As we argued in Chapters 1 and 2, both family forms and family time schedules have undergone considerable change in recent decades. There are pressures on how diverse and fluid family groupings come together and connect. There are clear pressures on family schedules created by the increased commitment of mothers to the paid labour market (Wajcman 2008). While Wajcman suggests that 'the perception that life has become more rushed is due to the real increases in the combined work commitments of family members, rather than changes in the working time of individual workers' (Wajcman 2008, 64; see also Southerton 2006; 2003), scheduling conflicts are a characteristic of contemporary family lives (Pocock 2006).

Media and communication technologies have become vital in the management of contemporary family time economies (Maher et al 2008). Encouraging and allowing children's media use has become a crucial way for parents to manage the tensions between increased supervision of children and work and care commitments.

> To occupy children at home, many parents—rich and poor—seek to fill their homes with media. To give children and parents some privacy, ever more media are located in children's bedrooms. To keep them in touch with friends, parents provide mobile phones and domestic internet access. If they are worried, guilty, rushed for time or flush with cash, the media—in one way or another- provide a ready answer, seemingly less the problem than the solution. (Livingstone 2009, x)

Although parents are often ambivalent about media use (Kline 1995; Livingstone 2009), the conditions of contemporary lives and media penetration means media is present in homes and offers time relief and alleviation to parents. In our *Family Time* study many of the families described their children's extensive media use in terms of work and family. Computer and television use was pleasurable for children, it 'keeps them entertained' so parents could do other tasks, or helped the kids be 'low maintenance' so grandparents could easily look after them. One mother, who worked in a school, described how computers were useful when bringing a sick child to work.

Alanna: If I know they're not that bad, but they're well enough to sit and colour for a while or go on the computer. So the school is fine, they have no problem with us bringing our kids; we don't do it all the time. But even if they've got a day off and when Courtney was littler she'd come into school with me and she'd play with everything

> and do colouring and whatever, play on the computer all day, and the school was fine with that. (Alanna, part-time administrative worker, John, full-time construction; three children)

Yet, this narrative of media use as alternate care privileges the negative and troubling aspects of media consumption as parental absence and distraction. Family media use has many other meanings too. Families are necessarily committed to developing children as competent media consumers. Whatever the media prohibitions and platforms adopted in different families, parents are seeking to encourage, train and teach children to consume well (Kline 2010b). Parents provide media options for children because they know children want and will enjoy access to media platforms. As in parental choices of gifts, parents try to give children desired objects that provide pleasure and enjoyment. Parents do use media to negotiate and smooth the scheduling difficulties and temporal gaps of contemporary family life too and they may be seeking to reduce their guilt over being absent from their children through media products (Livingstone 2009; Pocock and Clarke 2004). Yet information and communication technologies (ICT) also provide ways for families to connect with each other and be virtually present in new ways. Mobile phone use provides a key example of how media forms are taken up within families, they serve different purposes for individual members but contribute to connection and intimacy too.

MOBILE PHONES AND THE INCREASING 'MEDIATION' OF EVERYDAY FAMILY LIFE

In Chapter 2, we discussed mobile phones as gifts and goods: here we consider the familial practices of connection and relationship mediated by mobile phones as a way to reposition media in the threads and connections of everyday life. There are longstanding fears that mobile phone use and constant contact would allow 'work problems to colonize social spaces and times once reserved for family life' (Wajcman et al 2008, 636). Yet there is countering evidence that domesticated ICTs offer new opportunities for 'deepening strong ties' (Wajcman et al 2008, 636). ICT use has been shown to make relationships more connected, durable and continuing (Green 2002; Licoppe 2004; Wajcman et al 2008).

The mobile phone has become a vital everyday technology that is embedded in relationships between parents and between parents and their teenage children (Bond 2010; Wajcman et al 2008; Williams and Williams 2005). Using mobile phones provides a way for families to engage in everyday family practices of scheduling time, the domestic labour of shopping, transporting goods and people and everyday expressions of love and care through short and frequent calls and text messages. The multitude of mundane calls made or messages sent everyday such as 'where are you?', 'when will you get home?', 'how did your meeting/interview/conversation/test or sports day go' and smiley emoticons or 'x's representing kisses in text messages both express and constitute contemporary families. We argue mobile phone communication is simultaneously a 'family practice' and a 'display' of family (Finch 2007; Morgan 2011a). This media platform offers a vital way of creating quality relationships while physically separated (Wajcman et al 2008). The 'connected mode' where families can be constantly in touch enables creative new ways of doing family intimacy (Wajcman 2008).

Sherry Turkle argues that we are now 'tethered to our "always-on/always on us" communications devices' and the people and things we reach through them (Turkle 2008, 2). She says that urban teens are under pressure to be constantly available to friends by cell or instant message to share confidences and momentary feelings and experiences. Adults too are increasingly tethered to work and expected to be always on and manage the demands of email (Turkle 2008). Yet, we argue tethering in terms of family life is potentially a positive aspect of the communicative saturation of contemporary societies. If there are widespread fears about the loss of intimacy and connection in family life, the tethering aspect of social media technologies and mobile phones offer a counterpoint of connection and engagement between family members.

Wacjman at al (2008) found that most mobile phone use was for connection with other family members or significant others and that mobile phones offered opportunities for micro-coordination about meals and family activities. They suggest connection with significant others is a more prevalent impact of mobile phones in family life than is the sense of being tethered to work (Wajcman et al 2008). Mobile phones thus serve complicated contemporary family schedules. They support the sense that modern family time is organised around children's activities (Gillis 2003). Detailed analysis of handset logs found that mobile phone contact with family members rises in the afternoon when school ends and peaks before the evening meal (Wajcman et al 2008). Valentine (2006) found similar patterns in daily email use between parents and children where new forms of communication during the working days of each were made possible: projects, needed items for school and changes to family schedules were readily and quickly communicated.

Interestingly, the gendered care burden of family life is as evident in mobile use as it is in food provision—women more frequently maintain mobile phone contact with family members than men do.

> Women are more likely to use their mobile phone to contact their spouse around the time of the evening meal and their children after school hours. Men, on the other hand, are more likely to use the phone for job-related purposes and exhibit a more muted pattern of family contact around after-school care and mealtimes. (Wajcman et al 2008, 641)

In our *Family Time* study mobile phones operated in this complicated and connecting way. Mobiles were described as support for, rather than intruders on, family connection. Most of the builders worked very long hours and had limited free time with their families of an evening. In these families talking on the mobile phone was a way of staying informed and connected. In the Lennox family, mobile phone communication alleviated the absences of long hours.

Julia: Sometimes I just ring him up on his mobile phone to tell him things because I know that I might not see him that day much to talk about something. So I think I need to tell him that so I just ring him and tell him.
Interviewer: And you've got time during the day, bits and pieces?
Sam: Yeah, the phone is always ringing.
Julia: He has always got a phone on him so I can ring and say, "I need to tell you this because I might forget" or something. (Julia, home-based carer, Sam, full-time construction worker, two children)

Many of the nurses' families also spoke of the important role the mobile plays in family scheduling. Texting was particularly important for the Whittingtons.

Mary: You've got to text.
Matt: Text, text [. . .].
Mary: Just keep each other up to date, and I know some people think it's impersonal, but if you're crossing paths all the time and you don't get to have a conversation without an interruption from a screaming baby [texting is important]. (Mary, part-time nurse, Matt, full-time professional, two children)

Another couple described how they used access to each other's electronic diaries to request 'meetings' and family activities. The technologies enable these couples to address and centre the care needs of children and negotiate their family time economies (Maher et al 2008).

Pressures for availability through communications devices to the external world do impact on family relationships as family members communicate with outside networks. Yet we argue they also provide an important mode of family practices, of both doing and displaying family relationships (Finch 2007, Morgan 2011a). Technological co-presence can enhance intimacy, even as it simultaneously creates and reflects temporal pressures, as a woman in Chayko's research explained:

> I feel closer to my family and significant other due to constant mobile phone communication on a daily basis. I must speak to my bf at least 4–5 times a day and my kids usually once a day. I feel that due to this

> our relationships have stronger bonds, are deeper, and that we work out challenges quicker. The downside is I feel guilty when I turn the phone off . . . of course this is very rare. (2008, 12)

As mobile phones have been widely adopted and woven into family consuming, we can observe the complex ways in which they have been integrated into everyday family relationships. Phones enable the intrusion of work but they also offer new forms of connection not previously possible. They engender and enhance the complicated temporal schedules of contemporary families. As we explore in the next section mobile phones are an important element in children's transition to independence as they offer both parents and teenagers connection and freedom in family life.

PARENTS AND TEENS NEGOTIATING INDEPENDENCE

Receiving a mobile phone as a gift from parents in early adolescence facilitates the transition to independence. The mobile permits children to go out and socialise with friends outside the domestic sphere, an opportunity that 'would not be permitted without the phone-tethering to parents' (Turkle 2008, 9; Henderson et al 2002). As we discussed in Chapter 2, mobile phones are highly desired consumer goods that require on-going negotiation between parents and young people about use and cost. One important condition of the gift of the phone is that children will always take their parents call or respond to their messages. For some of the UK teenagers interviewed by Henderson et al (2002), the surveillance outweighed the freedom and they gave up their phones so their parents couldn't contact them all the time.

Williams and Williams (2005) argue that the mobile phone has become a key device for negotiations between parents and teenagers around boundaries. Parents invade their children's space via mobile phones to extend their authority and control. However the use of phones perhaps also facilitates greater intimacy and parent/child communication in line with newer and more democratic modes of parenting. The teenagers in the study felt that their parents were more lenient toward them because they had mobile phones. As Leon explained;

> Normally I have to be in by about 9 o'clock—well before it gets dark anyway. They check up on me for their peace of mind. They know they can get hold of you and that you're not isolated and if you need an ambulance or anything. I don't mind if it makes them happy, I don't mind. (Williams and Williams 2005, 325)

Texting was a particularly good option as it connected young people without direct parental intrusion (Williams and Williams 2005). Henderson and colleagues (2002) found similar acceptance of the tethers of the mobile phone amongst most teens in their UK study where greater freedom was exchanged for familial connection through the phone.

Intergenerational negotiations over phone use are complex. Kwongwon Yoon's (2006) account of the use of mobiles by young people in South Korea found that the phones allow for 're-articulation' and negotiation of complex traditionalizing and individualizing forces. While phones are individualizing technologies that may seem to diminish respect for elders and traditions, young people's use reflected both individual aspirations and responsiveness to existing familial obligations and older social norms. Mobile phones played a complex role for these young people in relation to transitions to adulthood. Yoon argues (2006) that the use and meaning of such technological objects cannot be assumed but must be carefully explored.

Turkle (2008) too urges a broad consideration of what mobile phones do in families especially in regard to adolescent and parental relationships. She considers the implications of mobile phones and teenage dependency on their parents. She argues that the mobile phone is a way for children to manage their anxieties and have their parents "on tap" (Turkle 2008). Therefore, the transition to autonomy and independence in navigating the city alone as a young teenager is no longer 'a rite of passage' which 'communicates "You are on your own and responsible. If you are frightened, you have to experience those feelings"' (Turkle 2008, 9). Turkle suggests this experience is now buffered by the 'on-tap parent'. This observation perfectly illustrates the multiple interpretations possible about the meaning of family consuming practices. There is a suggestion here is that mobile phones may be encouraging anxious connection between parents and children. Yet phones are feared also as alienating forces. They are alternately seen as supports to healthy independence in young people. It is not possible to adjudicate on which impacts and outcomes of phone use prevail: different families and different events will result in diverse effects. The contradictions and possibilities force us to recognise the complexity of phone use in families. At the very least, we are urged towards a more generous reading of family phone consumption as it reflects love and loss, the connection and separateness that characterises these early transitions to adulthood.

The literature tends to emphasise parental use of mobile phone contact with their children as surveillance but mobile phones may offer important ways of managing parental anxieties about teen independence too. For example in our *Consuming Families* study a 19-year-old university student Amanda, described how her father Simon managed his anxiety about his children's whereabouts by getting his wife to contact them on their mobile phone.

Amanda: My dad will stay up all night waiting for us to get home, like will not go to sleep unless the front door closes. He'll be next to

> my mum in bed going 'do you know where they are? Have they texted you?' 'No'. My mum will finally get up and go on the couch and he's like 'call them' and she'll call because he doesn't want us to think that he's stressing out. He wants us to think he's giving us our space so he makes mum call.

The father's mingled care and surveillance are apparent to his daughter, and the stratagem of getting the mother to call is readily recognised. As this discussion of mobile phone communications between parents and children suggests, mobile phone consumption is embedded in family life and family care. Phones enable the micro coordination of schedules, they support domestic labour and as we have emphasised they offer the opportunity for love and care, intimacy and more frequent connection. Mobile phones are a tethering device between parents and young people, or in some families an important symbol that contact can be made when necessary, as young people transition to more independence and time away from home. For some (both young people and parents themselves) mobiles offer a way to manage their anxieties about paths to independence. Yet as with other media use in families on-going negotiation over cost and times and locations for consuming are necessary. The following section on the disposition of screen time in family lives illustrates the diverse ways in which contemporary media is domesticated. Family patterns of use and adoption reflect individual desires and aspirations, parental regulatory strategies and tensions in family use. Media platforms such as computers and gaming technologies enable separate consumption in domestic spaces but also support new forms of family connection and play.

SUPERVISING SCREEN USE: NEGOTIATING COMMUNAL AND INDIVIDUAL CONSUMPTION

A widespread 'moral' panic about children's Internet use, and the effects this has on their social and physical development, has been identified by media researchers (Livingstone 2009; Livingstone et al 2012; Twenge and Campbell 2009). In addition to fears of threats posed by game violence, bullying and paedophiles there are concerns that young people are becoming 'media-obsessed, atomised and self-absorbed' (Chambers 2011, 71). Young people face multiple online risks including the risk of bullying and sexual harassment, access to pornography and extreme violence, racist and hate material, misinformation, advertising and stealth marketing, gambling, invasion of privacy and support groups for self-harm (Livingstone 2009). Yet the opportunities offered by the Internet are profound. They include access to global information, educational resources, technological expertise, opportunities for civic participation, employment, community engagement, social support, health advice, social networking, enhanced friendship links, entertainment, games and fun (Livingstone 2009, 30). The evidence shows that ICT use does not necessarily encourage social isolation or the breakdown of family relationships and friendships (Holloway and Valentine 2003, 155). But these media platforms do challenge families to explicitly discuss and negotiate family connection and individual freedom.

As Livingstone (2009) notes children, youth and their families are in the 'vanguard' of online activities and are the focus of popular anxiety and policy attention. Yet fears about media and the Internet are often an expression of wider concerns about contemporary childhood and well-being. In this context media consumption provides some freedom and the 'constantly connected', 'digital' generation are delighted to have media with them all of the time 'in their pockets and their ears, embedded—or part of the wallpaper—in most spaces they enter, whether public or private' (Livingstone 2009, vii).

To contextualise the integration of 'new' media into family life it is useful to consider how families integrated 'old-fashioned media' such as music and television into everyday consumption and into the home. Television is a thoroughly normalised and domesticated form of media. But Kline (1995) reminds us that television was the medium that initially and directly brought the market to children in the home. Chambers (2011) describes the promotion of television in the 1950s as a 'domestic technology that fostered family harmony' with images of nuclear families gathered around TV sets watching programs together. Television has long been presented as 'the glue that binds some families together' (Valentine 2006, 371). From the 1960s however as domestic media were miniaturised, communal viewing patterns were fragmented with the arrival of the second TV set in many family homes. This trend intensifies of course all the time with the emergence of multiple media platforms and competitive pricing making them accessible to most families.

Importantly, the relationship children have with television continues to raise an enormous amount of anxiety among parents, public commentators and child experts. Lumby and Fine (2006) argue that there has been a 'moral panic' about television and its effect on 'passive' children and a number of myths have gained currency which should be challenged. The first is that children do not use their imaginations when they watch television. Lumby and Fine argue watching television requires viewers to 'interpret fast-paced edits, narrative twists and turns and shifts between fantasy and reality' (2006, 94). A second assertion is that television is the cause of obesity yet there is limited support for a direct link between children's physical activity food consumption and television watching (Lumby and Fine 2006). Kline (2010b) suggests the relationships between television viewing and childhood obesity are complex and that television viewing is not necessarily directly linked to children's diminished activity. A third dominant myth is that advertisers have incredible power over vulnerable children, yet as many have argued assumptions about children's passivity and vulnerability needs to be more carefully explored (Buckingham 2011; Cook 2008a; Lumby and Fine 2006; Marshall 2010).

Parents use a variety of strategies to moderate the television watching of their children including restriction, co-viewing and active mediation where parents actively comment and provide their views on shared programs (Mendoza 2009). As televisions became smaller and more affordable it has become increasingly feasible and popular for children and teens to access a separate TV in their rooms.

How do we understand the multiplication of screens and changes to previous forms of family intimacy produced by the single screen? How are the conflicts and possibilities of individual media platforms understood and negotiated in family life? Many of the families in our *Family Time* study used access to multiple shared screens as a way of solving competition over access to media. One family, the Nugents, described their separate television viewing in the following terms;

Tom: We're not actually a homogenous [family], you know like we all function on our little planes.

Rita: If we are all home in the evening together, depends on what's on telly. Jessica's got certain programs that she particularly likes to watch, so [. . .] she can watch in her room, out of our hair. (Rita, full-time nurse, Tom full-time professional, two children)

Separate viewing offered a harmonious though compartmentalised version of family life. Yet the mother was quick to explain that the children also enjoyed and requested joint viewing too.

Rita: But yeah, there are certainly evenings where they'll say 'Oh, can we watch a movie as a family?', so we try and do that.

This type of complex family negotiation over sharing and compromising with television viewing and using domestic space also occurs with computer and other screen use in families. As family homes have progressively become multi-media centres, negotiation over competing spaces and times for media use has increased. From the 1990s onwards, it is argued, media entertainment for young people moved away from the living room to the bedroom and family life has become more compartmentalised (Chambers 2011; Livingstone 2007; 2009). Intergenerational negotiation over media use has intensified as parents attempt to manage and restrict their children's use of phones, computers, Internet and computer game use as well as the more traditional media of music and television. At the same time more democratic styles of parenting have also emerged and are valourised by childhood experts (Lareau 2003; Livingstone 2007). So parents aim to strike deals with their children about the timing and locations of Internet and computer game use (Aarsand and Aronsson 2009; Chambers 2011;

Livingstone 2009). As with the other forms of consumption we focus on in this book, families actively work to balance needs for individual expression and privacy (which is often demanded by teens) but also opportunities for family connection and engagement through consumption.

Research into ICT 'domestication' examines how technologies become 'tamed' and integrated into everyday life (Haddon 2007). This process of domestication occurs with all forms of technological development (Silverstone and Hirsch 1994) and the use of new ICT in home spaces always builds upon or supplements existing media and family practices (Haddon 2007). The use of ICT especially by teenagers plays an important role in transitions to independence and the multiple threads of belonging that characterise those transitions. Young people use mass media to make meaning and organise both public and private spheres within the home (Lincoln 2005; Reimer 1995). When we think about contemporary familial negotiation about media use and the placement of screens, it is useful to recall that teenage bedroom culture has a longer history. The bedroom is often the first space where teenagers can exert control, be creative and make a place of their own (Lincoln 2005). As Sian Lincoln found in her ethnography of teens in northern England, the bedroom 'is a space in which their cultural biography can be nurtured. Music particularly is used in the teenager's bedroom in diverse ways: volume, choice of music or associated resources all play a role in the creative control of the bedroom space' (Lincoln 2005, 400). In contemporary families teens continue to play music to claim domestic space and express their identity, though music experiences have been much enhanced by the Internet and new technologies (Lincoln 2005).

We argue that there are similarities between parents and children negotiating music inside and outside bedrooms and the negotiation of newer screen based media use. In terms of familial negotiation of contemporary media consumption, perhaps a picture of evolution rather than revolution is more accurate (Haddon 2007). In the following section we explore how computer gaming, like mobile phone use, simultaneously offers independent consumption and self-expression and opportunities for family connection. In each of these media domains, the currents of individualisation and connection are entwined, as families and family members make use of technologies to express both belonging and distinction.

NEGOTIATING COMPUTER GAMING

Parents' relative lack of skill and knowledge about ICT in comparison to their children is often highlighted as problematic in the literature (Aarsand 2007; Chambers 2011; Livingstone 2009). Such assertions tend to homogenise skills and family types: it is likely that parents have different levels of skill, depending on their own media use in their work and home lives. The location of computers and games consoles in the family home is a strategy used by some parents to manage and restrict their children's media use. When games consoles are located in the more communal or public space of living rooms and attached to the family television more negotiation is necessary than if the technology is located in the more private space of the bedroom. Locating ICTs in more communal spaces of the home also offers the parents an opportunity to display identities as 'involved parents' (Aarsand and Aronsson 2009). Such practices aspire in some ways to reproduce the effect of the single television in family lives, where media is one room, while accommodating new media possibilities too. Within contemporary discourses of the danger posed to children by gaming and the Internet, placing the computers and consoles in communal spaces and developing regulations for gaming operates as ready way of displaying involved parenthood (Aarsand and Aronsson 2009; Livingstone 2007).

Parents develop family regulations to limit Internet access, choice of games and types of games played (Aarsand and Aronsson 2009). Parents also skill up (Valentine 2006) creating new possibilities for intergenerational relationships. The parental regulatory function co-exists with the desire to connect through play and activities valued by children. Conversely children and teenagers may use various strategies to resist or avoid parental rules and pursue independent media consumption including hiding information from their parents, evasion and passive resistance (Livingstone 2007). Children can also use their expertise to control the social organisation of the games, claim communal space as their own and in some cases delay bedtime (Aarsand 2007). Aarsand and Aronsson (2009) detail an example of an eight-year-old boy playing an Xbox in the living room. His mother enters the room and tries to gain his attention but the child provides minimal verbal responses to his mothers' questions and remains focussed on the screen. The boy's body posture and his fixed gaze on the screen, operate to exclude his mother from the gaming space. Largely by ignoring her he manages to sustain his gaming space (Aarsand and Aronsson 2009). As Livingstone notes, normative expectations of 'the good parent' and 'the good child' are played out in such struggles over everyday media use and the organisation of domestic space (Livingstone 2007). Yet new opportunities for family connection are also offered by Internet and computer game consumption.

Family gaming opportunities have emerged on the market as an explicit way to support family togetherness and allow parents to interact with their children through the prospect of pleasurable shared media consumption (Chambers 2011). The generation gap with media expertise is frequently seen as a problem for parental online supervision and regulation. Yet Aarsand (2007) identifies generational differences as a resource within families. When children teach their parents or grandparents how to play a computer game they have the opportunity to perform their competence and skill and reverse the usual transfer of knowledge from one generation to the next, 'traditional knowledge asymmetries between children and adults are bracketed' (Aarsand 2007, 251; see also Valentine 2006). Adults sometimes use their lack of expertise and the digital divide to enter social intercourse with children, as a 'type of strategic act where children's competence is celebrated and where the child is cast at the centre of the attention' (Aarsand 2007, 252).

The development of family centred gaming began in the mid 2000s as companies strove to expand their markets beyond the main audiences of teenage boys and young men (Chambers 2011). Examples of new games marketed to families include Sony PlayStation's Rock Band® and the cross platform game 'Guitar Hero' (Chambers 2011). Nintendo Wii became the market leader in consoles offering 'family friendly' games and by 2010 a quarter of British homes had one (Chambers 2011). The games were designed to be easy to learn and group-orientated. They were specifically designed to allow mixed age and mixed ability groups to compete with each other. To encourage the participation of girls and women Wii offered a varied choice of new games and avatars with Wii Play, Wii Sports and Wii Fit (Chambers 2011).

Deborah Chambers analysed the representation of family gaming in advertisements for Wii and found that family camaraderie was emphasised. The commercials 'accentuate kinship bonding by showing teenagers and younger children playing sport video games with parents and grandparents in domestic settings' (Chambers 2011, 73). The targeting of the product to 'the whole family' is repeated frequently in the advertisements and children are placed in a central role and shown to be instructing or negotiating with adults in the games (Chambers 2011). Nuclear-style families are presented in the advertisements with parents, children and visiting grandparents playing or watching the game (Chambers 2011). Chambers argues that the 'relocation of video gaming devices in the family living room fosters the idea that parents can resume control over youth, with a sense of reintegrating "youth" within "family"' (Chambers 2011, 74).

The advertising suggests the Nintendo Wii offers a new opportunity for families to 'perform 'family togetherness' in a progressive communication technology context' (Chambers 2011, 75). Pugh (2009) marks the significant expense of such games, especially for working-class families but points to the 'intense emotions . . . of care, and of belonging' (2009, 13) that fuel family negotiations about such purchases. The translation into the family togetherness depicted in the advertisements is complicated in the everyday practices of different families. In Aarsand and Aronsson's (2009) ethnographies of game playing in middle-class Swedish families, gaming was predominantly a child-specific activity but it was located integrated into the communal media landscapes of families and parents 'joined or commented on children's gaming in hallways, spare rooms and living rooms' (Aarsand and Aronsson 2009, 504). Negotiation of media in communal spaces was often challenging and media frequently became the object of territorial disputes between adults and children about who could appropriate space for gaming and 'when and for how long' (Aarsand and Aronsson 2009, 505).

In contrast to the picture of family harmony presented in the Wii advertisements there is evidence that solitary play is more common than co-play between parents and children and teens in particular prefer to play solitary games and desire independence from their parents (Aarsand and Aronsson 2009; Chambers 2011). Moreover gender and generational hierarchies in families are played out through media consumption in the home. Men tend to dominate media technology within the home. In both the UK and USA men tend to symbolically and literally control the television set in living rooms and associated technologies such as VCRs and remote controls (Bryce and Rutter 2010). This means that access to gaming needs to be negotiated with men. For example in Aarsand and Aronsson's (2009) study one father interrupts his children's games to watch golf on the family television set and in another example the father allows his son to continue gaming 'for a little while' indicating that the gaming is time constricted and that the father controls both the space and the media use within it (Aarsand and Aronsson 2009). Though not a focus for the authors, the Swedish studies of negotiation over gaming provide examples where mothers were ignored by children seeking to continue their gaming. Fathers, on the other hand, were able to take control of the living room and children's gaming (Aarsand 2007; Aarsand and Aronsson 2009). Young people's media use is gendered too: young females are more likely to be frequent users of social networking sites such as Facebook while young males are more likely play computer games (Bryce and Rutter 2010; Tufekci 2008).

Nevertheless gendered patterns of technology use may be changing as the popularity of gaming among young women is growing. Bryce and Rutter go further to speculate that 'computer gaming may represent an activity in which resistance and renegotiation of gender stereotypes can occur' (Bryce and Rutter 2010). All of these insights suggest that gaming can operate in complicated ways in family life; and that different family members and diverse families will do media differently. Bearing these contradictions and currents in mind helps us to understand what media platforms are doing to family life and how families are integrating and domesticating them and how families are dealing with the opportunities and challenges media consumption presents. In the next section we examine the experience of social networking sites in family life. As with the other forms of media we have considered, fears about technologically fuelled narcissism and individualism abound, especially in relationship to adolescents. But social networking simultaneously offers new modes of self-expression, new ways of doing friendship and importantly new opportunities for family connection.

FACEBOOK, DIGITAL NETWORKS AND FAMILIES

Social networking sites have grown exponentially alongside the development of the Internet and they have become incorporated into the daily practices of millions of users worldwide (Ellison et al 2009). Facebook is one of the most popular and developed originally from an application for college students—other examples include MySpace, Friendster or LinkedIn, aimed at the development of professional networks (Ellison et al 2007). Facebook allows participants to present themselves through an online profile or wall and to make "friends" who can view and post comments on each others' pages (Ellison et al 2007). Although uptake has been phenomenal (and has spread far beyond the original target age grouping), there are contradictory assessments about whether social connection or alienation is being created or reinforced by Facebook and other social networking platforms. Attention to the 'narcissistic' tendencies encouraged by such platforms has been intense with consequent feared losses of intimacy and connection (Buffardi and Campbell 2008; Cowan-Jenssen and Goodison 2009; Twenge et al 2008; Twenge and Campbell 2009). The individualism of such technologies intersects with fears about family connections withering under the press of consuming forces and media saturation. Yet, such platforms clearly offer new ways of doing family and maintaining relationships between generations, even as they facilitate extra familial social connections.

Facebook has been shown to provide social benefits in terms of strengthening offline connections and staying in contact with large numbers of people (Ellison et al 2007). Ellison and colleagues (2007) found that Facebook was a way for college students in the US to develop their social capital and draw on resources from the networks they belong to. These resources include useful information, personal information, the capacity to organise groups and events and potential employment connections (Ellison et al 2007). Following Putnam (2000), Ellison and colleagues identify the importance of two types of social capital—'bridging' which involves loose or weak social ties to individuals who may provide useful information or new perspectives and 'bonding' social capital that involves emotionally close relationships (Ellison et al 2007). They found that Facebook use was connected to social capital accumulation and bridging social capital in particular (Ellison et al 2007).

Tufekci (2008) studied Facebook use in a US college campus and found that young people tended to use their real names and engage in high levels of self-disclosure. She argues that Facebook enables social 'grooming' where users can engage in gossip, small-talk and 'non-functional people curiosity' to improve their reputation and status. Social networking sites are about 'mutual acknowledgement, status verification and relationship confirmation' (Tufekci 2008, 547). To achieve this users engage in on-going impression management by linking to friends, displaying their likes, joining groups and adjusting their profiles (Tufekci 2008). She distinguishes between the *expressive* Internet of technologically mediated sociality and the *functional* Internet of looking up information, checking the weather or shopping. Expressive Internet users use the Internet to 'perform and realise social interactions, self-presentation, public performance, social capital management, social monitoring, and the production, maintenance and furthering of social ties' (Tufekci 2008, 548). Laura Robinson (2007) supports these accounts of Facebook and other online platforms as social and relational. Users, she argues, have to read complicated social cues and create online selves that are acceptable and engaging.

There has been extensive media attention to how parents should be regulating children's use of social networking sites. Much of this attention has been driven by fears about children's vulnerability. The advice given by Michael Miller (2012) in his self-help book *Facebook for Grown-Ups: Use Facebook to Connect with Old Friends, Family and Co-workers* typifies such an approach by emphasising the need for watchfulness both on media platforms and over children and teenagers more generally. He suggests that Facebook is an excellent way for parents to enhance their surveillance of their children (Miller 2012).

> Most young people use Facebook as a bit of a personal diary, posting all sorts of juicy details as to their private thoughts and activities: you can find out a lot about what your kids are up to just by reading their Facebook status updates. (Miller 2012, 71)

For Miller when teens are forging their identities online Facebook provides a window for parents to find out about their children's activities. However, this negative framing of social networking does not address the enhanced possibilities for familial intimacy. Indeed Ellison and colleagues (2009) see the enabling of 'lightweight social surveillance' and active and passive communication as a positive contribution of social networking sites. 'Before social network sites were popular, people used communication strategies like gossip and the holiday newsletter to maintain awareness of distant friends, old co-workers and far-flung relatives' (Ellison et al 2009, 7). It seems likely that keeping in touch with close family ties on social networking sites is occurring too but surprisingly little research has been published on the new opportunities offered by social networking sites in the family context. Internet users, particularly women, over the age of 55 are the fastest growing demographic on Facebook and in a study of retirees a primary motivation for signing up was 'persuasion by a friend or family member' and their most common activity was 'stay in touch with my friends/family' (Shyam Sundar et al 2011).

Anne West and colleagues conducted a small qualitative study of the views of UK university students on becoming Facebook friends with their parents and found complex negotiations were taking place (West et al

2009). Most students would not welcome their parents as friends because it would feel like an invasion of their privacy or because they did not want their parents, particularly their mothers, to view their pages. Yet others said they would not mind and did not have things to hide from their parents, as William explained 'the occasional photo of me looking really drunk . . . that's not stuff I really have to hide from my family' (West et al 2009, 621). Some would be happy for their parents to view their pages but described how they would experience an embarrassing collision of contexts if their parents posted on their pages. As Facebook uptake rapidly increases and diversifies, there is a suggestion that family connection may increase.

> I'm not embarrassed that my mum's on Facebook any more because there seem to be a lot more parents, oldies on Facebook. But at first it was just my mum, and I was pretty embarrassed by that . . . I just knew that it was something I didn't want my mum involved in, she could look at my photos, and that sort of stuff but I didn't want her actively partaking in it. Just because that's not what mums do. (West et al 2009, 621)

There is a need for more nuanced discussions of the daily activities of familial connection and communication that may be now occurring on Facebook. Daniel Miller's (2011) detailed ethnography describes how intimate relationships can be researched and initiated via Facebook and how relationship breakdowns are displayed. Yet his discussion of Facebook relationships between parents and children is limited and focuses on negative examples of children expressing anger toward their parents on Facebook or children in transnational families being upset by photos of their mothers (Miller 2011). The possibility that Facebook may enhance familial relationships is not addressed. Miller argues Facebook can support and enhance friendship rather than diminish it as 'close friends are now even more intensely in touch' (Miller 2011 167), but this positive potential of Facebook for family life is not canvassed. For us, it seems likely Facebook can be put to work in family relationships, allowing easy scheduling of family events, on-going instant connection and the amelioration of physical absences, as mobile phones have been.

When children become adults and may have a family of their own Facebook provides a useful mode of connecting and interacting online through sharing photos and updates. Andrew Mendelson and Zizi Papacharissie (2011) in fact propose that the typical features of Facebook photos demonstrate the centrality of connection and family in Facebook practice: photos are usually chosen to reaffirm social values of 'community, family and gender' (2011, 253). As in the domestication of other forms of media consumption Facebook offers an important and increasingly embedded mode of family display and connection. This potential is particularly important in family life when physical distance is in play.

TECHNOLOGY-ASSISTED TRANSNATIONAL FAMILY RELATIONSHIPS

The use of media by transnational families is the final, and perhaps most dramatic example we discuss of the mediation of everyday family life. Intimate relationships can now be 'built, sustained and accessed from practically anywhere at anytime' (Chayko 2008, 5). Transnational family relationships have benefited enormously from the development and accessibility of video-calls through VOIP, instant messaging and social networking sites. Wilding (2006) notes the significance of the transformation that ICT use has brought to transnational families but importantly she notes the continuities in 'the purposes and experiences of communication' and the ways in which families have rendered new technologies mundane in a short space of time (Wilding 2006). The core obligations of commitment, care and the effective distribution of resources (Silva and Smart 1999) are expressed in new forms. Families now use multiple technologies to communicate and understand what is going on for family members in other countries. Increasingly ICTs allow migration to be a reconfiguration of family relationships rather than a rupture to them (Baldassar et al 2007; Madianou 2012; Skrbis 2008).

Mirca Madianou's (2012) research on the experience of 'distant mothering' in Filipino transnational families provides rich information on the new possibilities of doing family at a distance. Drawing on her ethnography with Filipina migrants in the UK she shows how the practice and intensity of mothering at a distance has changed (Madianou 2012). The women migrate to care for their families by financially providing for their extended families and technology allows them to continue to play an emotional caregiving role from a distance. ICTs make it possible for some women such as Donna to engage in intensive mothering from a distance.

> Every morning at about 10pm GMT when it is 6am in the Philippines, Donna, a care-home worker on a student visa in Cambridge, video-calls her husband and two eldest sons, aged 12 and 10, while they are having breakfast and getting dressed for school. Early mornings used to be Donna's favourite time when she was back home. Now she will always make sure she is in front of her screen at that time to admire her sons in their school uniforms. This is the time when she asks about school and gives them advice on their homework. After a webcam session with her husband and sons, Donna video-calls her mother who looks after her eight-month-old daughter. She asks her mother about how her daughter slept and what she will eat. She sings songs to her daughter and they often play peek-a-boo. Donna can stay up for hours chatting to her mother and playing with her daughter, but the thought of her early shift finally forces her to quit the call and go to bed. (Madianou 2012, 287)

Donna also interacts with her sons via Facebook and through a café themed computer game. Madianou (2012) describes the difficulties and ambivalence that online connection brings to the mothers and the pain of not being able to physically be with and touch their children. Yet video calls mean that the women can still be recognised as mothers by their infant children in a way that was not possible before this technology. Elisa left her son before video calls were accessible when he was ten months old and returned two years later and found that he did not recognise her and cried when he was left alone with her (Madianou 2012). By contrast women such as Donna described can see their infants daily and reclaim their identity as mothers. The women talked about being valued and respected by their employers and by their families at home for the financial and emotional care they provide (Madianou 2012). Complications of women's work, care and time disposition that we discussed in Chapter 2 are heightened through physical distance but in part ameliorated through these new media platforms and enhanced access they offer to continued maternal intimacies. As Neila describes:

> Yeah, for me it's the right decision because if I was still there I might have lots of children, but my life might involve just staying at home and not having time for myself. I've [achieved] more here. As long as I support them, I give them what they need and I keep calling them. (Madianou 2012, 291)

For transnational families where members are located in various parts of the world ICT use offers everyday provision of familial love and care; adult children offer support to elderly parents, or new mothers are offered advice and anniversaries and birthdays are remembered (Wilding 2006). Transnational caregiving and the effective conduct of long-distance family relationships is challenging and family members struggle to manage family and traditional expectations, duty and obligation, longing and loss (Baldassar et al 2007; Skrbis 2008). Yet ICTs offer opportunities for more frequent and on-going communication and everyday family intimacies in such circumstances.

FAMILY DIVERSITY AND MEDIA CONSUMPTION

New forms of media offer opportunities for family connection, as well as the potential for distraction and distance. Family negotiations over different types of media consumption such as the mobile phone, computer games and screen use are a critical part of contemporary family practices but such negotiations always involve intersecting management of family resources and economic access. In this section we look specifically at how class difference and family separation define and influence family media strategies and negotiations.

There is somewhat contradictory evidence about the ways in which class shapes media consumption within families (Chambers 2011; Livingstone 2009). Paradoxically Livingstone and colleagues have found in their large scale research on the UK population that poorer homes were more likely to have both television and gaming in their households (Livingstone et al 2012). It is frequently assumed that poorer households will have inferior access to media products but perhaps this is an area where children from rich and poor homes have similar consumer items bought for them. Wealthier parents may exercise 'moral restraint' in media provision to align with their ideals of good parenting while poorer parents may exercise 'symbolic indulgence' and purchase expensive media goods for their children which are highly desired and important symbols of dignity and social belonging (Chambers 2011; Pugh 2009).

Children in less advantaged homes tend to have freer access to media consumption while children with more educated parents are less likely to have their own TV or video in their rooms but more likely to have their own books (Livingstone 2007). Some studies suggest that parents experiencing high levels of social and economic disadvantage are least likely to restrict their children's amount of viewing or discuss a program while viewing it with their children (Livingstone 2007; Mendoza 2009). Such shared media activity is often cited as an excellent parental strategy for shaping media literacy but requires economic and temporal resources to achieve. As we discussed in Chapter 2 regarding gifts and goods, social class and associated material resources play a significant role in how parents 'do' consumption in families. It appears that middle class parents are more likely to heavily regulate their children's media use than less advantaged parents, as Pugh (2009) also found in regard to goods. Yet the relationship between class and consumption is complex. It may be that working class parents provide more media consumption opportunities to compensate for other aspects of disadvantage or to enhance opportunities for children's belonging in their peer group by viewing highly valued programs (Chambers 2011; Gillies 2007).

The development of mobile media devices has coincided with changes in family structures characterised by high divorce rates, and the emergence of more post-divorce and new family forms (Chambers 2011). Chambers suggests that when children in post-divorce or multiple family households move between houses they may experience different rules about ICT use. Parents may have less control over their children's media consumption when they go to an ex-partners household and in single-parent households older children may have a stronger role in negotiating household rules (Chambers 2011). Media use becomes one of many fluid and changeable family practices in these new extended family situations.

In many post-divorce families mobile phones and other ICTs are used as an important way for parents and children to keep in contact while physically separated (Funston and Hughes 2006; Valentine 2006). As one father in Funstone and Hughes' study described the value of phones in his new family life.

> From personal experience I think mobiles are very useful because there is often tension between parents and calling a house phone can cause trouble so it's easier to call a mobile. (2006, 10)

But there are also potential downsides to the intimate access that technology allows to children's lives. It has been reported in the press that estranged parents are using video-calls with children on iPads and smartphones to gather information on the living situation of former spouses. Some women have reported that former partners a using video calls with their children as a covert way to 'spy' on the mothers' new partners and living arrangements. (Henry 2012). In seeking out the connecting and relational possibilities of new media, the harms must also be acknowledged. There is a need for more detailed research on differing strategies of media consumption in diverse families. The alienating or threatening aspects of new media shouldn't blind us to the potential for new media to sustain family life too. Though families face important challenges in media regulation, media consumption offers real opportunities for enhanced family communication and connection.

CONCLUSION

Media consumption is now embedded in daily family practices of communication between partners and importantly between parents and children. ICTs create challenges in families but also opportunities to do intimacy and display family life in new ways. The tension between individual freedom and connection and commitment to the family grouping is nothing new—as each form of new media is domesticated family members utilise them for both individuality and connection. Everyday wrangles over the use of domestic space and access to family resources remain a common feature of family life. Teenagers retreat to the privacy of their bedrooms, as they have for generations, to play music but now to also watch screens and interact with friends and the wider world via the Internet. Parents try and regulate their children's ICT consumption, both the content and the time spent consuming, in similar ways to their regulation of TV consumption. At the same time, parents may enjoy and benefit from the freedoms new media offer as they manage work and care tensions and struggles.

It is not surprising that as a new mode of technology is introduced to a family household that children and young people—the digital natives—show more interest and expertise in operating it. The generation gap in media interest and expertise is frequently cited as a potentially alienating force in family life yet we suggest that parents can and do skill up and turn media consumption to the sustenance of family relationships too. Mobile phone use within families offers a key example of the ways in which ICTs have been domesticated and offer new ways of performing everyday family practices. The mobile phone supports family scheduling and flexibility between partners and parents and children and opportunities for negotiation and connection. The mobile phone tethers young people to their parents but also facilitates the transition to independence. Both parents and children view mobile phones as security for young people as they spend more time away from home socialising with friends.

The exercise of power and resistance within families can also be clearly viewed in the domain of media consumption in families. As we would expect, family conflict and compromise are negotiated over access to media and children can find ways to resist their parents' attempts at regulation or hide their online activities from them. Yet media consumption does also offer new opportunities for family interaction and connection. Even in the traditionally fraught area of computer games, family gaming offers a way for young people to display their competence and connect with the older generation through gaming consoles designed for family living rooms.

Media consumption via television, games consoles and computers and communication via phones and computers offers substantial domestic entertainment and pleasure. For families who are physically separated either through divorce or through temporary migration or perhaps locally separated as most of us are every day, with independent work and study schedules, media consumption offers powerful new ways of doing intimacy and connection. Media platforms create significant challenges for families and they import market forces directly into the family home with consequent material and social pressures. But family use domesticates these technologies in particular ways, and family life is enhanced too. The panics about troubling media use make it difficult to see the positives and potential in the incursion of new media into families. But the consuming practices families adopt in relation to media technologies are a crucial part of contemporary family lives, and the conflicts and challenges in families about media use are important too. They define and distinguish family identities and shape forms of belonging and differentiation. In our next chapter, we look at food and contemporary food discourses in family life. In public discussions of family food practices, we find the same attention to consuming troubles that we have observed in media discussions. As we have done in relation to media, we work to illuminate the love, care and connection in family food.

4 The "Big" Issues of Childhood

Family Responsibility for Children's Weight

Helene Brembeck's (2005) provocatively titled article 'Home to McDonald's: Upholding the Family Dinner with the Help of McDonald's' is a great location to begin our consideration of food consumption in families. Brembeck (2005) goes directly to the issues that are consistently raised about troubling family food consumption in the West. Fears about rising fast food consumption and its consequent health impacts, about the decline of family meals and the consequent loss of sociality are all invoked in the title of her article. McDonalds, as Brembeck says, represents the antithesis of healthy eating practices; it is unequivocally bad food. The fast provision and the 'drive through' are emblematic of the threats to family life more generally. This is easy, and by implication, bad family consumption. Yet Brembeck's wonderful exploration of how families use McDonald's food and space to create and consolidate family life, the authenticity, creativity and joy she identifies in these commercialized family food exchanges, urge recognition of the complexity of family engagements with food and contemporary food practices. Families, and family meals, she suggests, can be made in McDonalds. The provision of fast food can be an enactment of care and belonging, an element of a good family life. In this chapter, we examine the intensifying concerns about excess food consumption in families, and consider how the fear of childhood obesity is changing family eating practices. As in our other contentious consumption topics, we contest idealised notions of parental, and especially maternal, control of children's eating to argue for greater attention to the complexities of family food practices. We use everyday examples to show how different families, and different family members, use food creatively and relationally. We focus on the care and connection of everyday food practices.

Food is simultaneously necessity and pleasure and family food relies on intersecting activities of production and consumption. In societies where the ready availability of foodstuffs means survival is no longer a critical question for most, the balance of production and consumption in family food is altered. Families are now often seen as sites where food is primarily consumed rather than produced, even though such an analysis obscures the planning, procuring and provisioning of domestic food production (DeVault 1991). Instead of working towards sustenance, families are seen to be at risk of over-consuming. There is fear that families no longer eat together or eat well, and that this change has created both social deficits (a loss of quality family time) and negative health outcomes. This fear of excessive family food consumption has found vivid expression in concerns about childhood obesity in affluent nations. Children, so the story goes, are getting fatter, consuming too much of the wrong food, sitting in front of screens rather running and jumping. Because childhood is a time of both vulnerability and development, children cannot be expected to rein in or regulate their appetites; they need to be protected from themselves. Parents, who should be managing children's development, appetites and ultimately their bodies, are failing their children and their responsibility to the future. The following sardonic quote from a mainstream Australian newspaper captures the flavor of such accounts.

> Our children consume poisonous chemicals because we are too busy getting rich to cook. The obesity epidemic surely tells us Nintendo and MySpace are cooler than a waistline. Teenagers do not accept responsibility or discipline. Gee, I wonder who they get that from. (May 2008)

Family responsibilities for healthy eating are tied to broader social and national goals too. Family food practices have long been identified with the health of nations and information about nutrition, about child feeding, and about rational housekeeping have sought to shape family life in ways that serve state ends (Reiger 1985, Jagger and Wright 1999). In contemporary Western households, the requirement to consume 'healthy food' and to ensure children's feeding optimises development and well-being has become more insistent in the face of extant fears about children's obesity and 'excessive' consumption. Families are asked to provide food that serves both their own children and longer term national and social goals (Burrows 2008; Fullagar 2008; Jackson 2009; Murphy 2003).

Elisabeth Murphy contends however that such obligations do not fall simply on the family; they fall most heavily and specifically on women. 'Mothers are invested with the moral and practical responsibility for making prudent choices' about food and nourishment (Murphy 2003, 455). As we argued in our opening chapter, concerns about child well-being parental responsibility are intimately linked to new family forms and changing gendered roles. The fact that women contribute most of the unpaid domestic work and carry most of the responsibility for family well-being defines women's food practices as a domain where mothers' presence and care must be expressed (DeVault 1991; Maher et al 2010b; Warin et al 2008a, 2008b). Changing allocations of women's time (discussed in Chapter 2) are also important here. When discourses of time famine, of food excess and necessary restraint overlay and interweave with obligations of love and nurture, women's food responsibilities become ever more complex.

In this chapter, we delve into family eating seeking out the constitutive nature of family food consumption as well as the risks associated with food. We look at the work food does in families and then consider who does that work. We explore the new responsibilities mothers have for managing and maintaining children's bodies when food is everywhere and excess is made visible in the bodies of overweight children. We argue that familial conflicts are a vital part of family foodwork and that we need to recognize the dynamism and complexity of family food practices, especially in terms of children's power to resist, mediate and critique family food practices. Food practices, conflicts over eating, children's food refusal and exchanges of treat food in family are central in the connections of family life. Belonging, identity and nurture are achieved through food in families.

For us, food practices are great exemplars of David Morgan's idea of 'family practices' (2011a) where the everyday activities of family offer vital insight into family change. Morgan suggests the routines of daily life need to be carefully considered; in his view, the routines and 'repetitions of family life consist of a mixture of the more habitual or traditional and the more rational and purposive' (2011a, 28). Routines illuminate change as well as traditional and persisting patterns. Family food practices can be viewed particularly as practices where the habitual and the rational and purposive are consistently coming into contact with complex and uncertain effects.

The provision of food is an everyday occurrence, but is also a set of practices shaped by the economic resources of different families, patterns of employment, changes in agriculture and retail and by dynamic knowledge about what constitutes a 'healthy' diet. The forms of food produced for purchase are inextricably linked to family needs and demands, reinforcing the multi-directional flows between households and markets. Food practices reflect family priorities and values as they are mediated by social and economic constraints (DeVault 1991; Zelizer 2005). They are a 'lens through which changing ideas of "family" might be displayed' (James and Curtis 2010, 1167; see also Jackson 2009), as they are consumption practices that directly sustain family lives but carry wider relational meanings and salience. As in all of the consumer issues we consider in *Consuming Families*, food practices both make and threaten family life.

FAMILY FOOD: THE WORK IT DOES AND WHO DOES THE WORK

The daily foodwork of families encompasses local familial practices and is embedded in wider social discourses about food and families. Food contributes to the physical well-being of family members, but is central to the creation of family identity and is deeply relational (Backett-Milburn et al 2010; DeVault 1991; Phillips 2008; Silva 2010; Valentine 1999; Wills et al 2011). Food is an 'everyday accomplishment' (James at al 2009b, 7) of family life, where the social and material are linked. The provision of nourishment is key but so too are the 'social interactions necessary for carrying out food provisioning' (Phillips 2008, 106). The ways in which families do food together are vital in constructing family life. Food, commensality and familial connections are all inextricably linked (Brembeck 2009; Curtis et al 2009). While, as David Marshall says, 'much of our engagement with food is unspectacular and inconspicuous' (2005, 69), it is nonetheless central in family relationality and in how people create relationship structures. Proper meals make proper couples (Marshall 2005) and proper families (James et al 2009a).

> '[T]here are cultural discourses about proper and improper families. These ideas are pursued by [family members] through conscious and unconscious reference to the current political hegemony that feeding one's family well is a visible and public sign of good parenting. (James and Curtis 2010, 1177)

Jan Phillips' (2008) rich account of a trip to the grocery store with her son shows the complexity of food consumption in families and details how food works to create, maintain and remake social relationships within families. 'Grocery shopping', she argues, 'is first and foremost an opportunity to accommodate or enact family through the routine recurring work of consumption' (2008, 92). As she further explains, shopping, preparation, decisions about menus, places to eat, and times of eating, are all practices where family is constructed and enacted. Even grocery lists have been identified as crucial in how families make and negotiate everyday food decisions and create family cultures (Bassett et al 2008). Rebecca O'Connell (2010) says:

> [F]ood has been recognised as a medium through which family relationships can be negotiated and constructed. (2010, 564)

Amanda, one of our university student informants from the *Consuming Families* project, reflected on the constructive nature of family food (and alcohol here) practices in defining her family life and key family events.

> [M]y grandfather's from Ireland and my dad's been raised consuming a lot of alcohol where grandma was born in Norway so she came over—so Christmas for us is we drink like the Irish and eat like the Scandinavians. (Amanda George, 18 years old, lives with her mother, father and younger sister)

Any discussion of the work that food does in families, however, must recognise the importance of gendered patterns of care in food provision. As we earlier observed, the responsibility for the management and provision of food is not equally shared between parents. Women are consistently found to do more food work and are held to be more responsible for the provision of food (Beagan et al 2008; Cook 2009a, Cook 2009b; DeVault 1991; Kendrick 2008; Maher et al 2010b). Megan Warin and colleagues argue that 'food . . . is directly linked to what it is to be a mother' (Warin et al 2008a, 107).

> [A]ny discussion of food and bodies in the context of families must incorporate an analysis of the meanings around motherhood and femininity, for in 'western societies, the purchase and preparation of food for the family is the major responsibility of women'. (Warin et al 2008a, 98)

In their examination of fairness and foodwork, Beagan colleagues (2008) link women's greater responsibility for the emotion work of the family to their greater responsibility for foodwork; it is feminised labour for family well-being. The importance of food in creating family life and love (Burridge and Baker 2009), and women's specific responsibilities for producing and sustaining care and connection are captured in the following newspaper comment.

> My last meal would be a grilled cheese sandwich and a bowl of tomato soup—the meal my mother used to serve us when we were sick as kids. It tastes like love to me. (Osborne 2010)

Daniel Cook (2009a) has argued that mothers' involvement in child feeding must be understood beyond debates about nutrition and divisions of domestic labour. Cook interviewed mothers in the US about their child feeding practices and ideas, and found, as did DeVault (1991), that food expressed and created intimacy in families. Though 'nutrition and health emerged as an on-going accomplishment or aspiration' (Cook 2009a, 323), food exchanges between mothers and children demonstrated the 'everyday interplay between the provisioning of food, the policing of nutrition, the enactment of care and encounters with consumer culture' (Cook 2009a, 318). Cook uses the term 'semantic provisioning' to describe women's foodwork in families, arguing that women's activities as the procurers and preparers of food need to be understood as a form of provisioning. This work of provisioning:

> interweaves 'market activity' proper (i.e. purchasing) with social-emotional ends and contexts like caring and providing for family members, with an emphasis on how women's efforts transformed purchased goods into meals thereby creating and sustaining 'family. (2009a, 322)

Cook's analysis reminds us of the role of consumption and specifically food consumption in creating both family cohesion and family health. Food is a material and vital ingredient for family survival and is simultaneously central to the generation of the social relationships necessary to ensure that survival. Food creates family connections and belonging. When mothers provide the food that they are obligated to offer for children's physical needs, they are simultaneously constructing care and building family—giving material expression to key intimacies and commitments of love, care and responsibility. DeVault (1999) describes such practices as 'the expressive uses of food that give weight to caretaking activities' (1999, 54). Lisa's comment in the *Childhood Obesity* study when asked how she planned meals captures this love and relationality.

> Probably the top thing I think of is will the kids eat it because you know nothing makes me feel better than seeing my children eat dinner. (Lisa, partnered, PhD student, two children)

The sense that maternal love and care are mediated and expressed by food practices however becomes more complicated as fears about consuming practices that 'diminish' family life enter into the frame. Alan Warde (1999) says convenience foods, for example, are seen as problematic because they don't demonstrate the required degree of attentiveness and effort. Fears about snacking, and a failure to do the 'family meal' (Brembeck 2005; Curtis et al 2010; Marshall 2005; Mestdag and Vandewyer 2005; Warde 1999), seemingly reflect wider breakdowns and failures in family life all across the West. As we argued in Chapter 2, concerns about family time are consistently invoked in discussions of contemporary family life and 'meal times' are often a key concern in such accounts. But Warde (1999) urges a more thoughtful recognition of how time pressures evident in contemporary families may change family food practices rather than simply destroy the connecting threads of family eating (see also Jabs and Devine 2006). Warde (1999) argues we need to attend to the family scheduling pressures that may create new types of food practices. Different families might use food in different ways to sustain and support their lives. Convenience food may serve families and family life rather than diminish it. Curtis and colleagues (2010), for example, found that food practices often identified as problematic, such as snacking, are being used to create family in new ways.

Family resources will determine access to foodstuffs, the meaning of different types of healthy and 'treat' foods, and how women distribute food within families. Though individual decisions are privileged in contemporary consuming discourses, resources and opportunities define *how* people decide and what they can choose (Brannen and Nilsen 2005; Gillies 2005; Vincent and Ball 2007). The cost and availability of certain types of food impact on the foodwork mothers do. Concerns about scarcity and waste, for example, have been found to have greater impact on food decisions in less well-resourced households (Green et al 2009). But such concerns should not be automatically accepted as representing family deficiencies. There has been considerable emphasis on the perceived inattention of working class families to healthy food (an emphasis critically examined by Gillies 2005 and McDowell 2007). But many studies have found that working class families do have aspirations for healthy lifestyles and diets even if such diets are differently expressed than in middle-class households (Backett-Milburn et al 2010; DeVault 1999; Wills et al 2008).

We would argue there is evidence that all families, and mothers in particular, seek to provide food that nourishes and supports their children's well-being, both physical and emotional. Gillies' qualitative research on marginalized mothers in the United Kingdom found that the women were simultaneously engaged in sheltering, clothing and feeding children on meagre resources but also soothing and compensating for the day-to-day experience of disadvantage (Gillies 2007). Junk food offered opportunities for pleasurable consumption from which children living in straitened circumstances are otherwise excluded. Tubbs and colleagues (2005) also found low income mothers used food treats to show love and care to children. Discussions of family and maternal foodwork need to attend to the universal invocation of responsibility and care, and the specificity of its expression in different family and mother-child relationships. In particular, a careful and generous consideration of how families, and mothers in particular, aspire to feed children and the constraints they face is important to understand contemporary family food practices. Rather than demonizing family food practices, it is important to explore how families do food and what everyday practices mean and achieve.

As Marshall (2005) identifies, it is how food is used in family life that is important. We cannot simply assume that changes to older habits and practices signal decline. One of our concerns in *Consuming Families* is that assumptions about the negative effects of family consumption are widespread and may be inhibiting our capacity to see how families productively and actively mediate consumption in their family practices. Fears of excess consumption and troubling patterns in family food practices, and in many other spheres of life, may divert attention from family creativity and resilience. Concern about snacking, convenience food and the decline of the family meal mobilise wider assumptions about the loss of familial intimacy. But we argue these fears may be limiting our insights into the efforts families, and especially mothers, are making to use food creatively and lovingly in family life. In the following section, we look at how mothers understand the call to be responsible to feed their children well, and how differently situated women talked about how they work to achieve this objective.

IT'S MY RESPONSIBILITY': MOTHERS AND HEALTHY FOOD

In the following comments from mothers in the *Childhood Obesity* study, women from very different social locations all willingly assumed responsibility for feeding their children well, but material resources shaped the expressions and priorities of this goal. Importantly, the injunction for health, to which we turn more critically in the second part of this chapter, was central to their construction of maternal food responsibility. Fathers and state institutions such as childcare and even surprisingly the regulation of fast food advertisements were all deemed to play a secondary role to mothers in providing nourishment for children. Women remained at the forefront of planning and providing family food (DeVault 1991; Beagan et al 2008). Their ready assumption of individual responsibility demonstrates one of the key contradictions shaping discourses and experiences of healthy family food consumption. Women are made responsible for good child feeding, their planning, preparation and choices are important in securing their children's well-being. This is a heavy burden and mothers' putative failures (fast food or overweight children) attract significant criticism. Yet mothers willingly accept full responsibility for their children's health as the following comments from the women in the *Childhood Obesity* study show. In *Consuming Families*, this is one of our key observations: families (and in this case, women in families) make concerted efforts to get consumption for their children right.

Ella was 26 years old and had three children; the oldest of which was eight. Ella's first child was born when she was very young and she had no post-secondary schooling. Ella was clear that she cooked healthy food and that her children learned to eat it no matter how long the processes of eating and food education took. This attention to health was important for their future well-being.

> [Y]ou're going to give them the food sort of like . . . I don't know, the way I see it is hopefully when they do leave home they're used to eating their meat and their vegetables and their you know just their . . . and fruit and water and stuff like that, so when they do move out of home they probably will want to . . . they're used to it you know what I mean, hopefully. (Ella, partnered, full-time primary carer, three children aged 8, 7 and 2 years)

Ella's own commitment to healthy family diet was cited in contrast to her own mother's use of pre-prepared food and the bad impact it had on her teeth. Her mother and sister were very overweight too and she was really keen that this problem didn't emerge for her children. From 13 years of age, she had lived with her grandmother for some years and learnt about the preparation of good food. She felt this time had set her up well to give her children a better start than she had.

Petra was similarly unequivocal about her job as a mother. While she used the term parent, Petra was raising her children alone and it was clearly her own responsibility to which she was referring.

> You're the parent. You take responsibility for your children's well-being and you give them healthy foods because that's what's right. (Petra, single, full-time primary carer, three children aged 16, 9 and 2 years)

Megan willingly assumed her role as the provider of healthy food for her son.

> [I]t's up to me to decide what's good for him and what's not and being his carer, like being in charge of him kind of thing. It's up to me to make sure that he is eating healthy and that he's not just eating whatever he wants, whenever he wants. It's all about [the] responsibility I guess of being a mother. You know you've got to keep your kids healthy . . . They have to have all the healthy foods so that their bodies grow the way they're meant to grow and all that stuff. (Megan, single, full-time primary carer, one son)

Jane too was quite clear about her maternal responsibility to ensure that the food is healthy, but also to regulate other undesirable forms of consumption that might impact on her children's health.

> I don't believe it's anybody else's responsibility. [. . .] I firmly believe that about ads on telly [sic], you know people saying that they shouldn't have these McDonald's ads on telly or the McDonald's toys and all that sort of stuff. Well at the end of the day that's my responsibility to make sure that my child isn't [. . . eating it]. You know, when they start harping on about going to McDonald's I have to say 'well you can't go or we can go or the reason we can do it is this, but we're not doing it every week or every day so'. (Jane, partnered, small business owner, two girls aged 11 and 4 years)

Rosie articulated her responsibility more directly in relation to public health discourses. She expressed willingness to take responsibility but felt she was 'bombarded' with information and obligation.

> I'm one of those people who thinks that really that's the kind of thing parents should be onto themselves. It's pretty hard to avoid, especially when your kids are little and you're seeing the maternal and child health nurse all the time. You get bombarded with pamphlets and information and I guess its out there sort of in the media too, this childhood obesity and you know this message that you need to feed your children properly and get them moving and you know limit screen time and all that sort of thing. (Rosie, partnered, high-level administration, four children aged 7, 6 and twins aged 3 years)

Even children understand maternal responsibility as this comment from the interview with the Alessi family in our *Consuming Families study* shows.

Maila, in conversation with her 13-year-old child, says that at least some of the meals she makes are adequate and healthy and asks for ratification from the child.

Maila: I make a good effort with dinner; you've got to give me that. (Alessi family, mother Maila to son Tim)

James et al (2009b) have observed that even young children are active judges of family food practices and Maila's appeal to Tim invites his assessment of her cooking. Holly's comment from the *Childhood Obesity* study below best captures the ways in which mothers understand their job as doing their 'best' for children in terms of diet (Beagan et al 2008; Maher et al 2010b).

Interviewer: Well it sounds like you have kind of formulated your own understanding of what would be the right amount, the right food and also the right amount of activity. It's certainly something you're aware of.

Holly: Yes I am aware of it and I try to do my best. It would be easier if I had some guides to know if what I am doing is enough.

Interviewer: Do you experience anxiety around or a sense of responsibility around your children's diet?

Holly: A sense of responsibility yes, anxiety no. No, I don't get anxious about what I am going to feed them I just, but then. (Holly, partnered, public servant, two girls aged 7 and 5 years)

Holly denies she is worried her food responsibilities, but she is clearly not sure whether her daily practices were good enough. Efforts to achieve a healthy diet for children were evident (see also Beagan et al 2008; Milburn 1995), but these women were still worried. We argue this uncertainty about good enough family food consumption is linked to the broader fears about excess consumption and family responsibilities. Mothers' foodwork occurs in the context of uncertainty about 'good enough' provision and little social support or praise for their consistent efforts. In the next section of this chapter, we turn to two commonly invoked 'failures' of maternal responsibility in foodwork: the 'lost' family meal and fears about childhood obesity. These fears target families for failing to restrain problematic food consumption. Again, the proper role of mothers is central to this fear. If women are responsible for food, the lost family meals story becomes one about the changing use of adult women's time (Bianchi et al 2006; Bianchi 2001; McDowell, 2007, 2008; Craig 2007, 2006a, 2006b), as we explored in Chapter 2. Children's expanding bodies become a site where fears about loss of love and connection in contemporary family life and excess consumption are materialised.

THE LOST FAMILY MEAL?: MOTHERS OUT OF THE KITCHEN

The 'threat' to the family meal has been omnipresent in childhood obesity debates, (Jackson et al 2009; Lupton 2004; Maher et al 2010b). A brief selection of media articles from an Australian study (Maher et al 2010b) illuminates key themes that have been apparent in articles and headlines all across the Western world (Bahr Bugge and Almås, 2006; Boero 2007; Gallegos at al 2011, Marshall 2005; Mestdag and Vandeweyer 2005; Warde 1999). The supposed alienation in contemporary family life is often connected to the demise of the family meal. In these discussions, the suggestion is often that the changing structure of family life and mothers' absence through employment is putting pressure on family meals and therefore children's health. Such assumptions reinforce the cultural tenet that family food is women's business. Examining assertions about the family meal in Norway, Annechen Bahr Bugge and Reidar Almås state 'many of the claims about the modern Norwegian meal pattern may be seen as criticism of the working woman' (2006, 206). While there are countering discourses about employed motherhood as responsible motherhood (McDowell 2008, 2007), employment is often seen to have a negative effect on women's capacity to discharge their food obligations.

In the following headlines, assertions about the protective value of the family meal are quite clear: 'Family meals cut teenage fatness' (UQ News online 2005), and 'Family meals a recipe for fit kids' (O'Brien 2008). The term family here does invoke the valued sense of connection and belonging in family life, but women's preparation of and responsibility for family food is always present. In the articles, when direct questions about family meals are asked, they are all directed to women. In an article entitled 'Working Mums have fat kids' (Masters 2007), women are presented as failing, even though it is recognised fathers are getting off lightly.

> It gives new meaning to the term bringing home the bacon- a groundbreaking Australian study has found one in five children are overweight because of the amount of time mum spends in the office. Meanwhile the modern dad suffers no guilt over his child's weight because they have less influence over their child's eating patterns. Realistically, although in principle it is not fair, fathers usually get let off the hook where food preparation is concerned, Sydney University's obesity expert Dr Michael Booth said. (Masters 2007)

Another conservative commentator was quite explicit about mothers' real responsibilities as homemakers and food providers.

> Couples who can afford to have one parent stay at home or only work part time—usually the mother—are more likely to involve their

> children in formal after-school exercise. In families where both parents work full-time, they often have less energy after a long day to prepare nutritious meals or sit down together. (Francis 2008)

Reflections on the difference good maternal food practices could make to children's health eating were often cited. Research findings were backed up by evocative examples of maternal diligence in relation to family meals.

> Every hour of TV watched and every meal not eaten together as a family raises the chance of obesity. Mother of two, Simone Matlock works hard to ensure her daughters have regular family meals. 'It's a wonderful time to get everyone together to chat, so we make sure the TV is off', she said. 'And the girls are really lucky that at least half the time their dad is back from work, so we all eat together'. (O'Brien 2008)

> They might prefer to be in front of the TV or Playstation, but Brisbane teenagers are likely to be healthier if they eat meals with mum and dad. Eating together will enable the parent to have better knowledge of the child's food choices and amount that they tend to eat, Dr Mamun said of the study, which appears in the latest edition of American journal, Obesity Research. The study found having a healthy maternal attitude to family eating and diet was more important than the frequency of shared meals. (UQ News online 2005)

The use of screens as alienating and negative in family life, one of key themes in Chapter 3, subtends the food articles too. Likewise fears about women's absences from home, which we explored in Chapter 2, are integrated into discussions about 'lax' food practices too.

> "Health education is getting through to kids, but [it is] mothers who are not taking note because they have a guilt complex"; [Korn says] modern mums equate the word well-being with happiness as if happiness is all that counts or is at least more valuable than discipline, responsibility or overall health. Working parents are often too busy or too tired to explore the alternatives. (Ostrow 2008)

All of these articles link the loss of family meals to women's lesser time for care, reinforcing expectations that women should continue to shoulder the prime burden for producing healthy food even when they are doing paid work. Although sometimes the language of 'parents' is used, as in Petra's comment earlier, mothers are clearly the targets for responsibility. It is evident that more processed food is being purchased and less time being spent in domestic labour including cooking (Jabs and Devine 2006; Mestdag and Vandeweyer 2005; Warde 1999). Women's paid work is part of this trend. But many argue there have been no significant declines in the time families actually spend eating together (Jackson et al 2009; Curtis et al 2010). It is also clear that other forms of communal eating are still occurring and the meaning of the 'family' meal' and family eating as connection are still important to people, even when they are hard to achieve. Yet the story of decline dominates media accounts and feeds in Western societies into widespread fears about negative health outcomes for children, most commonly childhood obesity, to which we now turn.

CHILDHOOD OBESITY AND FAMILY FOOD

In national and international research and policy forums, childhood obesity is identified as one of critical public health challenges of the 21st century. The term 'epidemic' is routinely applied to a crisis understood to be enveloping the Western world, and sometimes the developing world too, despite the persistence of malnutrition in such contexts (Caballero 2005). The longer term impacts from increased rates of childhood overweight on national economies from higher health burdens is recognised as both high and preventable (WHO 2012). The particular vulnerabilities of childhood and adolescence are part of this global dialogue about childhood obesity.

> Unlike most adults, children and adolescents cannot choose the environment in which they live or the food they eat. They also have a limited ability to understand the long-term consequences of their behaviour. They therefore require special attention when fighting the obesity epidemic. (WHO 2012)

The implication that children and adolescents cannot choose the food they eat is important in the push for national strategies to address the negative health impacts of children's obesity. Yet, the statements that children and adolescents 'cannot choose' and 'are limited' in their understanding invoke the vulnerability of children as consumers. Children's carers and families are mobilised by such calls to regulate consumption and embed competent consumption practices for the future. Public policy discussions about effective preventative strategies for childhood obesity often focus on the role of the family in managing children's food intake with fears about children's overweight being central to public discussions in the developed world (Burrows 2008; Fullagar 2008; Gard and Wright 2005; Kline 2010a; Lupton 2004; McNaughton 2011).

Importantly in terms of our central concern about consuming families and individualisation, childhood obesity is one of the locations where the private sphere of the family has been easily penetrated by the state (Gillies 2011). Yet this intervention requires a complex balancing act as Fullagar observes, 'self management of healthy lifestyles in advanced liberalism, however, raises a key dilemma for state sponsored agencies' (2008, 111) for they have to achieve regulatory outcomes from a distance. In an individualised society the maintenance of ideals of individual choice is important while state goals are being pursued. It is here that families and particularly mothers come into play. States recognise that children cannot be held responsible for food production and consumption themselves, so family approaches to food, food management and family eating are important in the socio-political landscape of childhood obesity. Mothers are situated as directly responsible for food practices and the preservation of children from overweight (Herndon 2010; Jackson 2009; Maher et al 2010b; Warin et al 2008b).

Yet, the story of children's incapacity to 'choose' the food they eat must be contested. Children's control and influence are revealed in everyday accounts of family food, both anecdotal and evidence based (Marshall and O'Donohoe 2010; Wills et al 2008). Children's tastes, preferences and food refusals are a critical part of everyday family food practices. Children's eating habits and behaviour change family food practices in complex and important ways (Marshall and O'Donohoe 2010; Lindsay et al 2012). Parents rarely control adolescent eating practices: independent food consumption is a key transition in adolescence in Western societies (Backett-Milburn et al 2010; Chitakunye and Maclaran 2008; Wills et al 2008).

In the following section of this chapter, women from the *Childhood Obesity* study describe the conflicts between their responsibility and their children's food independence. These women were very concerned about their children's health and weight. They worried about 'heavy', 'chunky' or 'chubby' children; a number visited health professionals with fears their children were overweight. They were active and interventionist. Yet, while they willingly accepted responsibility for children's food, they acknowledged that they actually had little everyday control over children's eating. Rowena describes the conflicted negotiations in her daily foodwork, especially with one of her children.

> Breakfast in the morning, so breakfast in the morning for example, Michael of course won't eat cereal and we've tried many, many, many times, this is from like a baby to feed him cereal. So we did all the Farex and all that sort of stuff; refuse, refuse, refuse. We tried, you know obviously he will eat Nutri-Grain which is shocking by itself but you know as far as getting him to eat Weet-Bix and milk whereas my other child will just eat Weet-Bix and milk every morning for breakfast because I tell him to basically so its just, I don't know, and I tell him to do it too. Maybe you know you need to be a bit stronger and stuff, I don't know. (Rowena, partnered, medical specialist, two boys aged 3 and 6 years)

Prue talks about daily food struggles with her daughter Melanie.

> It's like a battle since birth really. Since she was born we calculated how much mls of milk she has drunk for the day and since then we have never stopped. She is not a very, she is not a baby that eats everything. (Prue, partnered, works in finance, one girl aged 2 years)

Prue laughed at a later point and said Melanie's appetite was like 'the Melbourne weather', very variable. This sense of struggle around the everyday management of children's eating was really common for these women. Most women in our study found getting a child to actually consistently eat a healthy diet was a challenge. Children's agency is not fully expressed in shopping or active choice about foodstuffs, but their daily practices at the table gave them considerable power.

Mothers in this study talked about 'fussy' eaters, about stresses around food refusal, about the times when they simply gave children what they wanted (preferences for white carbohydrates such as plain pasta and white bread, for example, were reported by a number of mothers). Anna's discussion of her child's reluctance to eat and the strategies that she adopted to manage reflect this on-going complicated negotiation of maternal foodwork. Her child was a fussy eater and she did her best to offer him a variety of foods and not provide unsuitable options, but she really worried about her son's eating. First Anna said,

> the Maternal nurse would say, 'oh if he's not wanting to eat, let him be hungry for a few days, he'll automatically [eat]'. [. . .] But given the choice Raj won't eat for a week you know. That stresses me. (Anna, partnered, postgraduate student, one boy aged 2 years)

Anna resolved this dilemma after further advice from her maternal health nurse and after a visit to the general practitioner, when milk with vitamin supplements added seemed the best way forward.

> She said 'try new foods, but then on those late nights just give him milk'. I know it's not the best thing to do, but at least that day if he's not eating, milk is there with the supplements. So there's something that's gone in. (Anna, partnered, postgraduate student, one boy aged 2 years)

Marie was facing similar struggles, offering supplements and 'desperately trying to hide pureed vegetables in his pasta, which works sometimes and not at other times' (Marie, single, high level administration, one boy aged 3 years). Sarah and Marie both ruefully concluded that maternal control over children's eating was a myth.

> I used to laugh at people who said 'I can't get my kids to eat vegetables' or 'I can't get my kids to eat this' or 'I am cooking 3 different meals a night', you know. I just thought that was just insane because they

eat what you give them, you know. (Sarah, partnered, academic, three children aged 10, 8 and 4 years)

People will say my children eat everything that's put in front of them and then you actually observe and you think well that's not the case at all. So, so I think that . . . people are not really that honest about it. There is so much spin put on everyone's lives now that it's like you're not a celebrity, your life is a shambles great, so is mine, but I think there is that thing now there is that thing where people want to appear to have everything under control, you know. (Marie, single, high level administration, one boy aged 3 years)

In drawing out the daily feeding practices of these women, we see the complexities of family food consumption where children's choice must be accommodated alongside the mandate for healthy eating. These women are all very willing to try to achieve healthy outcomes, but faced real conflicts and struggles in their daily experiences of feeding their children. Marie's comment also references her experience of the surveillance directed to contemporary families in relation to consumption (Gillies 2011, Morgan 2011a). Admissions about the 'shambles' of daily life and 'bad' everyday eating habits are not really acceptable in social discourse. Daily struggles have been observed by other researchers, too. Milburn (1995) in Scotland similarly found that parents struggled with the obligation to create healthy lunchboxes and their simultaneous need to give children food they would eat at school. Food compromises and conflicts are everyday occurrences (Curtis et al 2009, Wills et al 2008) with children's desires and preferences holding considerable power. Children have considerable power and agency in family food practices, as we explore in the following section.

MAKING CONTEMPORARY FAMILIES WITH FOOD

Control over children and children's eating is increasingly recognised as provisional. While discourses about parental control and stratagems designed to achieve it, (Gabb 2008; Morgan 2011a) resonate with parents, children are now seen as active participants in family cultures, food and other material and social practices (James et al 2009b; Marshall 2010). New discourses of healthy eating influence parental behaviour but also reach children in school classrooms and then make their way into homes. Children may adopt moral assumptions about food (James et al 2009b) and proper types of family eating. The 'democratized' family food decisions observed by Marshall and O'Donohoe (2010) see children as active in food consumption decisions. Children's intertwined agency and vulnerability impact every element of family food practice from shopping, through preparation to eating and the attached familial meanings to types of food, shared or individual food practices and assumptions and perception of proper bodily size and habits. In fact, if one of the key aspects of contemporary good parenting is to create competent child consumers, tastes and preferences *must be* respected (Cook 2008a, 2009b; Kline, 2010b). And this respect and negotiation should be understood as part of family care and connection too, not reduced to the failure of parents to adequately discipline children's appetites. Listening to children's food preferences and likes and working with them is part of love and care.

We would argue that family food practices must necessarily take account of individual members and their choices within the family context. Food preferences, habits and identities reflect both collective and individual consuming practices: they create individual and family outcomes. Kathleen Backett-Milburn et al argue that:

> Not only is the collective identity of 'family' being created through everyday food choices and eating behaviours in the home but so also are the individual identities of family members. (2010, 303)

Gill Valentine (1999) encourages fuller recognition of the agentic nature of children's involvement in family food practices. She explores how different families respond to the preferences of children, and how children's decisions and preferences change family food patterns. One family in her study, for example, moved to vegetarianism on the basis of the decision of one eight-year-old child. She stresses the dynamic and complex nature of food practices within different families and the importance of paying 'attention to processes of conflict, compromise and decision-making within contemporary households' (1999, 497). Wilk's (2010) account of how teenagers experience the 'family meal'—they generally loathe it!—cautions against assumptions about the shared meanings of particular food practices, especially as Gallegos and colleagues (2011) found the teenagers in their study did really value the family meal.

Even judgments and ideas of responsibility move in more than one direction as our earlier comment by Maila Alessi seeking approval from her son in the *Consuming Families* study showed. In the following discussion from the *Childhood Obesity* study, Margaret talks about one of her sons Liam who was taking responsibility for family food production. The show *Masterchef* inspired Liam and his mother Margaret had bought him one of the cookbooks as a gift. This gift had created some significant changes in the family diet, with Margaret now being exposed to new types of healthy food that she wanted to encourage in her family.

Margaret: The real good stuff does taste yuk. I suppose you have to grow into the taste. And then I read a study thing that said if you attempt to eat it, the more times you attempt to eat little bits of it that you will eventually find you like it.

Interviewer: Do you know where you read that?

Margaret: No, I think it was on like . . . I think like one of those chef books or something, like Master Chef thing, because I got my son one, it might be in one of his cook books but it said you really need to taste it and you might say yuk but, or my son told me, he learnt that at school. I didn't read it, he did, there you go. (Margaret, single, full-time primary carer, five children aged 13, 10, 7, 3 and 2 years)

Margaret's aspiration to create a better family food context for her children than she herself had—to introduce the 'yuk' good stuff—is evident here as is her willingness to learn from a range of sources about family food, including her children. These multi-directional flows were evident in family discussions in our *Consuming Families* study too. Complex and dynamic intergenerational negotiations of food practices within family groups characterized food practices and instances of conflict and tensions were commonplace. The Dawson family shared a commitment to healthy eating, but one of their children, 16-year-old boy Michael resolutely refused to eat what the other family members did.

Interviewer: If we can start broadly talking about food, if you were describing a healthy diet to someone how would you describe it?

Liam: One that's low in saturated fat that has a good balance of carbohydrates and protein and is balanced also in terms of the amount of consumption and is designed to a lifestyle rather than just looking at quantity of food. It depends what the person does, what their makeup is and what their activity level is to determine what might be healthy for that person.

Sue: I see it with lots of grains and nuts and fruits and vegetables and certainly quantities, not too large in quantity. But a good balance of

Interviewer: So portions?

Sue: Yeah, portion, that's a better word, portion sizes. Not too many saturated fats.

Liam: And a balance of white meat and red meat and vegetables, of course. We live with someone who's mostly vegetarian so we have to consider that as well as part of it.

Meredith (daughter): And Michael who doesn't eat anything.

Liam: That's a big challenge because Michael really has a limited type of food that he likes so then trying to have something that's healthy for him is a real challenge.

Sue: Huge challenge. He's what you'd call a white eater so that's quite difficult and quite challenging, to give him something that you believe is going to keep him healthy, and he's a

Interviewer: Do you try and mash things in secretly?

Sue: No.
Liam: Can't do it.
Sue: Used to be able to do that when he was little, or send him to his favourite aunty's or something like that. She'd be able to get something into him because he wouldn't want to offend her but not with—no, he's too smart, he knows. No, just more offering him—try to offer him—I have orange juice for him all the time because he's not great at grabbing a piece of fruit. Offering him lettuce, cucumber and carrot because they're three things he will eat so squeezing in what he will have as much as possible.

The food strategies this mother used from early childhood—repeat offering, disguising food or mobilising the extended family to assist—can't readily be implemented with a 16-year-old boy, even though she continues to try. Interestingly the only family member who did not participate in the study was Michael, the 'white eater' who now has a part-time job at McDonald's, a particularly strong symbol of resistance to the healthy family food culture driven by his mother. Indeed when asked to describe unhealthy food his mother Sue immediately replies 'Maccas' [McDonald's]. In a separate interview the 18-year-old daughter offers detailed descriptions of her brother's power in family food negotiations.

Claudia: My middle brother has one of the worst diets I've ever seen in my life. He just eats white food so he'll eat pasta by itself, he'll eat anything with potato, he'll eat chips. He's obsessed with lollies and he won't have sauces or anything. If he gets a burger he won't have mayonnaise on it or any kind of sauce, he's just very, very picky about his food and he doesn't like hardly any green vegetables and yet he's as skinny as a stick and tall. He's probably the most different diet out of all of us, the rest of us are pretty easy going.

Later in the interview the daughter describes how angry the young man will become if the food he wants to eat is not available.

Claudia: A lot of the time he has to get his own special meal because otherwise he'll crack it. Usually mum will have to make something separate for him. A lot of the time she'll just make it something like DIY, something like tacos or souvlaki or something like that where we can make our own so he won't get annoyed so, yeah, we have to be easy-going with him.

The George family comprises a mother and father and two daughters, the oldest of whom, Amanda, participated in the interview. The mother, Lena, 'is an amazing cook' and runs a catering business and also does food planning and cooking for the family. Amanda is 'a big believer in the diet pyramid' and subscribes wholeheartedly to her family aspirations to eat well: she hates fast food. But she engages in her own forms of food refusal and challenge within the family, while her mother continues to work on the diet of her adult daughter often using emotions to get her daughter to eat particular foods.

Amanda: I hate silverbeet. My mum keeps trying to make me eat that, and broad beans. My dad started growing them because my dad decided to be a vegetable farmer and started growing them and all of a sudden we have the abundance of silverbeet and this abundance of broad beans and I just hate them, I hate them so much. Cauliflower as well, not a fan

Interviewer: Do you have an input into what is bought?

Amanda: If I turn my nose up enough it generally stops getting put on the menu. I'm still working on the silverbeet and the mushrooms but mum buys cauliflower maybe like once a year and just tests it out. [. . .] it's really important to my mum that we like her food. If you say to her 'that's awful' it's almost a self-esteem thing. She gets really upset. It's kind of cute. She gets really upset actually.

In the Baker family, discussions about healthy and unhealthy food play out in complicated ways. The family is comprised of a father, Dan, two daughters Lucy and Sophie (one aged 14 and the other aged 12) and a younger son, Hamish. They live in a middle-class central suburb of Melbourne and describe their efforts to have a healthy but 'balanced' approach to food.

Interviewer: What about an unhealthy diet? You've already told me a little about what you think is unhealthy but what would you classify as an unhealthy diet?

Dan: Maccas, always Maccas. The first words you always think of are McDonald's and unhealthy. We do love KFC as our treat thing but we only have it probably once a month, I suppose it would be. We used to have it a bit more but once a month, but all those takeaway sorts of things. Anything cooked in very heavy oils so a lot of restaurants, the food is beautiful but you look at the plate and there's oil everywhere. Apart from that we're terrible sweet tooths so we know all the sweet tooth—so we try to limit it as much as we can. What do you reckon is a bad food?

Sophie: Kentucky Fried Chicken.

Dan: It's so yummy though.

Interviewer: What do you think is unhealthy about the KFC? Do you know what's in there that's not good for you?

Sophie: Well my sister Lucy has told me—I'm not too sure if this is true—but KFC doesn't really mean Kentucky Fried Chicken, she told me it was kids fattening centre.
Dan: Is that from Lucy?
Sophie: Yes.
Dan: Oh God.

Unexpectedly in this case Dan, the father is describing KFC as 'yummy' while the 12-year-old daughter Sophie activates the common highly negative judgement of this fast food. Dan's 'oh God' comment, expressing worry, guilt and impatience, reflects the complexity and difficulty of family food interactions. Pugh observes that, 'like working mothers, consuming parents feels bad' (2009, 85). Later, Dan describes how he purchases and cooks food that he knows the children will eat to avoid conflict over food.

Dan: Yeah you're pretty good (to one daughter). These two are quite fussy. This one's tough to get his veggies down sometimes. I've kind of sifted out the foods they don't really like to keep to a continuous pattern so that I know that they'll eat it and that it's good. I probably don't do enough variety with their food in as far as in global types of foods but then I know that there's enough variety in the stuff that they have each week. For example, they're not really great on eating steak, they don't like the chewing of steak, but if I do beef strips into either the rice or a stir-fry or a stroganoff, they'll eat that because I'll make it with a type of sauce rather than just steak and just putting it into tomato sauce. Probably the bad sorts of foods that you guys, which isn't really that great, is—they don't mind sausages which aren't really that high quality but they like sausages.

In the Egan family, comprising of mother Deidre and her 14-year-old boy/girl twins, Eliza and Adam, contested discussions about meals and snacks reveal the complexity of intergenerational food negotiations. In particular, Adam's refusal to eat breakfast and sometimes lunch is an ongoing issue and causes to Deidre who claims to have 'given up'. The son makes references to issues of health, time and personal preference in explaining why he won't usually eat breakfast.

Interviewer: If you can take me through your meals, so what would you enjoy for breakfast? What kinds of foods would you enjoy?
Deidre: This household ain't too big on breakfast.
Adam: Yeah, maybe my sister has a piece of toast with Nutella but me and mum don't really eat breakfast.
Eliza: We have a banana if I have bananas.
Deidre: I just get up, get dressed and leave.

Eliza: We always have a cup of tea.
Adam: Yeah.
Deidre: We always manage to get a cup of tea in. It depends how—mornings aren't very good for us because we don't seem to move quick enough but on the weekends [name] will get up and make bacon and eggs if I've got bacon and eggs.
Adam: I try to make larger breakfasts on
Deidre: Yeah or he might make pancakes.
Adam: Or an omelette.
Deidre: During school days—but what I've started to do is when I get to work, because I don't have breakfast, at about 10:30 I buy a Gippsland yoghourt and I try to have that in the morning so it's more like a brunch than breakfast.
Interviewer: Moving onto lunches, I guess
Deidre: Oh yeah, here we go.
Interviewer: What kinds of foods do you like for lunch?
Adam: I don't eat lunch either.
Interviewer: Really?
Deidre: Yeah we had big issues with—but, yeah, I've given up now; it's not like there's no food in the house.
Adam: It's just that I
Deidre: No, but that's a lie. Sometimes you do have lunch. If I have something nice that I've cooked the night before left over Adam will somehow manage to make time in the morning to eat it, like shepherd's pie.
Adam: No, it also comes down to how much time we have. If I get up at 7:30, which rarely happens, I will make lunch but—you know.
Deidre: And what do you put in your lunch?
Adam: I usually just make a sandwich with some cold meats in it, that's about it.
Deidre: Which is rare.

Clearly both the mother's food choices and the son's irregular eating patterns remain emotionally charged and ongoing issues in this family. Each of them strive to eat healthy food but feel constrained by the foods available in the house, preferences for unhealthy food and lack of time to prepare and eat meals during the week (see Jabs and Devine 2006; Warde 1999). The son is active in critiquing parental food choices, while the mother is challenging the emphasis on health over making sure at least something is being eaten. The multi-directional flows of judgement between parents and children are evident, challenging both ideals of parental control and children's vulnerability. Silva and Pugh say in fact that 'parenthood imparts a sense of being constantly under the gaze of another, namely their child' (2010, 619). Adam's disapprobation is clear in the following exchange.

Interviewer: Coming back to food again are there any foods that you think you shouldn't eat and are there any particular times when you think 'I probably shouldn't have this'?
Adam: Chocolate and not in the mornings.
Deidre: Why?
Adam: Because it's
Deidre: I like chocolate and chips.
Adam: No, but it's not
Deidre: Why not have that in the morning?
Adam: Because it's early in the morning and
Deidre: At least I'm eating breakfast.
Adam: Yeah but it's an unhealthy breakfast.

In our *Consuming Families* study, parents (usually mothers) had the power to select and purchase particular foods, to stock cupboards and cook particular meals depending on access to money and availability of fresh food in their local area (Lindsay et al 2012). While parents may no longer have cultural backing to enforce children's consumption of particular foods, mothers in particular worked on children's food preferences seeking a healthy diet for their children. Remarkably some 18—20-year-old children, as in the George family, were still having their diets actively managed by their parents.

But parental power was tempered by the food preferences of different family members, the need to 'keep everyone happy' and the prospect of complaints by family members or food refusal. Parents reported making purchasing and cooking decisions based on what they knew children would eat, as in the Dawson family where one of the daughter's vegetarianism influenced family dinners (see also Valentine 1999). While children and young people had little direct autonomy to choose and purchase foods for themselves, parents responded to children's preferences and demands in creating family diets. Conflicts and complaints shaped shopping and family eating habits. Some children were critical of family food choices; some explicit statements about healthy food (and unhealthy food) sometimes emanated from children. These tensions and contradictions make clear the 'multi-directional' flows (Ekström 2010) in family food consumption decisions. But these discussions and negotiations are also part of making family life. Opinions about food, about eating together and what's good to eat are part of family culture and communication. They define and distinguish what is important, what is allowed and what is difficult. Adam and his mother Deidre are doing family work even in their conflict and trouble.

CONCLUSION: FAMILY FOOD DIVERSITY

Images of overweight children act as visual representations of over-resourcing, affluenza, and excessive consumption in our society. Discussions about childhood obesity often draw on fast food, Play stations and cars: symbols of the social and material development beyond subsistence that characterises contemporary 'post-scarcity' societies (Buckingham 2011). Gard and Wright (2005) suggest that 'obesity discourses reveal a particular kind of anxiety about food [as] an undesirable side effect of modern western life' (2005, 539), but the persistent association of children's weight with screen time (Kline 2010a), the use of portable electronic devices and other consumer goods consuming suggest that the anxiety conflates food with other troubling patterns of consuming behaviour. Social responses to the body of the obese child may be shaped by collective questions about whether families and mothers in particular are adequately discharging their obligations to manage children's consumption. The public discussions of children's excessive flesh and mothers' insufficient care reveal childhood obesity to be more than simply a 'health' issue. This is an important contemporary site for the airing of fears about women's aspirations, and the social changes they entail. It is linked to the broader story of families bearing the brunt of consuming forces, as fears that materialism and excess diminish the relational links in the family abound.

But we argue that in discourses of childhood obesity particularly, a wider and more generous account of family food consumption is necessary. The negotiation of healthy and appropriate food and the actual feeding of children entails addressing basic needs, responding to the imperatives of taste and culture, engaging with nutrition and health messages, and drawing on ideas about ideal bodies and good food all at once. All of these imperatives and strategies operate at an individual everyday level but are also driven by a deeper desire to ensure optimal health, well-being and longevity in the child. These practices are deeply relational; they are part of the creation and ongoing maintenance of intimate family life. Talking about food preferences is part of recognising and accounting for family differences. Compromising on food choices to accommodate likes and dislikes is nurturing. Conflicts and disagreements over food are part of the interconnection of family life (Curtis et al 2009). Negotiations of 'special foods' or 'treats' are central in familial expressions of love and care (Gillies 2007; Tubbs et al 2005).

Mothers are agents and actors in the provision of food, but their choices, actions, and practices are circumscribed by gendered roles, economic circumstances and social expectations. Children are active in creating family food practices and in determining how they eat and how their parents eat and feed them. In fact, as Cook (2009b) has identified, families are now responsible for creating competent child consumers, which requires the recognition of individual consuming tastes and preferences. Therefore the 'sanctity of the choosing self' (2009b, 116), and in this instance, the choosing child is paramount. Cook (2009b) has challenged the assumption that families are simply acted upon by childhood obesity that flows from the outside, which is awash with excess sugar, fat and food, urging a more complicated account of how and why families eat as they do, of the role mothers have and of tensions inherent in contemporary family food consumption.

Our two qualitative studies reveal the complexity of family consumption decisions and how and why they are made. Warde asks us to recognise the 'compassionate commingling of domestic labour with foodstuffs as families engage with contemporary time and cost pressures' (1999, 518). Curtis and colleagues (2010) urge greater recognition of the productive and constitutive uses of family food, beyond panic and a fear that family life is being consistently diminished through changing food practices.

> [F]amilial constructions of children's snacking and their other food and eating practices are managed within the ebb and flow of everyday family lives so that, rather than negating the importance of family food and togetherness, they become 'constitutive of [the] inter-generational relations and generational identities' (Curtis et al 2009, 92) through which the idea of 'family' is itself constructed on an ongoing and everyday basis. (Curtis et al 2010, 301)

Family food practices have many layers and meanings. Love, responsibility, resistance and conflict are present in equal measure. Aspirations for health entwine desires that children eat something and that everyone can enjoy food together. Maternal responsibilities intersect with children's refusal and independence in regard to taste and consumption. 'Treat foods' may be moments of respite and pleasure in otherwise difficult days. Rather than rush to judgement about familial failures, we need to be attentive to how food is being used by families (Marshall 2005), and within families by different members to do the work of both belonging and distinction. Family food practices need to recognized as care as well as potential threat.

Food consumption practices create the same individual and communal tensions for families, as do other spheres of consumption such as goods, the disposition of family time or media use in family contexts. Practices of consumption are expressions of individual identity and aspiration, but are also normative (Southerton 2001). Within families, consumption practices reflect communal priorities and care and produce conflicts and dissent. Our reading of family food practices has emphasized the complexity and creativity in family food work. We have looked for the threads of care and connection in family food negotiations that are too often characterized as parents 'giving in' or failing children. In the following chapters, we seek out the constructive aspects of consumption in even more contentious consuming contexts: alcohol and sex.

5 Youth Drinking and Family Alcohol Cultures

In 2008 Sheriden Bowen aged 15 hosted an underage Halloween party at her home in a middle-class Melbourne suburb. She sent out invitations to over 50 people via text and Myspace. Her parents supplied food and soft drink and guests were allowed to bring alcohol. Everyone was drinking. A fight broke out with gate-crashers and Justin Gallagan a 16-year-old was punched on the left side of the jaw, fell to the ground and hit the back of his head. He regained consciousness and was taken home by friends. He was placed in a chair to sleep and was found on the floor by his mother the next morning and he died the following day after unsuccessful surgery to relieve the swelling of his brain. Christine Bowen, the mother hosting the party, heard about a boy being hurt but did not know who it was and faced the 'sickening dilemma' of whether to ring the parents of boys who did attend the party at 2 a.m. and ask them to check their sons. She decided not to call because this would cause a 'state of terror' among parents (Russell 2012).

How should we interpret this example of a teen party gone wrong? There is no doubt that this example of unregulated alcohol consumption and consequent violence and death intensifies an established public anxiety about teenage binge drinking. How do we understand the Bowen decision to allow alcohol at a party for young people? How should young people be initiated into consuming this 'adult' substance and what responsibilities should families take for teen drinking? The case also raises questions about the diversity of family approaches to alcohol. If there was more community support for teen abstinence could the party have been alcohol free? Alternatively if all parents understood and accepted that their children would be drinking could the mother have called them in the early hours of the morning without fearing negative repercussions? As with all of the consumables we address in this book we feel it is valuable to look beyond the public panic and tendency to blame young people or their parents. We explore the diverse family negotiations and approaches to young people's alcohol consumption in an effort to understand how families are managing the difficult terrains of teen drinking and engendering responsible alcohol consumption.

Alcohol permeates the social lives of the majority of adults in advanced western countries but also causes great harm in terms of chronic disease, dependence and accidents (Babor et al 2010). For young people, drinking is primarily about pleasure, social belonging and a symbol of maturity. The legal age of drinking—18 in Anglophile countries and 21 in the US—and the wide consumption of alcohol by the adult population, means that consuming alcohol has inevitably become a marker of adulthood.

In this chapter we explore how family alcohol cultures are negotiated and how young people learn to manage their consumption as they seek pleasure and sociality with friends and family. Underage access to drinking is a contentious issue for families to negotiate and consuming practices in both public spaces and in family homes are fraught. As most alcohol research is framed by public health approaches and therefore focuses on the risk and harms caused by consumption, there is limited information on the ways in which families are constituted by alcohol consumption. It is difficult to reconcile everyday consumption practices with public health warnings and see how drinking, a taken for granted part of everyday life and celebration in many families, can be understood as creative as well as toxic in family life. We draw here on diverse sources including our own studies to open up the dilemmas families face and reveal at least in part, how and why diverse family alcohol cultures are being created. We move beyond the paradigm of regulation, and 'failures' around teen drinking, to consider how this difficult consumable is woven into everyday family experiences. In the first section of the chapter, we consider the new external regulatory frameworks for alcohol that families are facing as they negotiate alcohol in their family homes and lives.

NEW ALCOHOL STORIES FOR FAMILIES AND THE STATE

There is a dynamic relationship between the alcohol market, State regulation and family life. In recent decades in many Western countries the State has retreated and relaxed liquor licensing laws to allow for urban renewal and the development of night-time economies. This has created new opportunities for the intersections of sociality and alcohol. Many young people now actively participate in socialising in the new leisure spaces created in city centres. Demographic and labour market change has contributed to an extension of the 'youth' life stage as it has become harder for young people to enter the full-time labour market. Most spend a longer time in education, which requires living within the parental home for longer and life stage transitions such as partnering and childbearing occur later in life (Furlong and Cartmel 2007; Heinz 2009; White and Wyn 2008). The 'student/worker' group is steadily growing as increasing numbers of young people combine tertiary education with flexible paid work (White and Wyn 2008). Those who are better off or live at home with their families, have fewer responsibilities and more disposable income to spend on recreation and going out drinking than previous generations of young people (Chatterton and Hollands 2001).

The provision of alcohol has always involved big business. In the UK large, corporate venue operators have transformed drinking from a community-based activity to a profit driven lifestyle activity as companies compete for the youth leisure dollar (Chatterton and Hollands 2001). In many Anglophile cities around the world, café style drinking has developed (Chatterton and Hollands 2001) and venues are able to stay open for long hours. Patrons are no longer required to purchase food when drinking alcohol in cafes or other venues (Lindsay 2005b). Alcohol companies enthusiastically target young people with new products and brands designed especially for them. 'Designer drinks' such as alcoholic lemonades and strong ciders have high alcohol by volume, softer tastes and use advertising images that young people identify with (Brain et al 2000). These drinks have become very popular with very young drinkers (aged 13–16) and young female drinkers in particular (Brain et al 2000). Public drinking spaces were traditionally male dominated and women were largely excluded from them. Now women's consumption is encouraged by more diverse drinking spaces, higher levels of customer service and in the provision of broader range of alcohol products (Chatterton and Hollands 2001; Lindsay 2005b). This feminisation of contemporary nightlife and heavy drinking has heightened public concern about teen drinking and the figure of the heavy drinking, sexually provocative and available 'ladette' from the UK context has become a kind of 'folk devil' in the public panic about alcohol (Dobson 2012; Henley 2011).

At the same time there has been a remarkable domestication of alcohol consumption that occurred alongside the development of the night-time economy (Valentine et al 2010a), though this has received much less public attention and concern. Alcohol is now cheap and accessible and this has supported the domestication of drinking. More alcohol being is being consumed in suburban houses than in pubs or clubs. In the UK for example, more alcohol is sold through liquor outlets than public drinking premises and women in particular identify the supermarket as their preferred local liquor outlet (Valentine et al 2010a). Children in families are clearly exposed up close and personal to their parents and older siblings drinking. Young people themselves are also consuming alcohol in family homes. 'Pre-drinking' at home before going out to socialise, thus minimizing cost at venues has become common practice. Yet families are mobilised in alcohol discussions mostly in relation to the control of young people in the night-time economy and in fears about controlling youth binge drinking. The transitions to adulthood in which alcohol is seen as important are not fully accounted for in contemporary drinking discussions and the consequent parental responsibilities. In the following section we examine how young people talk and feel about their alcohol consumption before turning to family responses and reactions to teen drinking. We aim to illuminate the consuming tensions embedded in the contemporary regulatory context in which families try to negotiate safe and acceptable drinking with their teenage children.

DRINKING OUTSIDE THE FAMILY: THE NIGHTCLUB AS A RITE OF PASSAGE

In many parts of the world consuming alcohol is seen by teenagers as a symbol of adulthood (Sulkunen 2009) and a way of creating symbolic capital, displaying maturity, making friends and enhancing their popularity (Hoel et al 2004; Jarvinen and Gundelach 2007). In the West consuming alcohol is normalised and acts as a central component of social life. Young people emphasise alcohol's pivotal role in socialising—'in facilitating conversation, enhancing pleasurable activities, increasing confidence (particularly when interacting with members of the opposite gender) and creating a friendly atmosphere' (Grace et al 2009, 23). By contrast choosing not to drink can lead to social exclusion (Jarvinen and Gundelach 2007).

It is frequently argued that drinking alcohol is a 'rite of passage' but analysis rarely goes beyond this brief statement. Jeremy Northcote's ethnography of the Perth nightclub scene in Australia is an exception. He provides a compelling argument that nightclubs provide a transitional context for young people to experiment with adult identities.

> Nightclubs are viewed by young adults as establishments where the roles of adulthood can be enacted in a socially sanctioned manner, and in this respect clubbing can be understood as a means of assisting them to bridge the divide between the structural roles of childhood and adulthood. (Northcote 2006, 6)

Northcote describes the complex social processes occurring within nightclubs. On the one hand there is the characteristic 'carefree, hedonistic excitement of youth and popular culture' and the opportunity to 'party like there is no tomorrow' (Northcote 2006). On the other hand there is the anxiety-producing task of impression management to look confident in a large crowd of strangers and venture on to the dance floor. According to Northcote 'the importance of expressing to onlookers and fellow dancers that one is a free and sensual (even sexual) being can be an essential component of affirming an independent, adult status' (Northcote 2006,10). In this context, alcohol, drugs and cigarettes are used to alleviate self-consciousness and insecurity.

Meeting people for possible romantic and/or sexual relationships is a common aim of young people attending nightclubs. In the *Alcohol Consumption Contexts* project socialising with friends and the opportunity to meet others from similar backgrounds were the main attractions. Peter described an inner city club as follows.

Peter: Yeah, it's just the vibe really, yeah.
Interviewer: Yeah?
Peter: You just have a few drinks and then the music starts and you sort of get into the mood and you just dance and have a few more drinks and you're looking at the chicks. And when you see people that you know that you didn't go there with and you start talking to them and you talk to other guys. You just talk to everyone.
Interviewer: Yeah. [laughing]
Peter: And it's just yeah, like a friendly environment. There's no like real heroes and all that sort of stuff. Everyone is pretty cool and they're there for a good time, so yeah. (Lindsay 2006, 45)

Similar comments were made by Michelle, who enjoyed the friendly crowd and easy interactions between women and men at her favourite nightclub.

Michelle: Yeah. Just we know a lot of people there, so you get to know a few people, and we keep going back. We just go there to dance mainly. So, socialise.
Interviewer: That's good and is it because the Planet has a few dance floors and various areas?
Michelle: Yeah, a lot of rooms and everything. You just walk around and you meet new people, too. People try and pick you up on the way around.
Interviewer: Yeah. [laughing]
Michelle: It's fun. Meeting new friends. (Lindsay 2006, 52)

Drinking alcohol for these young people is intertwined with growing up and engaging in the rituals of contemporary courtship. For many young people meeting romantic, sexual or potential life partners occurs in public drinking spaces such as the nightclubs. Yet this complicated and seemingly benign account of young people drinking sits in direct contrast to the dominant narrative of excessive teen drinking and a damaging 'culture of intoxication' across contemporary Western countries. This 'panic' defines the alcohol culture parents and young people are working in as they try to manage consumption practices in the 21st century.

THE PANIC ABOUT YOUNG PEOPLE AND 'DETERMINED DRUNKENNESS'

There is nothing particularly new about young people getting drunk but there is evidence, and a strong community understanding, that alcohol is now the drug of choice and young people are being socialised into a more intense culture of intoxication (Measham and Brain 2005). Such assessments are linked to wider fears of excess consumption in the West. Prominent UK researchers such as Fiona Measham and Howard Parker have argued that alcohol and illicit drug taking should be understood as interlinked and as reflective of more general cultures of hedonistic consumption (Measham and Brain 2005; Parker 2005). These researchers argue that 'determined drunkenness' is a new mode of socialising and escape in our contemporary consumer society. By the turn of the century in the UK and elsewhere the use of 'party drugs' declined and binge drinking became the new substance of choice (Measham 2004). This UK research has been echoed in research on young people in European countries.

Although national differences in approaches to alcohol remain, there is evidence that contemporary young people drink more heavily and have a clearer focus on drunkenness as a desired outcome than previous generations (Jarvinen and Room 2007). Young people highly value the bodily, psychological and social pleasure alcohol consumption provides (Szmigin et al 2007). In the *Drinking Biographies* study, alcohol was seen as effective in changing both mood, social interaction and to some extent, personality (Lindsay et al 2009). Alcohol was used as a 'social lubricant' to enhance sociality and confidence. Young people enjoyed the 'social togetherness' enabled by drinking and the positive effect alcohol had on their social skills and confidence. It gave them 'courage to talk to people', 'confidence', it made them feel 'less inhibited' or 'affectionate' and enabled 'fun' with friends' (Lindsay et al 2009, 375). Most of the young people in *Drinking Biographies* talked about the positive physical effects of drinking although these were sometimes contradictory—some used alcohol to energise themselves while others used it to relax (Lindsay et al 2009). Many described the positive effects that alcohol had on their mood, linking alcohol to happiness. Nick and Ying both said that alcohol made them happy and Hugh said alcohol provides the 'laughs'. Others spoke about alcohol making them or allowing them to feel 'giddy', 'silly', 'tipsy', 'warm' or 'fuzzy'. For these young people drinking was a positive and pleasurable bodily experience at once making them more like themselves by enhancing sociality and confidence but also making them less like themselves by offering a release from the usual constraints of everyday life (Lindsay et al 2009). Other research has confirmed that young people see drinking as 'stress relief' and a pleasurable release from everyday activities a facilitator of social interaction and belonging (de Crespigny et al 1999; Grace et al 2009).

It is worth noting that in Australia the evidence about the danger posed by the 'culture of intoxication' is paradoxical—some harms are on the rise but overall youth drinking rates have remained steady for the last few decades (Livingston and Room 2009; Livingston 2008). The increasing numbers of young people ending up in accident and emergency departments of hospitals is potentially linked to an increased emphasis on intoxication. Drinking shots of spirits ensuring a rapid path to intoxication has become common practice for some groups of young people (de Crespigny et al 1999; Grace et al 2009; Lindsay 2006). The image of young people intentionally and determinedly getting drunk on nights out has become an accepted framework to which families are called to respond.

Although young people increasingly pursue hedonistic consumption and intoxication they do also actively pursue their own strategies to manage their consumption and the negative outcomes and harms associated with drinking (de Crespigny et al 1999; Grace et al 2009; Lindsay et al 2009). To manage the negative and enhance the positive outcomes young people actively stage their alcohol consumption, when and in what circumstances they will get drunk (Lindsay et al 2009). They consciously 'control' and 'de-control' their consumption and make on-going decisions about their drinking as they time, balance and coordinate their consumption with their friends in particular locations. As Measham (2006) has argued from the UK context, young people are engaging in 'controlled loss of control' when they drink to excess (Measham 2006). Similarly, Szmigin et al (2007) have argued that 'calculated hedonism' is a useful description of youth drinking in the UK.

How are parents and families managing the culture of intoxication perceived to be defining youth drinking outside the home? 'Pre-drinking' or drinking shots of spirits or other alcohol at home before going out to public venues, for example, has become common practice. The purpose of this consumption practice is to meet and drink at a private home to ensure intoxication, save money and create the 'right mood' before going out to licensed venues (Grace et al 2009, 25). But there is little direct insight into how families negotiate such pre-drinking in the family home. Some parents do view the youthful focus on rapid intoxication and determined drunkenness as quite different to their own drinking styles as young people. As one mother in a UK study says:

> What worries me is that they go out to get drunk . . . That's what they do, they don't go out to drink socially and then end up drunk, that's the main cause to go out . . . so that does worry me and I do think they drink such a lot, this binge drinking . . . It's not a little amount, it's every weekend and it's excess isn't it . . . it's definitely more than when we were young (Valentine et al 2010a, 921).

In the face of parental uncertainty and ambivalence about what drinking is safe and about how to achieve good family alcohol approaches, the regulatory context and the changing requirements for parents are particularly important. In the next section of this chapter, we examine the new regulatory schemas governing youth drinking and how families are positioned in relation to controlling consumption. These wider contexts shape family negotiations, conflicts and efforts to achieve good outcomes.

PUTTING THE FAMILY TO WORK TO MANAGE YOUTH DRINKING

Public health prescriptions calling on families to manage the alcohol consumption of young people have become increasingly commonplace across Western countries. A brief comparison of Australia and the UK is useful for illustrating the interactions of, and dynamic tensions between, consuming families and the state over 'good' consumption of this commodity. Australia has recently tightened its legal controls over underage drinkers and tightened consumption recommendations in comparison to the UK. An increased emphasis on abstinence and prohibition on alcohol consumption is observable in policy at both national and state levels in Australia. In 2009 there was a re-orienting of the alcohol guidelines by the Australian government (NHMRC 2009). This re-orientation redefined 'risky' drinking. Risky drinking was previously more than four drinks in a session for men and more than two drinks per session for women; the new guideline proscribes more than two drinks for women and men. Adolescent well-being was a particular focus and these NHMRC guidelines now specifically promote abstinence from alcohol consumption by those under the age of 18 (NHMRC 2009).

Although both Australia and the UK cite 18 as their legal age of drinking, they have different laws regarding underage consumption. In Australia it is illegal for those under 18 to purchase alcohol or drink alcohol in a public space while in the UK it is legal for 16–17 year olds to consume alcohol in a public venue if an adult accompanies them. In many states of Australia, there are secondary supply laws where it is illegal for adults to supply alcohol to young people without permission from their parents or guardians. This type of law was introduced in Victoria in 2011 and would make the provision of alcohol at the Bowen's Halloween party described at the beginning of the chapter illegal. In the UK there is no such law though it is illegal to provide alcohol to children less than 5 years of age. Australia has recently strengthened health advice about the adverse effects young people drinking and the UK has introduced such advice for the first time (Valentine et al 2012). It is worth observing though that the tone and content of this advice is quite different in each country.

Advice from the UK Government (DirectGov 2012) is relatively gentle, and more directly in line with contemporary modes of negotiated parenting. The website states 'It's difficult to know when to let teenagers drink' as there is no 'right' age' and suggests a series of tips for negotiating with teenagers including 'set clear boundaries for your child and be consistent about them', 'encourage your child to stick to lower-strength brands and not to drink too quickly', 'try not to overreact if your child drinks against your wishes, or drinks too much' and 'if your child has drunk excessively, explain how you feel and encourage them to talk about why it happened' (DirectGov 2012).

Advice from the Australian Government covers similar ground but affects a more strident tone emphasising the high-risk nature of consumption and the need for detailed communication with teenagers about alcohol related risks such as drink-spiking and young people collapsing. Tips from the Australian government website include, 'explain the risks of alcohol and focus on the immediate harmful effects of intoxication' and 'discuss family rules about drinking alcohol'. While there are gestures towards more democratic and collaborative family discussions, such as 'Most young people expect and appreciate some ground rules. . . . If teenagers are allowed to drink alcohol, set limits about how much, how often and the type of alcohol. . . . Allow teenagers to take part in setting the rules as this encourages them to take more responsibility for their actions', the emphasis and expectation is clearly that parents actively manage teen consumption. 'Once you agree on rules enforce them, but talk about "withdrawing privileges" not "punishment"'. The website also calls on parents to 'Discuss the laws in your State or Territory about alcohol possession and consumption'. (Australian Government 2012)

In the Australian guidelines, there are clear tensions in expectations of parental responses to teen drinking. Collaborative and democratic parenting is partly valourised. The development of consuming competencies in relation to this difficult substance is encouraged:

> Discuss what they can do to reduce harm—eating food, drinking slowly, using mobile phones to check in with parents, making arrangements to get home safely, and having a buddy system with a friend. (Australian Government 2012)

But the regulatory paradigm—where parents act as agents of the state and work to prohibit drinking—dominates the advice. Although there are acknowledgements that many young people begin drinking before the legal age, this is couched in terms of troubling new patterns of youth excess consumption.

The emphasis on prohibition for young people under 18 in Australia and under 15 in the UK does not mesh with the 'common-sense' teaching young people to drink at home approach taken by many parents (Jayne et al 2011). While public health interventions on underage drinking promote abstinence, this approach stands in stark contrast to the everyday tensions that families manage on alcohol use and common beliefs and practices in the West (NHMRC 2009; Valentine et al 2010b). For example in the US where at 21 the legal age of drinking is the oldest, the majority of children under 12 years of age have tasted alcohol. This 'sipping' of alcohol usually occurs under parental supervision in the family context (Ward et al 2010). In Australia the average age of drinking a full serve of alcohol is 14.5 and over half of teenagers aged 14–16 had an alcoholic drink in the last month (Ward and Snow 2011). In the UK the average of first drink is lower again at 11 years old (Valentine et al 2012). There is some evidence that the age of beginning alcohol consumption has been getting lower with successive generations (Roche et al 2008; Valentine et al 2012), an example perhaps of 'age compression' (Buckingham 2011) or children getting older younger that undergirds most of the consumption panics we discuss in this book.

The contradictions between the public health messages, the panics about youth bingeing and family practices are evident. They are often read as parental failures in their responsibilities to drink responsibly and to ensure that children in their care do the same. But families are facing complicated and difficult tasks in managing alcohol and teen transitions, as they always have. Messages of prohibition and control oversimplify the role of alcohol in families and the complexities of contemporary family life (Jayne et al 2011). They may obscure our capacity to see how hard families are trying, often in quite different ways, to get the regulation of alcohol right in their homes. It is possible that the new emphasis on abstinence may even work against parents' efforts to minimise harm and socialise their teenagers into moderate consumption. One young man in the *Drinking Biographies* study described how when he was at high school it was common practice for party invitations to indicate a drinking limit of two drinks at the bottom of the invitation. This suggested a consensus had been negotiated among parents that they would supervise moderate drinking by older teens at the parties they hosted. Further anecdotal evidence comes from a local government youth network meeting in Melbourne that confirmed the practice of parents supervising consumption at underage parties following school events was relatively widespread till very recently. Now that new liquor supply laws have been introduced in Victoria, Australia the practice of stating acceptable drinking limits on invitations has been curtailed and many schools have banned 'after' parties. For the families in our *Drinking Biographies* and *Consuming Families* studies, these changing regulatory paradigms in tension with everyday family practices are the landscape in which they negotiate the consumption of alcohol.

David Morgan says:

> [F]amily actors are looking in two directions. The one is to the business at hand the everyday . . . while the other is towards more public discursive constructions of mothers, fathers or parents. (2011a, 69)

The requirement for parents to look in two directions, toward the child to be cared for and their child's desire to belong in their peer networks and towards the noisy and panicked public discussions of teen alcohol abuse as they negotiate alcohol with young people is clear. The tensions and conflicts in such complicated negotiations cannot be understated. In the following sections, we examine how contemporary discussions about 'good' drinking practices invite families to manage and respond to teenage drinking. We look at variable family practices, tried by parents and assessed by teens, to see how the everyday regulation of this contentious substance is experienced in family life.

FAMILIES MANAGING THE INTRODUCTION OF ALCOHOL

When it comes to alcohol consumption family strategies and the processes of bargaining and negotiation parents engage in with teenagers have not been fully documented. Yet we know that parents are major suppliers of alcohol to teenagers. Children's consumption is dependent on and embedded in social relationships with parents as well as peers and parents often act as gatekeepers or facilitators of purchasing through a process of negotiation or bargaining (Buckingham 2011). For young people without an independent income it is likely that the consumption of alcohol is also embedded in family relationships and subject to substantial negotiation and bargaining. An Australian study of parents of 14- 16 year old teenagers found that parents were more likely to supply alcohol to their children if they believed they were drinking alcohol already and if they were monitoring their children's alcohol consumption (Ward and Snow 2011).

There is a significant body of quantitative research that offers some insights into the impact of family variables on youth drinking patterns. Parents have been found to be influential on youth drinking; teenagers are less likely to drink if their parents disapprove of drinking, if parents set house rules about drinking, if teenagers have effective parental support to abstain and if there is parental monitoring to reduce the likelihood of drinking (Barnes et al 2006; Jackson et al 1999; Kelly et al 2011; Kloep et al 2001; van der Vorst et al 2006). There is also some quantitative evidence that higher quality relationships within the family are associated with less alcohol consumption (Kelly et al 2011). In some of these studies, family variables had a weaker relationship to consumption than peer drinking variables (Bahr et al 2005; Kelly et al 2011). Children's attitudes toward drinking and intentions to drink *are* shaped by their parents' patterns of consumption (Ward et al 2010). One New Zealand study found that preschoolers whose parents were regular drinkers could identify different types of beverages by smell (Noll et al 1990). In a UK study most children aged 5–12 could also recognise different types and brands of drinks that their parents or relatives drank (Valentine et al 2012). These examples illustrate that children are keen observers of both their parents' consumption practices and wider familial alcohol approaches. But these predictive analyses of what impacts families might have on teen drinking and its outcomes do not capture the complexities of negotiation, discussion and even conflict in family life.

There are few qualitative studies available on family processes of negotiating, allowing or supervising teenagers' alcohol consumption. Notable exceptions are the recent studies by British geographers Valentine, Jayne and colleagues (Jayne et al 2011; Valentine et al 2012; Valentine et al 2010b). Their work demonstrates the tensions and contradictions that parents experience in transmitting safe drinking practices and creating acceptable alcohol cultures within their families. They found that parents were happy to 'introduce children to the pleasures and dangers of alcohol' in the home which they perceived to be a safe environment (Jayne et al 2011a, 1). According to their survey data when parents reflected on their own induction into drinking and changing family drinking patterns across generations most parents felt that the range and amount that parents drank at home had increased, that the amount that mothers drank had increased and the amount of alcohol that parents drink in one session had also increased (Jayne et al 2011a). Parents clearly felt unsettled and impacted by contemporary cultures of intoxication and fears about their own excess consumption.

But their quantitative and qualitative data produced some quite contradictory findings about how these fears were managed and expressed in family life. In the survey most parents claimed that children should be in their mid-teens before experimenting with alcohol and 75% indicated their children had never tasted alcohol. In the qualitative study, however, the majority of the children (aged 5–12) had been offered or tried alcohol at home or at a family event. This perhaps reflects the complexity of negotiating consumption in families and the tensions between ideals that good parents restrict their children's drinking, and the more permissive outcomes of everyday negotiations on the ground. The authors reflect on changing discourses around parenting and the expressed desire by parents to have more open, 'closer' and less hierarchical relationships with their children (Jayne et al 2011a). As one of the mothers in the study explained;

> I want to be more relaxed with my children. Because I think . . . I mean there are loads of things I didn't tell my mum when I was growing up, loads of things which I wished I could, and I wouldn't want my children to feel that way, which is why I think I want to be more open and more relaxed . . . I want them to be honest. (Jayne et al 2011a, 5)

In this statement, contemporary aspirations for more collaborative and democratic parenting can be seen, an approach supported in part by public health guidelines that emphasise discussion and education. Rather than critically identifying the gap between the desire to restrict alcohol intake for teens and family actual practices of introduction, it is worthwhile seeking to understand what underpins family drinking practices and what parents are hoping to achieve as they negotiate this contentious form of youth consumption. We have found that there are a variety of family approaches to introducing children to alcohol. At one end of the continuum is the supervised introduction to drinking where parents purchase limited amounts of alcohol for teens. Sarah, a participant in the *Drinking Biographies* study, recalls this approach and sees it as a successful harm minimisation strategy for her.

Sarah: When I was young I sort of—15 or 16—if I wanted to have a drink they'd let me have some vodka and lemonade or something. It would be like a finger of it, but they let me have a little bit and always let me try their wine, which usually I didn't like, but they always let me try it. [. . .] When I went to parties in high school my parents would buy me alcohol, but they'd only let me take two bottles. They knew that I was going to drink but they set the amount, so they felt comfortable with what I was drinking. Which I think was a good system, rather than just saying you can go to the party but we're not buying you alcohol, in which case I probably would have had—you know, friends would have given it to me, or whoever's hosting the party would have had mixer drinks and I would have just drunk that instead.

When I had mine I was quite happy to drink my bottle of Strongbow, or whatever, and stop when I had finished. I think they set a good example with—except for one friend's parent, I never saw my parents drunk, so I think they set a good example in that sense.

Sarah's family accepts teens will drink, appears to facilitate teen drinking by purchasing alcohol, but Sarah's parents are hoping this practice will support Sarah's longer term safe drinking and her development as a competent consumer. Her consumption is actively negotiated with her parents. In Sarah's case, the outcome worked for her and she did not go beyond the limits set by her parents. At the other end of the continuum are family approaches that limit underage consumption and promote abstinence. These approaches follow the law and are supported by public health and government guidelines. Alex's parents followed a restrictive consumption approach.

Alex: To be honest, my parents—my mother particularly kind of demonised alcohol, and that was really not something that sat well with me. She was very much no 'We're not giving you alcohol until you're 18', which while I understand is trying to do the right thing, but felt like the least useful way to go about it. [. . .] My parents were pretty restrictive on most things, and I think rather than that having developed a positive alcohol culture that says, 'There's nothing wrong with alcohol but you need to be responsible with it', it's actually said that—both that 'Alcohol is the devil' and 'it's something that doesn't actually need to be respected', because you've got to that point now [you are 18] and

> now you're free to do whatever you like, rather than actually having gone all the way along with 'This is a thing and this is how it works and this is what you need to do to be respectful of it and respectful of other people'. Great parenting. [. . .] It was really tough to be out with people and say 'no, I can't drink because my mum won't let me', rather than actually be able to say, as I can now,' no, I'm not drinking because I don't want to'.

Alex feels his parents took the wrong approach, which left him unprepared to negotiate his consumption and hampered his social life. The abstinence approach Alex's parents took is supported by laws restricting underage purchasing and reflects recent public health assessments of the very significant harms consequent upon teen drinking. He is deeply critical of his parents' excessive regulation prior to 18. Alex considers his consuming competencies were delayed and diminished by that approach. Alex's comment offers a valuable insight into the complexity of individual and collective practices as they emerge in family contexts. Alex, in the end, does feel able to make safe choices about alcohol, but this capacity was produced in adversity and conflict with his parents, rather than through direct negotiation as Sarah experienced.

In our view, the abstinence and supervised introduction approaches use different logics but can both be seen as protective family consumption strategies. The abstinence approach sends a strong message that alcohol is not condoned, as many teens have limited access to money apart from their parents, supply may be effectively limited. The supervised introduction approach may also be effective through sending a strong message that responsible drinking is has a limit and that limited amount is set by the parents. Alternatively teens may resist their parents' alcohol management strategies and drink whatever alcohol they can get their hands on from whatever source or come to their own conclusions about regulating their intake. Parental strategies are variable and will have variable effects.

It is clear that the pursuit of more honest and open parenting shapes contemporary family negotiations about consumption; this way of doing parenting and family is relevant to all of the domains we discuss in this book. It is especially challenging for parents when difficult substances such as alcohol (and sex the focus in our next chapter) are being consumed. Parents weighed the fear of permissiveness in allowing drinking and the possibilities of protecting through abstinence in their approaches to family drinking. There was no single or simple way but many do see active supervision of young people's drinking at home as safe and preferable to the risks young people faced consuming alcohol to excess in town centres. As one father in the UK study described;

> I'd rather do it that way [allowing his son and friends to drink in his home], then I know what he's doing and then hope that by doing that, it

> will open a link of trust between us both . . . once they're out the front door, you're not going to know until you get a knock on the door from the Police or whatever, saying 'He's been found drunk'. You know, I'd be quite happy to supervise him. (Jayne et al 2011a, 6)

Valentine and colleagues (2012) argue that the social distance between adults and children is being reduced so that children are allowed to observe the adult practices of their parents and are invited to engage in adult practices, such as trying alcohol. Now that alcohol has become increasingly domesticated, drunk by women and men in the home, the family has become a primary site for socialising drinking behaviour in young people (Valentine et al 2012). As Myles a father explained 'the kids know that if you're going to be criticising them you're a hypocrite . . . it's not a secret from my children that I've drunk to excess' (Valentine et al 2010a, 923).

Most parents model alcohol consumption practices to their children though they make distinctions about what kinds of drinking is displayed. The majority of parents felt that it was acceptable to drink in moderation in front of their children and have a drink with a meal. Indeed many of the parents described their own drinking at home as a form of relaxation that could be undertaken in the domestic space without the need to organise childcare or go to much effort. One of the mothers described how alcohol was a part of familial life:

> It's a family treat, a meal, a celebration . . . I can certainly picture him [son] in the right environment having a beer with us or certainly by the time he's 16. (Valentine et al 2012, 784)

In this study the children were well aware that alcohol played an integral part in family hospitality and how friends and family bring alcohol to their home when visiting and vice versa (Valentine et al 2012). Although most of the parents restricted their children's exposure to public drinking, children were sometimes unintentionally exposed to their parents heavy drinking and drunkenness, particularly during parties or family holidays (Valentine et al 2012).

Understandably parents who drink more tend to be more permissive about alcohol consumption by their children and children fetching and pouring alcohol. Some families allowed and encouraged children to imitate adult drinking rituals.

> These included giving children non-alcoholic cocktails modelled on their parents' alcoholic drinks, teaching children how to drink shots of water, and asking children to serve alcohol at home. In such ways, parents' desire to create open, democratic, familial relationships means that children develop an intimate knowledge of adult life. (Valentine et al 2012, 787)

Interestingly parents also unintentionally used soft drinks to model their views on alcohol. In many of the families in Valentine et al's (2012) study soft drinks were regarded as bad for children's health- bad for their teeth and leading to hyperactive behaviour. Children we allowed to have soft drink on special occasions or as reward for good behaviour. This paralleled the ways in which alcohol was regarded for adults as potentially bad for their health and leading to 'abnormal behaviour'. A 'reverse morality of drinking' was constructed in families where good behaviour is rewarded with a drink that could be potentially bad for health (Valentine et al 2012, 787).

Our own research suggests that there is no consensus on how alcohol consumption should be managed within families. We found a variety of approaches to introducing children to alcohol. The Dawson family in our *Consuming Families* study for example have three teenage children and prohibit alcohol consumption while their children are under the age of 18.

Liam: In terms of attitude we definitely are responsible drinkers and we've been really tough on the kids from an alcohol perspective. Our line has been you don't drink until you're 18. [. . .] We've never condoned drinking so if the kids have gone to a party and they've had a drink well, we can't stop that but we don't give the kids alcohol . . .

Sue: We never supply it.

Liam: . . . for them to go to a party and we've always said to them 'we don't want you to drink.'

Sue: And we've almost always made them come home from a party too, so we follow through on it and make sure that they're not in someone else's care and getting drunk.

Yet they feel social pressure when they are compared to more permis sive parents.

Interviewer: You were saying that you never supply the kids with alcohol; do you know any families who do this and have a different attitude?

Liam: Yeah.

Sue: Yes, it's a real challenge because so many parents do and from the age of 15 or 16. It makes it tough for the families that want to do the right thing.

The 18-year-old daughter in this family confirms her families approach to underage drinking but also their more open negotiating approach now she is at the legal drinking age.

Meredith: I guess because my brother's 17 and he's turning 18 in three months so there's always that discussion on whether he's allowed to drink or not. Obviously my parents are firm on the idea that you don't drink until you're 18 and other families have different ideas to that. Alcohol we talk about a fair bit and even I still talk to my parents about alcohol these days, just about how much you should drink and 'don't drink as much tonight because you haven't been feeling well'. My parents still talk to me like that and 'make sure you don't have too much because you have to come home' or if I'm going to the city they don't like me drinking as much because you're in the middle of the city and it's quite far out. We're always talking about 'having your senses when you're drinking' and 'having your wits about you' and things so we still talk about that.

By contrast the 18-year-old son Sam from the Ingles family in the *Consuming Families* study describes a very different family approach to underage alcohol consumption where drinking was allowed and openness about consumption was encouraged. Yet he has also experienced negative judgements from others for drinking while underage at a family function.

Sam: If you've got two parents who have grown up amongst Australian culture I know that there is so much guilt and so much like 'Don't do it', so much prohibition placed around it and it actually pisses me off to a huge extent. I remember one Christmas in particular, I was 16 years old and it was Boxing Day. I was having a few drinks with family and my brother's, now wife's, family was there [. . .] I remember getting absolutely just destroyed, being told [that] I shouldn't be drinking, I shouldn't be doing this. I'm just like 'Get out of my life, you're not my family'—in fact at that point they weren't even married then—'Why should you have the right to be telling me what I can and can't do?' I've grown up in a place where it's a choice, where it's something that shouldn't be so much prohibited.

Sam feels strongly that secrecy about underage alcohol consumption is problematic for managing negative drinking outcomes.

Sam: Amongst certain friends, there would be times where we couldn't tell their parents we'd been drinking or if we'd told their parents we'd been drinking they would have many negative repercussions. Until they turned 18, that would be the point where you could actually talk about it, sort of the proper, legal age, but

> apart from that you couldn't discuss it at all and it was actually quite sad because you go out some nights and have friends that would get absolutely legless and you can't bring them home, you have to take them back with you and you can't tell their parents, you've got to nurse them back to health. It's actually ridiculous, especially when growing up during year 12.

Sam sees the abstinence approach as linked to Anglo-Australian culture which he contrasts with 'European' approaches to induction to alcohol.

The available research therefore presents us with a complex and heterogeneous picture of family alcohol cultures. Families are making considerable efforts to manage and assist their children to be safe in relation to alcohol. Yet, the best way to achieve good consumption is not clear and families differ in how they approach the difficult task of transitioning to safe consumption through the tumultuous teen years. In the following section, we describe the complex social patterning of drinking within families according to gender and life stage.

THE AMBIGUOUS PLACE OF ALCOHOL IN FAMILY LIFE

Alcohol occupies an ambiguous role in families; it is both inside and outside, both embedded in and independent of the family. For parents and other adults, drinking is increasingly embedded in everyday family life. In contrast to previous generations adults, both fathers and mothers, are now likely to drink at home. Alcohol is now a highly visible part of everyday family celebrations. Yet drinking is also an independent activity for young people—consumption is conducted outside the home with friends at parties, in public spaces or in the night-time economy and kept secret from parents.

Though there is some evidence of convergence in the consumption of alcohol by young women and men gender differences continue to shape drinking preferences, risk of harm and importantly moral judgement about alcohol consumption for people of all ages (Chatterton and Hollands 2001; Greenfield and Room 1997; Holloway, Valentine and Jayne 2009; Taft 2001). Till the 1980s public drinking spaces were 'coded as male' and respectable women were located primarily in the home and most did not drink (Holloway et al 2009; Room 2010). Men of all ages continue to drink more than women (National Alcohol Strategy 2001). Contemporary young women do however have greater access to night-time socialising than previous generations and young single women without children and domestic responsibilities tend to drink more heavily than others (Banwell et al 1999; Jonas et al 2000). When women have children their socialising patterns change substantially and they reduce their drinking and confine it more to the home than in public venues (Holloway et al 2009). Gender may shape how families seek to manage the consumption of their children with different rules or advice for sons and daughters. For example in the UK, parents continue to feel there are different risks for their daughters and sons posed by public alcohol consumption—daughters were seen as sexually vulnerable and in need of more protection than sons yet sons were perceived to be at risk of violence (Jayne et al 2011).

In addition to gender differences drinking styles are differentiated according to age and life-stage, so family members are likely to drink different types of drinks and at different quantities and frequencies. The general pattern for in Western countries is that most young people begin drinking while underage. Drinking sessions are infrequent but a relatively large quantity is consumed. On reaching the legal age of drinking and through the early 20s young people move to sustained heavy drinking in terms of both frequency and amount consumed. As noted earlier young people these days are often living at home during this life stage. The move into older adulthood involves 'maturing out' into drinking styles which involve more frequent drinking but reduced amounts drunk per session (AIHW 2004; Casswell 2002; Lindsay et al 2009; Roche 2008).

Drinking preferences and drinking locations tend to vary according to the age of drinkers. One notable difference between the Australian and the UK drinking contexts for underage drinkers is that in the UK young people tend to drink in unsupervised outdoor locations (Coleman and Carter 2005) while in Australia drinking at home, at friends houses and at house parties is more common (Roche 2008; White and Hayman 2006). When young people reach the legal drinking age they choose to drink in both domestic and public locations such as pubs and clubs (Roche 2008). Drink choices also tend to vary according to the age of drinkers. In Australia for example, underage drinkers prefer to drink spirits by themselves or pre-mixed along with beer for young men. By age 18 regular strength beer becomes more popular for men alongside spirits and by age 21 young women add bottled wine to spirits in their preferred list of drinks (Roche 2008, 52). Both parents and young people are aware of these socially expected transitions in alcohol consumption from youthful exuberant spirit drinking to the more settled beer and wine drinking styles of parents at home.

Getting older and related life transitions and increased responsibilities tend to shape alcohol consumption patterns (Harnett 2000; Maggs and Schulenberg 2004). For young people leaving home and living with peers is likely to increase consumption (Casswell 2002). The residential college at university is a particularly "wet" context where young people drink heavily and often (Raskin White et al 2006). Paid work also has an impact on drinking but it is no simple relationship. In some cases work may act to increase consumption by introducing young people to heavy drinking networks and providing funds and access to the night time economy—particularly for young people still living at home (Lindsay 2001; McMorris and Uggen 2000; Raskin White et al 2006). By contrast the demands of work can decrease consumption for some groups of young people and for older adults. Entering relationships has an impact on consumption—research suggests that marriage is likely to decrease consumption (Casswell 2002; Eng et al 2005) and having children decreases consumption and tends to locate drinking more frequently in the home, particularly for women (Holloway et al 2009).

Importantly the young people in the *Drinking Biographies* study imagined their drinking would change across the course of their lives (Lindsay et al 2009). Most of the participants in the research began drinking while underage at secondary school. Teenage socialising was characterised by weekend house parties in family homes, with cheap alcohol products (such as pre-mixed drinks and cask wine frequently referred to as 'goon') and easy access to alcohol either through parents, older siblings or friends or using fake ID or passing as an older customer (Lindsay et al 2009). The ages 18–21 were described by participants as a time of increasing frequency of drinking and amount consumed as young people enter a more 'socially open space' which they expect to pass through, into the next stage (Harnett et al 2000). For example, Keith, a 20-year-old justifies his current drinking as appropriate for his life stage

> I think this is my time to shine kind of thing . . . I'm giving these years to do it. Whereas like when I finish like at 26, 27, it's like I won't be as fast paced as I am now in my teens and early twenties. (Lindsay et al 2009, 47)

Between 18 and 21 years of age, the frequency of drinking increased and most drank more and drinking in domestic settings increased. Social lives included house parties and the frequent round of 18th and 21st birthday celebrations. The price and access to alcohol is a significant driver of consumption for people of all ages and for young people on lower incomes engage in pre-drinking or consuming alcohol at home before going out is now common practice (Wells et al 2009).

Despite the public panic about underage youth drinkers, young people tend to drink the greatest amounts as young adults over the legal drinking age (from 18–20). It is likely that some of this 'heavy' drinking and its effects would be readily observed by parents and other family members but much of it would be conducted with other young people away from the gaze of parents. There is some evidence that parents play a moderating role in their adult children's alcohol consumption. Our recent research on young people in the *University Drinking* study has found distinct drinking patterns according to where university students live. Young people who live at home with their family or with a partner tend to drink at less hazardous levels and display fewer alcohol problems than those who live at college or in shared houses. Jessica describes how living at home is a more regulated drinking environment than living in college and 'doing their own thing'.

Facilitator: Do you think uni students living in colleges would have different alcohol consumption patterns than you and your friends?

Jessica: I think so. The couple of people I've met who do live in college say that every night is a party. Every week it's a bunch of young people who don't have any adults around, more or less, who are independent and doing their own thing. From what I've you know, the way she's described it to me, there is a lot of drinking, basically, because they can. They don't have to worry about getting home or anything, because they all live there together so it's not a problem (Student living at home, Melbourne).

The study by Anne West and colleagues (2009) about UK university students and Facebook also provides some information on family dynamics around alcohol consumption. Although not explicitly addressed by the authors, it seems young people did not want their parents to be Facebook friends because they wanted to keep their drinking secret from them. Many of the middle-class young women in this study spoke of wanting to protect their mothers and from images that would upset them. For example Lorna said

> I wouldn't really want her knowing what I was getting up to! I think that would be a step too far in the friends/family boundary . . . mums care on a different level, they care about your safety and your health and all that kind of thing. My mum might be quite distraught if she saw some of the photos! . . . mums would be more inclined to check it and invade your privacy, because they care more about what's going on. (West et al 2009, 622)

A young man in the study reported that his friend's mother had posted embarrassing advice and comments on his consumption behaviour such as 'Oh my God, you were so pissed last night'(West et al 2009, 621), an effort perhaps to moderate their adult children's drinking from a distance. In these examples, real (and imagined) attempts by mothers to care for their adult children were made while young people tried to hide their intoxication.

The deep involvement of families in facilitating and managing alcohol consumption is implied in young people's stories of domestic drinking. The transition to adulthood (and the legal drinking age) is celebrated in 18th and 21st birthdays and families are usually centrally involved in the organisation and management of them. Yet there is a need for more research on how families negotiate the consumption of alcohol after their children reach the legal drinking age—when consumption peaks but increasingly young people remain living at home.

The young adults in the *Drinking Biographies* study could imagine how having their own families would decrease their consumption and most envisaged drinking less frequently and smaller amounts by the time they are middle aged, particularly if they have children. They foresee a transition to 'structured drinking' in the future such as drinking with dinner or the occasional celebration (Harnett 2000). Sarah, a 20-year-old living in Melbourne Australia explains how she might use alcohol in 20 years time:

> I mean depending on whether I had a family or not. I probably wouldn't want to drink so much around my kids if I had them, more so probably on special occasions like I think you have a responsibility to your kids and you should always, you don't want to be impaired when you're taking care of them. (Lindsay, Harrison et al 2009, 47)

These projections forward into their own family lives are important reminders that families play multiple and complex roles in youth drinking. Concerns about the night-time economy and cultures of intoxication mean that parent-child exchanges about alcohol are caught up in the heat and trouble of excess consumption and intensifying regulatory pressures. Yet these young people are evaluating what their parents are doing (and sometimes criticising as did Alex) and imaging the changing role of alcohol in their family lives. Even when they are drinking too much, they are worried about what parents might think and try to hide some of the evidence. It is critically important to address the harms of alcohol, in its use by young people and their parents and in the next section we look directly at how alcohol consumption is particularly harmful in some family contexts. But we also need to think more fully about what parents are trying to achieve in their negotiations with their children and to consider the wider context of family connections and relationships as they shape drinking cultures and practices.

FAMILIES AND HARMFUL CONSUMPTION

Some alcohol consumption problems such as alcoholism and family violence emanate from within families themselves and cause substantial personal trouble. For young people in these situations, escaping your family is a useful risk reduction strategy. Living in a family with someone who is drinking excessively and alcohol dependent is extremely stressful for family members. Reviewing numerous international studies Orford and colleagues (2010) identify that family members commonly struggle with their relative becoming disagreeable or aggressive, they experience conflict over money and possessions, experience worry about the relative and uncertainty about the future and ultimately find the disruption to everyday home and family life stressful (Orford et al 2010).

There is a substantial body of research on the links between alcohol consumption and experiences of violence in the family context (Klostermann and Fals-Stewart 2006; Hanson et al 2006). Intimate partner violence is recognized as a major public health issue which, despite the advances of second wave feminism, remains common and is apparently intractable (Hegarty, et al 2000). Women remain substantially more likely to be victims of partner violence than men (Graham et al 2008; Hegarty et al 2000).

In the *Drinking Biographies* research family or relationship arguments and/or violence was mentioned by 8 of the 30 women in the sample and one of the 30 men (Lindsay 2012). Most of these participants avoided violence by steering clear of their drunken fathers and attempting to avoid antagonising them. It is notable that two of the women in this research who had experienced extreme alcohol related family domestic violence had made determined efforts to avoid incidents by escaping their families and dramatically changing their socio-spatial contexts by moving towns and changing their networks and socialising with non-drinkers (Lindsay 2012).

For example, Natalie was a 23-year-old woman from Geelong who studied full-time and worked part-time. She was in a committed relationship and planning to get married. Alcohol had played a volatile role in her family life and had led to violence and fighting and general unhappiness over the years. Natalie rarely drinks these days because of her new-found Christian faith and her negative childhood memories and her own bad experiences drinking too much a couple of years ago.

In the interview Natalie described her upbringing in a family-owned pub before her parents separated. She recalled the distress caused by family violence and verbal abuse by her father toward her mother even after her parents had separated.

Natalie: It's when they step over that mark with an extra glass of scotch and coke that it turns really unhappy and in tears and violent . . . if they're drinking they're happy and it's all good and then they turn violent, like that's the last thing that you're going to remember so . . . Yeah. I think my family just don't know when to stop drinking, like you can hit a point where you're really happy and believe you're tipsy but they just want to keep going and going and going and that's where it's stupid, like it's quite embarrassing or whatever.

Between the ages of 16 and 20 Natalie drank regularly and sometimes heavily and had a few negative experiences throwing up, passing out and almost being sexually assaulted herself. In more recent years Natalie has changed her socio-spatial context through meeting a new partner, shifting towns and now socialising with Christian friends. Alcohol now plays a very small role in her life. 'My whole life has kind of transformed differently so it's not an issue at all.' Her Christian faith has given her much to live for and it has allowed her to develop new social networks 'a whole new social scene' and create some distance with her family' (Lindsay 2012).

Though it is not the focus of sustained discussion here it is worth noting that alcohol abuse and dependence are clustered with a range of social problems such as poverty, trauma, abuse, domestic violence and mental health issues (Hanson et al 2006). In these cases, alcohol deepens family misery. The negative impact of alcohol use on indigenous families in Australia and in other post-colonial settings is particularly extreme. Though rates of abstinence are substantially higher among indigenous than non-indigenous populations, rates of problematic drinking are also high (AIHW 2011). Conflict in indigenous families is related to alcohol consumption and a high proportion of assaults against women are committed by intoxicated male partners (Kelly and Kowalyszyn 2003). In addressing alcohol consumption in family life, it is important not to minimise the harms. And in situating young people's drinking in family contexts, we must acknowledge that there are aspects of contemporary drinking culture that are dangerous and damaging. The branding and marketing of alcohol has produced multiple and complex effects and many young people are being drawn into forms of consumption that are troubling. Families are responding very differently to these challenges: resources, education, and culture all shape how parents negotiate these difficult consuming transitions and conflicts. In our view, it is important to recognise parents' efforts to devise and implement alcohol strategies and practices that assist and protect their children. While there are many approaches, for the most part, it is clear parents are working towards what they think will keep their teens (and young adults) safest and assist them to manage alcohol themselves across the lifecourse.

CONCLUSION

Alcohol consumption is deeply relational—it is used to celebrate and symbolise the importance of relationships and connections and it is a symbol of gratitude and care. For many families alcohol is a taken for granted part of sociality; like taking a bottle of wine or beer when invited to social events by family or friends (Valentine 2010b). Family celebrations such as 18th or 21st birthdays in Western countries almost always include alcohol as they mark the transition to formal adulthood and are often organised and managed by families. These family celebrations are important occasions for family 'display' to friends and relatives. Yet for young people drinking is an act of separateness and independence from family. Alcohol symbolises maturity, the transition to adulthood, and importantly it also symbolises belonging to their friendship group. In a world where major transitions to adulthood such as living independently, partnering and parenting have become delayed, or interrupted, socialising in the night time economy remains open and accessible to most young people. The night-time economy is a largely youthful space where the young are active agents in consumption and major targets of alcohol promotions. Yet the visibility of young people's drinking in public spheres has created panic and trouble. Parents are called to actively negotiate alcohol consumption with their teenagers—through role modelling behaviour, setting rules and boundaries. In some, and perhaps many cases, parents seek to alleviate harms and build connections with their teenagers by actually supplying alcohol to them or allowing them to drink at home. The negotiation of alcohol within families continues as young people reach the legal drinking age and move into their early 20s where their alcohol consumption peaks.

Families clearly play a crucial role in the transition young people make to social adulthood via alcohol consumption but they do so in a changing and difficult context. The remarkable domestication of alcohol consumption that has occurred relatively quietly alongside the development of the night-time economy since the 1990s means alcohol is present in new ways in the home. Alcohol is now highly accessible and cheap and is identified by parents as a pleasurable and relaxing part of family life (Valentine et al 2010a). The 'social distance' between parents and children has reduced so that new parenting approaches now emphasise openness and communication rather authoritarian rule making (Valentine et al 2012). Therefore the increase in familial democracy coincides with children's intimate exposure to their parents and relatives drinking in the domestic context.

At the same time, States are concerned with public health and order. Families are asked to regulate and control drinking: parents are often blamed for setting a bad example or for allowing teens too much autonomy. All of these concerns about alcohol are real and they do merit attention: the parents in our *Consuming Families* study did worry about how to best manage these difficult issues. But the worry itself, and efforts of different parents that include negotiation, prohibition or managed introduction, shows parental love and care that is recognised by young people. In family alcohol cultures, there are no ready answers, but in our view, more attention to everyday practices in this difficult terrain, attention to what families are trying to achieve and why, will be more illuminating than emphasis on family failures and misjudgements. This need for more nuanced and careful consideration of family hopes and aspirations underpins our consideration of family practices in our final chapter in which we explore how families manage and consume sex.

6 Seeing It and Doing It

Young People, Families and Sex

In the 21st century, young people inhabit an increasingly sexually open world. New media platforms and changing social mores means that we see more, and know more, about sex. There are widespread fears that the balance has been tipped; that young people know too much, too soon and are driven toward 'adult' sexual practices long before they are ready. Parental obligations in this changing landscape are complicated. Providing knowledge and openly discussing sex are markers of new democratised parenthood, but parental regulation and restriction are also demanded especially in relation to the purported 'sexualisation' of Western culture. In this chapter we discuss the community outrage over the 'sexualisation' of children and young people negotiating 'raunch' culture. We examine sex as a consumer commodity that now mediates both short and long term relationships for young people but may well be influencing parents' relationships too. We trace new freedoms but also new threats to wellbeing in young people's sexual lives and how these are negotiated within families. How are parents and families called to respond to these pressures of sexualisation? How do they care for children and young people during the emergence of their sexual lives?

Young people's sexual habits always provoke deep cultural anxieties. In Western culture, as with alcohol consumption, sex marks an unofficial entry into adulthood and contests over age-appropriate sexual practices are longstanding. Sexual knowledge, symbolism and sexual experience have been profoundly commodified over the last few decades and the transition from childhood to adulthood is being re-negotiated in this area of consumption as it is in other areas. Western societies have moved rapidly from the closeted approaches to sex and sexual desires that characterised the early parts of the 20th century towards greater openness about sexuality. New sexual freedoms have emerged in the context of more fluid intimate relationships, changing gender norms, and these freedoms have been supported by the development of media technologies (Buckingham and Bragg 2004). In fact, the social currents that have created change in family life have been integral to the opening out of sexual life too. While families are often positioned as guardians against sex, especially for young people, families are constructed through sexed and gendered relationships. Young people's observations of, and ideas about, sex are framed and produced through familial experiences as well as in the broader social domains. New openness about sex and sexuality has been in part produced by family fluidities and change.

This sense that the relationship between family life and sexual identities and experiences is both intimate and intricate seems important to us. Many of the panics about sexualisation, as we discuss below, are framed as sexualisation being pressed upon young people from outside forces; through media, social networking, peer pressures and in the availability of sexualised consumer goods. The appetites of young people are being exploited by market forces with ensuing damage to vulnerable youth and to our social fabric. But in this terrain, as in the others we have examined in *Consuming Families*, there are multi-directional and dynamic flows of information, practices and identity construction. We cited Silva and Smart earlier who suggested that families are 'not just a passive bedrock for wider structures, but a redefined, fluid context for intimate relationships' (Silva and Smart 1999, 2). This insight seems particularly important in relation to sex, which is always already in the family as well as outside. In this chapter we look at contemporary sexual panics in the context of family life. We acknowledge the real challenges that families face in the context of free-flowing sexual information and greater access to potentially harmful sexual material. But we are interested in how families respond to and engage with these sexual currents as they seek to provide love and care to young people. In the first section of the chapter, we detail the extant panics that define sexual life in contemporary Western countries.

WAY TOO MUCH, WAY TOO SOON

In the early part of the 21st century, there are widespread fears that the commodification of sex has gone too far. Although openness and good 'health' information are acknowledged as valuable, the consuming appetites that produce excess in other spheres: goods, alcohol, media – are active in terms of sex too. We see too much sex; images are highly sexualised and sexual practices are described and depicted too explicitly. There are concerns that representations of sex have been hijacked by the pornography industry and ever more extreme and exploitative images are being used to sell products. Put 'innocent' children into the mix and the public panic about sexuality becomes particularly intense. As Rovolis and Tsaliki (2012) argue;

> We live, the argument goes, in a culture saturated and depraved by uncontrolled sexuality, in which childhood innocence is debauched by media and consumer culture within which the availability of sexual information to children is rarely treated as positive. (2012, 165)

Even a casual perusal of a daily newspaper will frequently reveal a consistent and increasingly shrill call for parents to wake up to the purported exploitation and theft of innocence by the market and take urgent action to protect their children from the threats of 'sexualisation' or 'pornification' or 'sexploitation'. Psychological studies point to the dangers facing children of the media effects of increased explicitness about sex (Warburton and Braunstein 2012). Popular books aimed at educated parents argue that children are 'growing up fast and furious' (Warburton and Braunstein, 2012), their innocence has been 'consumed' (Brooks 2008) or 'stolen' (Giroux 2000) and that parents need to be aware of *The Lolita Effect* (Durham 2008) so they can combat the early sexualisation of girls or with *Honey, we lost the kids* (McDonnell 2006), that competent parenting has been lost to the media and needs to be regained. The panic about young people and sexual consumption is intense. These books and the popular press suggest profound failure on the part of parents to identify risk and protect their children. Often a range of issues are conflated which operate to incite and mobilise parental fear as parents are called on to act now! The blurb from *The Lolita Effect* nicely illustrates common rhetorical devices in this genre.

> We live in a culture where major chain stores sell junior panties that read "Who needs credit cards . . . ?" and where primetime shows contain elements of underage sex and sexual violence. Toddlers play with dolls dressed in fishnets and miniskirts. Television, movies, Web sites, and video games almost exclusively feature young women with Barbie-doll body types. We are continuously assaulted with the message that youth is hotness and hotness is essential. [. . .] The horrific trickle-down effects of a media culture obsessed with sexy representation of young girls are changing the meanings of childhood and adolescence. Incidents of child pornography, child sex trafficking, teen pregnancy, sexual violence, and sexually transmitted disease are on the rise. There has never been a time when mass media was more influential on our daily lives-and more dangerous to its consumers. (McDonnell, 2006, blurb on bookcover)

Importantly in these panics, and in the protests they provoke, the role of parents as social actors and as socially responsible, are consistently invoked. The vulnerability of children to new sexualised consuming pressures is a consistent focus. These fears have vivid expression in the public concern that children, and girls in particular, are being encouraged to present themselves in overtly sexualised ways through the fashion and beauty industries. Books written for popular audiences such as Ariel Levy's (2005) book *Raunch culture* and Pamela Paul's (2005) book *Pornified culture* point to new emerging forms of female sexuality, that, in seeking to throw off the double standard and assumptions about women's asexual nature, have adopted highly sexualised expressions of femininity. But rather the delivering young women power and freedom, these forms of femininity in fact recreate young women's sexual availability and pressure younger children into raunch culture from an early age.

Policy targeted reports documenting these trends, such as *Corporate Paedophilia: Sexualisation of Children in Australia* (Rush and La Nauze 2006) and from the UK, *The Sexualisation of Young People* (Papadopoulos 2010) have had extensive media coverage and attracted popular support from anti-sexualisation lobby groups. The *Corporate Paedophilia* report paints a dire picture of advertising and marketing systematically abusing both children and public morality. Rush and La Nauze (2006) argue that there is increased pressure for children to adopt a sexualised appearance and behaviour. Their key examples are girls posing as sexual models in advertisements and girls being encouraged to adopt sexualised behaviour by television programs and music video-clips in particular (Rush and La Nauze 2006). Girls magazines such as *Barbie Magazine*, *Total Girl* and *Disney Girl* targeted at tweenies are viewed as problematic because they contain material related to adult beauty practices, fashion and celebrities (Rush and La Nauze 2006). Rush and La Nauze (2006) argue that there are three major risks posed by premature sexualisation for girls. The first is increasing body image dissatisfaction and associated incidence of eating disorders. The second relates to lowering the age of intercourse and the third is that a sexualising media may play a role in making young girls more vulnerable to paedophiles.

Assertions that we are facing increased and damaging sexualisation, as these reports suggest, have been challenged and critiqued by sociologists and media studies academics. Some have argued that rhetoric overwhelms reality and fears about sexualisation are not supported by rigorous evidence (Bragg et al 2011; Smith and Attwood, 2011). Many of these sexualisation reports have been criticised for using evidence that is selective and one-sided, generalising and oversimplify issues, ignoring feminist academic work on the media, gender and the body and lacking an historical or cross-cultural understanding of sexuality (Bragg et al 2011; Egan and Hawkes 2008; Hawkes and Egan 2008; Smith and Attwood 2011). Bragg and colleagues argue that one of the major problems with the debate about sexualisation is the lack of a 'consistent definition' of sexualisation and acknowledgement that there are diverse views and reactions toward sexual imagery (Bragg et al 2011). They argue that in the more polemical work on sexualisation there is a conflation between beauty products, sexual imagery and pornography and intended audiences. The concepts of 'adultification', 'sexualisation', 'sexploitation' and 'pornification' are applied indiscriminately to t-shirts and children's makeup kits as well as to harder core images and products (Bragg et al 2011, Hawkes and Egan 2008; Smith and Attwood 2011).

Gail Hawkes and Danielle Egan (2008) take a critical view of the concept of 'sexualisation' and argue that in political campaigns sexualisation is seen as a monolithic and universal process that is viewed as uniformly damaging. In the sexualisation discourse children and girls in particular, are constructed as passive, innocent and asexual. According to Egan and Hawkes (2008) the problem with the sexualisation discourse is that it reproduces negative assumptions about gender differences and works to disempower girls. The hegemony of the discourse means that there is no space for the sexual expression of girls or the possibility that young people might 'negotiate their sexuality in a manner that both reflects and resists hegemonic marketing messages' (Egan and Hawkes 2008).

Notwithstanding these voices of contest, activism against sexualisation has increased in the last decade. Protest groups against sexualisation have emerged in the last few years and are having traction in gaining media attention, closing down advertising campaigns, getting products removed from sale and raising community concern about the issue of sexualisation. These organisations specifically call on parents to join the social movement against sexualisation; they make explicit the requirement that parents actively manage and restrain their children's engagement with sexual commodities. The Collective Shout organisation offers a good example of this invocation of parental responsibility to regulate. It was formed in 2009 in Australia and the slogan is 'For a world free of sexploitation'. They describe their activities as follows;

> Collective Shout is a grassroots campaigns movement mobilising and equipping individuals and groups to target corporations, advertisers, marketers and media which objectify women and sexualise girls to sell products and services.
>
> Collective Shout names, shames and exposes corporations, advertisers, marketers and media engaging in practices which are offensive and harmful, especially to women and girls, but also to men and boys. (Collective Shout 2012a)

One of the founders of Collective Shout is Melinda Tankard Reist, the author of popular books on sexualisation and porn. The Kids Free 2B Kids organisation traverses some similar ground but is focussed more closely on the concerns of parents. This organisation particularly focuses on psychological harms and purported damage to the psychological development of children. The founder and Melbourne mother of two, Julie Gale, argues that sexualisation undermines her parenting. She explicitly calls for action from parents to lobby advertisers and corporations directly;

> We parents play a key role in what we allow our children to see, watch and wear. However, our parenting is being undermined by the powerful forces of advertisers and marketers, who have multi million dollar budgets and use sophisticated psychological techniques.

> It is time for parents—in fact, all adults—to take the initiative and decide what sorts of images we want our children to see.
>
> It is time for corporations to be held accountable for the psychological and emotional harm that comes from sexualised advertising and marketing.
>
> It is time corporations listened to the child development professionals who work with children and see the impacts.
>
> We have crossed a line. It is time for action! (Kids Free 2B Kids 2012)

In these impassioned political campaigns 'sexualisation' is both naturalised and presented as a very bad form of consumption. Parental views are homogenised and parental responsibilities are clear: children shouldn't see or be exposed to these consumables. Parental control, as with campaigns on food and alcohol, is presented as vital and desirable. Market forces are undermining 'good and responsible' parenting. It is not our objective here to adjudicate on sexualisation, or to dismiss the genuine anxiety many parents feel about strong sexual imagery and access to explicit sexual material. Indeed, Angela McRobbie (2009) argues that we are facing a resurgence or reinvigoration of sexualisation in culture that may be subverting the social and political gains for women and girls achieved through feminist activism. But the stridency and emotion of the debates about contemporary youth sexuality and the sexualisation of younger children means that it is very difficult to get a sense of how young people and their parents might actually be negotiating consumption in this domain. Danger, harm and exploitation are the dominant stories, censorship and government regulation has failed and parents must be called in to take responsibility for mediating and regulating their children's sexual consumption.

In this noisy environment, we are interested to explore how these pressures on young people and their families around their children's sexual knowledge and transition to adulthood are experienced within families. In the next section, we chart a brief assessment of recent changes in youth sexual practices and the way these are shaped by wider social patterns of family change and inequality. This account of change is important because sex doesn't exist in a social vacuum and neither do other troubling modes of sexual consumption—sexualised products, sexting and accessing pornography. Although there is copious literature on the potential harms of consumption in this field and numerous advice books calling parents in to actively restrict manage their children's sexual consumption, there is limited research focussing on how different families actually negotiate young peoples' emerging sexuality and sexual consumption in everyday life. How do the embodied intimacies and bodily co-presence of family life (Gabb 2008, Morgan 2011a) shape young people's experiences and family approaches to sex? From diverse academic sources, we draw out threads and insights into how parents are negotiating the everyday consumption of sexual information, images and goods with their children. These negotiations occur in a fluid and complex social sexual landscape, where there has been considerable change in the last several decades. As with food and alcohol, approaches that emphasise the need to regulate, overwhelming threats and parental failures obscure the efforts parents make toward love and care in this difficult sphere of family consumption.

YOUNG PEOPLE AND THEIR FAMILIES: NEW SEXUAL FREEDOMS AND OLD CONSTRAINTS

Prior to the sexual revolution of the 1970s having sex was highly risky behaviour for young people both socially and physically in Western countries. Sex before marriage was frowned upon, and the sexual double standard was the norm; having sex could enhance young men's reputations but seriously damage the reputation of young women. The consequences of sex such as pregnancy, or sexually transmitted infections were stigmatised and experienced as deeply shameful. Young heterosexual women in particular carried the burden of dealing with unwanted pregnancies. If they could not marry their partners many organised dangerous 'back yard' terminations or adoptions (Lindsay 2005a). Homosexual sex was highly stigmatised and anal sex was illegal (Lindsay 2005a; Weeks 2007).

In the new millennium the social and sexual landscape has changed dramatically. Sex is less regulated and in some ways less risky for many young people in Western countries. More young people are having sex outside of marriage and more are having sex at younger ages (Tolman and McClelland 2011). Social mores have changed and sex has become part of everyday youth socialising relationships and courtship (Bailey 1988; Powell 2010; Tolman and McClelland 2011). The feminist and gay rights social movements have mobilised for legal and social change in sexual relationships (Weeks 2007). Homosexual sex is now legal and health and social support services for same sex attracted young people are steadily increasing. For heterosexual young people, effective contraception is widely available and pregnancy terminations are legal and available through the public health system in most Western countries (Lindsay 2005a; Moore and Rosenthal 2006).

The changing social location of sex, is produced in part by changing family forms, new public health imperatives and through changing media landscapes, a core theme in this chapter. Public health has become more interested in sex in response to the HIV/AIDS pandemic of the 1980s and efforts to control other forms of sexually transmitted infections. HIV/AIDS in particular made young people's sexual relationships more visible as governments and others sought to minimise health risks in the population. There is now much more detailed and reliable data on the diverse and changing patterns of young people's contemporary sexual practices and detailed information on the meanings young people attribute to their sexual experiences (Lindsay 2005a; Moore et al 1996; Moore and Rosenthal 2006; Tolman and McClelland 2011).

In general young people's sexual lives are now freer but these wider social changes have not been entirely positive and some changes have not gone far enough. Sex remains a site of love and intimacy but also of coercion and risk (Lindsay 2005a). Young women must deal with a more complex and contradictory double standard (Powell, 2010). On the one hand they need to maintain their social reputations and avoid whore/slut labelling but on the other hand popular media encourages young women to not only have sex but also become sexual experts. Young men also struggle with their sexuality and social pressure to be viewed as sexually experienced. In general young people's sexual relationships have become more acceptable. Many parents, particularly those from Anglo and non-religious backgrounds, are accepting of young people's sexual relationships and allow them to sleep with partners in the family home (Hartley 1993, Smith et al 2003a). By contrast, other parents do not accept sexual relationships outside marriage, causing considerable guilt and stress for their children (Lindsay 2005a).

Sex is now a normalised part of pre-marital relationships for most young people (Bailey 1988; Powell 2010). New terms have been developed by young people to describe their contemporary sexual landscape and 'casual' or 'sex-only' encounters as the 'hook-up' or 'fling' and the partner as a 'fuck-buddy', 'a friend with benefits' or someone they are 'seeing' (Powell 2010, 30). Longer term relationships described as 'a relationship' or 'a boyfriend' or a 'committed' or 'serious relationship' are still valued (Powell 2010, 30).

Same sex relationships are increasingly visible and supported, and the Internet provides a safe place for same-sex attracted young people to connect with each other. However, homophobia remains widespread and at the extreme end has dire consequences. Same-sex preference has been linked to increased drug and alcohol consumption and youth suicide. Sex is a major theme in popular media targeted toward youth audiences (Buckingham and Bragg 2004). The increased openness and sexualisation of youth culture paradoxically may give some young people less choice about being sexually active as virginity becomes stigmatised. Sexual coercion and unwanted sex remain relatively common experiences. In general, sexual relationships remain difficult to negotiate, they are a site of pleasure as well as danger, and young people must deal with contradictory pressures on their intimate lives (Lindsay 2005a). Anastasia Powell's research shows that a revised version of the sexual double standard is in operation for young Australians. Men's promiscuity is judged positively with the term 'player' but women's promiscuity continues to be viewed negatively with the term 'slut' (Powell 2010, 43). Yet women are expected to be sexually active as one student in this research explained.

> It's like you're either frigid or a slut, like, you shouldn't be having sex that much, or you should only be having a bit. It's such a fine line.' 'Yeah, like there's standards between what is and isn't okay. (Powell 2010, 41)

The new sexual rules for women illustrated in the American television show *Sex in the City* offer what Powell terms a 'false freedom' where women who have many sexual partners continue to be judged negatively by their peers as one 19-year-old woman said:

> I call it the Samantha syndrome . . . its still a bit new that girls are being so liberal and talking about sex. I am all for the 'Samanthas' that do talk about it but it can hurt if you find out that you're being very liberal and open about your sexuality, and it turns out people are talking about you behind your back. I have seen it happen in my group. (Powell 2010, 50)

The young women in this study were sceptical about the positive side of sexual freedom outside of love relationships. 'Everyone's gone through a bit of a slut stage but it's watching people regret it that just sucks' (Powell 2010, 50) from a group interview with 15-18 year old females.

The social divisions of class, ethnic background and sexual identity have an important impact on sexual practices, choices and constraints (Moore and Rosenthal 2006; Tolman and McClelland 2011). In terms of social class, young people with lower levels of education, lower levels of income and blue collar occupations were more likely than others to have had intercourse before the age of 16 (Rissel et al 2003a). Class emerges as a strong influence in teen pregnancies and decisions about unwanted pregnancies. It is apparent that working class and underprivileged young women are more likely to get pregnant and more likely to bear children at young ages. By contrast middle-class young women in the US and Australia are more likely use contraception or terminate a pregnancy (Coory 2000; Santelli et al 2000; Smith et al 2003b). Ethnic and religious backgrounds also shape young people's sexual lives in particular ways. Young people who hold strong religious views are less likely than others to engage in sex outside of married relationships. The racism that permeates society also permeates representations of sex. For example in popular culture, black men are frequently represented as predatory and black women are represented as promiscuous. There is a need for more sustained comparative research on the impact of cultural background on sexual practices (Lindsay 2005a).

Despite the increasing acceptability of same-sex relationships 'coming out' as gay or lesbian remains a fraught process. This is particularly the case for young men as dominant versions of masculinity are defined against homosexuality. Family members and friends can be deeply homophobic and being same-sex attracted can challenge these core relationships. But reactions are diverse and many same-sex attracted youth have positive feelings about their sexuality and find supportive peers and/or family (Hillier et al 1998; Lindsay 2005a; Weeks 2007).

Contemporary parents are likely to have enjoyed some sexual freedom and to have had a number of sexual partners over their lifetimes

(Rissel et al 2003a, 2003b). A large minority of heterosexual parents today are not married themselves, and may be re-making their families by ending or initiating new relationships. Parents in same-sex relationships and their families are increasingly viewed as ordinary rather than threatening. All parents, heterosexual and same-sex, experience increased fluidity in personal relationships (Lindsay and Dempsey 2009). As divorce and separation have become normalised (Beck-Gernsheim 2002) children are in a position to observe their parents, the parents of their friends and other adults negotiating new sexual relationships. Yet despite all of the public concern little is known about how parents negotiate the responsibilities of parenthood and deal with the increasing visibility of sex in the West. As always, the embodied intimacies of family life are an important part of these negotiations.

NEGOTIATING SEXUAL RELATIONSHIPS IN THE FAMILY HOME

As young people stay at home longer, now often well into their 20s, new areas for negotiation emerge such as young people having sexual relationships within the family home but little is known about how this is being negotiated or managed by diverse families. Amy Schalet's (2010) work comparing the views of Dutch and US parents to their children's sexual relationships documents quite distinct cultural approaches in these Western countries (Schalet 2010). Her work offers an important example of the specificities in discussions about sex and of the diversity of family sexual practices. In the US parents tended to emphasise teen sexuality as dangerous, that teens experience 'raging hormones' that are difficult to control (Schalet 2010). There is a strong feeling that adolescents should separate from home before they begin sexual activity so US parents actively discourage sexual activity and respond to the idea of sexual relationship in their house negatively with the expression "Not under my roof!" (Schalet 2010, 20).

Dutch parents tended to normalise teen sexuality and felt that young people can assess for themselves when they are physically and emotionally ready for sex. They were willing to adjust to and accommodate the 'sleepover' so they could exert more informal social control (Schalet 2010). For example a Dutch father in the study had the following views about the possibility of his daughter having a sexual partner stay the night. 'She is sixteen, almost seventeen. I think she knows very well what matters, what can happen. If she is ready [for sex], I would let her be ready'. Karel would also let his daughter spend the night with a steady boyfriend in her room, if the boyfriend had come over to the house regularly beforehand and did not show up 'out of the blue' (Schalet 2010, 16).

By contrast an American mother had forbidden sexual activity at home by her son. Rhonda tells her kids that premarital sex 'at this point is really dumb'. It's on the list with shoplifting, she explains, 'sort of like the Ten Commandments: don't do any of those because if you do, you know, you're going to be in a world of hurt'. Rhonda responds viscerally when asked whether she would let her fifteen-year-old son spend the night with a girlfriend. No way, Jose!' She elaborates: 'That kind of recreation...is just not something I would feel comfortable with him doing here' (Schalet 2010, 17).

Little is known about the views of parents in other Western contexts such as the UK or Australia. However, the Australian national survey of high school students suggests that teen sexuality is domesticated as 28% reported they last had sex at their house, 37% last had sex at their partners' house and 23% last had sex at a friend's house (Smith et al 2009). We do know that parents have an influence on the relationships of their children and are a trusted source of advice on sexual issues. In the Australian national survey of high school students, mothers in particular were often used as sources of information on sexual health (56%) and were viewed as trusted sources of information (69%). By comparison fathers were used by 31% as a source of information and were trusted by 48% as a source of sexual health advice (Smith et al 2009). Many high school students are also confident in talking to their parents about sexual issues; 47% reported feeling confident to very confident in talking to their parents about sex, 52% were confident they could talk to their parents about contraception and 56% were confident they could talk to their parents about sexually transmissible infections (Smith et al 2009). Young people's responses in this survey make it clear that families are active in discussions about sex. Such communication suggests that the vision of sexual forces pressing on the family from outside needs to be complicated by recognition that sexual forces are active inside the family too. When children and young people experience media images and ideas about sex, they are already sexual citizens. Family practices will shape and inform sexual practices too.

In Anastasia Powell's research on the sexual experiences of young Australians aged 14–24 some of the women identified parents as a positive influence on their relationships. As one young woman said in a group interview:

> Yeah, I think parents do play a big role in things in relationships: my parents were a good model and talked about things. I think the parents talk to you a little bit about relationships and so their views sometimes become your own views. (Powell 2010, 49)

Yet in this same study other women spoke about their parents being out of touch with contemporary sexual relationships where young people are likely to have experienced 'casual' or 'sex-only' encounters as well as 'longer-term' or 'committed' relationships (Powell 2010, 30–31).

Although these studies point to evidence of a new openness about sex in some families, and do support the sense that family approaches to sex are important in shaping the experience of young people and children, they also raise the difficult questions of youth transitions and consuming competencies. Much of the fear about openness about sex in the public sphere – about how much should children see and how much should they do– is embedded in worries about children's capacities to choose carefully and consume wisely. As in all of the contentious consumption domains we have explored in *Consuming Families*, the vulnerabilities of children subtend public panics about consumption. In the following sections we explore the contemporary marketisation of young people's sexual lives and the complex ways in which parents seek to manage the consumption of sex by their children and teens. We imagine how the themes of autonomy, independence, connection and self-expression might resonate for sex as they do for the other domains of consumption we have explored in this book. Our exploration here is grounded in the sense that the framing of both public and academic debate in terms of risk and harm means that information about family interactions and negotiations is muted or absent (Doring 2009). As in the sphere of alcohol, prohibitions and panics create pressures for parents and young people as they move towards adulthood and sexual maturity.

THE NEW MARKETING OF SEX AND THE REACTION OF PARENTS

For young people there are great pleasures involved in accessing and participating in popular culture. Young people's sexuality has been a major theme in the mass media since the 1960s. Popular music provides a background for dancing, meeting people and initiating sexual relationships. Magazines particularly those directed toward young women give advice on how to look good and how to conduct sexual relationships and most television soaps and movies directed to the youth market have sexual relationships as a central part of the storyline (Buckingham and Bragg 2004). The mass media has played a large role in exploring relationships, promoting sexual freedom and in the case of magazines and television, has provided an accessible avenue for sex education (Buckingham and Bragg 2004). Yet there is a strong public anxiety that the media, and the market that sustains it, has gone too far in using sex to sell goods. There is a substantial body of research which demonstrates that youth sexuality is represented, promoted and commodified through numerous mass media channels including music videos, television shows, movies and youth magazines (Arnett 2002; Reichert and Lambiase 2006; Walsh-Childers et al 2002).

In contemporary media young people are frequently represented as highly sexual beings and these representations are negotiated by families in diverse ways (Buckingham and Bragg 2004). Henry Giroux argues that corporate culture positions young people 'as both the subject and object of commodification, as objects to buy and be sold in the marketplace'(Giroux 2000).

Over the last three decades, young sexual bodies have become a prominent money generating element of consumer capitalism. and teenage sexuality is represented as amoral and out of control (Giroux 2000, 1998), but also deeply attractive. Teenage models are presented as objects of desire to sell fashion and other products. As Giroux argues;

> In the profit-driven world of advertising and fashion, the image and culture of youth are appropriated and exploited for the high pleasure quotient they evoke. The body in this 'fashionscape' does not represent the privileged terrain of agency, but rather serves as a site of spectacle and objectification, where youthful allure and sexual titillation are marketed and consumed by teens and adults who want to indulge a stylized narcissism and a self that is all surface. (Giroux 1998, 34)

Rosalind Gill argues that sexual advertising reinforces the sexual hierarchies and inequalities and whiteness is presented as the desirable ideal (Gill, 2009). Young women are shown as submissive and vulnerable in comparison to young men and heterosexuality is illustrated as hegemonic. Gill (2009) outlines how advertising may appear transgressive on the surface but offers limited subject positions where middle-class whiteness, male power and heterosexuality are promoted (Gill, 2009).

Despite the concern over sexual marketing there is limited information available on how these sexual images of young people are read or negotiated within families. We can gain insight into some parents' reactions in the public campaigns to which we described earlier. Mossimo created a 'peep show' underwear advertising campaign that ran in Australia in early 2012. The campaign involved shop window displays with the words "Peep show" and "take a peek inside" accompanied by images of men and women in lingerie. In one image, the woman is pulling at the man's underpants so that they are coming away from his waist. The campaign was supported by a 'Facebook app' encouraging young people to post similar images of themselves on the Mossimo website. There was a tide of public complaint, mobilised in part by Collective Shout, and parents complained to the national Advertising Standards Bureau (ASB) that the sexual imagery and use of pornographic tropes had gone too far. The following quotes illustrate parental concerns.

> In the shopping centre setting up a display that mimics the adult sex industry is offensive and inappropriate for children to see. To encourage people to peep at women in their underwear is not appropriate . . . (ASB 2012, Case no: 0075/12, 1).
>
> These windows are in plain view of children and provide complete approval of something that is illegal. It takes away the choice I get to make as a parent regarding the view my children should be allowed to make but

> it also made me feel the complete objectification of women. On the one hand I am being encouraged as a parent to protect my children from this sort of thing on the internet and provide strict parenting controls to protect and value my children but in a shopping centre they are being confront with something that not only provides a distorted perception for women but ok's [sic] doing this in secret. (ASB 2012, Case no: 0075/12, 1)
>
> This is entirely unacceptable material for display to the general public. (ASB 2012, Case no: 0075/12, 1)

The response by the Mossimo company to the ASB suggested that its core customers were young people who consume independently of families and had apparently not considered that younger children may engage with their 'peepshow' advertising. To quote the company response;

> Mossimo is a cheeky, irreverent and light-hearted brand! In the same vein, the Mossimo Peepshow Facebook campaign is a cheeky, irreverent, light-hearted and slightly controversial promotion that is consistent with Mossimo Underwear's brand positioning. Like any brand, Mossimo is continuously focused on developing better and more effective ways to talk to and engage its core customers, in this case 16–30 year olds. There is plenty of research that demonstrates that social media avenues like Facebook and Twitter have well and truly replaced traditional forms of advertising as the most popular and frequent means of communicating within this demographic. Mossimo believes that the Mossimo Peepshow Facebook app represents the best way to talk to its target audience in a language and a medium with which they are both familiar and use regularly. (ASB 2012, Case no: 0075/12, 2)

Mossimo are clearly stating here that the best way to target their market of 16-30 year olds is by being 'cheeky', 'controversial' presumably by using symbolism similar to that used in the sex-industry and by going online. Interestingly protesters to their campaign also went online. Some young women protested on the campaign website including 'naughty Nicole' who posted a picture of herself holding a handwritten sign "Mossimo peepshow = sexist rubbish' and this picture received the highest number of votes on the site for her photo according to the Collective Shout website. (Collective Shout 2012b)

Going a step beyond common marketing of sexuality are pornographic images being used on various products marketed to teenagers. One example of this is the US CityBeach clothing chain which sells soft porn t-shirts and pencil cases to teenage boys in Australia and internationally. There is a wide variety of magazine like images of women in skimpy clothes exposing their breasts or buttocks. Sometimes these are presented with graphics inspired by heavy metal music or tied to alcohol consumption or all three with the '187 Drink, F*ck, Fight' t-shirt which shows a large breasted woman in underwear as the central image (Citybeach 2012a, Citybeach 2012b).

The Collective Shout organisation has campaigned vigorously against the company selling these t-shirts and products with some success. They secured media coverage of community concern over the pencil cases in the Herald Sun when a year 8 teenage boy took one to school and the teacher advised Collective Shout. (Michael 2011; Collective Shout 2012c)

In this story of the 8-year-old boy, and the other campaigns we have explored, the public response and protest is important and often invokes parents and parental responsibilities. But families and the daily negotiations of family life around bodies, sex, and nudity are never canvassed in any detail or complexity. In the reported story of the pencil case, the family story is absent. Who helped him buy it? Was the pencil case an acceptable purchase or a contentious one? These are the everyday questions about sex in families that are obscured in the current debates about sexualisation. Different family approaches to, and thinking about sex, nudity and consumption are silenced in intense public currents where 'wrong' consumption is plain and not open to questions. Diverse practices and thinking about sex, and sex in family life, cannot be readily acknowledged. The marketing of sexualised products, especially to younger children, necessarily involves the market interacting with families. Playboy products for girls under 12 are not generally independently bought: these commodities invoke family decisions and rely on family resources. In the following sections of this chapter, we have chosen to focus on three key examples of sexual consumption—consumption of 'sexualised' goods, the practice of sexting on mobile phones and pornography consumption—to examine challenges for and responses by families to the visible intensification of sexual marketing. In exploring these topics, we are interested in seeking out evidence of how different families may be negotiating the consumption of sex.

NEGOTIATIONS OF SEXUAL COMMODITIES WITHIN FAMILIES

It appears that market pressures around adult and sexual imagery and goods and responses to them are being negotiated within families in diverse ways. Mari Rysst's (2010) ethnographic research with 10-year-old Norwegian girls provides some insight into these processes. The girls in Rysst's study wanted to appear kul (cool) rather than sexy and had to negotiate with their mothers before being allowed to buy clothing. 'Central to the negotiations are colours and how much of the body is to be shown by tight clothes or skimpy fabric, and the price of the clothes' (Rysst 2010, 82). There was substantial intergenerational negotiation into what were viewed as age appropriate by mothers as the following quote from one girl illustrates;

> Me and Ellen [her best friend] were in a shop for clothes [Popin, a shop for women], and there were many clothes that fitted us, and then

> mummy and Grete [Ellen's mother] thought they were rather nice, but they didn't think we should have them, because we became sort of too grown-up. That it became rart ['odd']. (Rysst 2010, 82)

This sense of 'inappropriately grown up' was expressed by an Australian mother too when her daughter purchased a playboy bunny necklace at the Diva jewellery chain store. The mother described her outrage on the Collective Action Facebook page.

> My daughter and her best friend went to Diva while we were out. They returned and proudly showed me their purchases: mood earrings with the peace symbol on them and matching necklaces with their birth months. They were really excited to be doing the 'best friend matching necklace' thing.
>
> Unfortunately, I then had to explain to them that they needed to take the necklaces back as they actually said 'Miss November' and had the playboy bunny on them. I was really angry about a) this being in a tween jewellery shop b) I had to explain to my 10 year old about playboy magazine—something I wasn't planning on discussing for a few years yet c) I had to explain to her that, in wearing the necklace, adults would associate her with a specific playboy bunny—again, not a conversation that was in my pre-teen repertoire.
>
> The argument that it's everywhere doesn't cut it. My daughter could have seen this on someone older and been oblivious to the context, but in not only making it available to purchase, but specifically targeting her age group, Diva has forced my ten year old to face the fact that not only do people want to overtly sexualise her, but they want to pornify her. (Collective Shout 2012d)

In this case the mother took offence at the product and chose to educate her daughter about sexualisation and pornography even though she felt she was too young and by implication, too innocent, to be given this information. As we argued in relation to alcohol, these diverging parental responses of prohibition in some cases and dissuasion in others and sometimes conflict are often simply represented as parental failures, or successes in terms of regulation and restriction. But such evaluations don't include the worry, the effort and the care parents expend in managing these consumption decisions. The purchase of the pencil case for the boy and the return of the necklaces are two different parental strategies to freely available sexual material but they both reflect forms of parental care. It seems to us that social mores around sex are in flux, sexual imagery is more prevalent and parents and children are negotiating new norms, expectations and hopes around sexual behaviour and sexual safety.

Parental diversity in approaches to sexual material and imagery is important to recognise. Sara Bragg and colleagues found quite different reactions to the Collective Shout parents in their qualitative research on sexualised products and the perspectives of children and parents for their report to the Scottish parliament (Bragg et al 2011). Their focus was on sexualised consumer goods rather than media images in Scotland and the parents and teenagers (aged 12–14) offered complex and nuanced views on the topic. Most of the parents and children felt that beginning secondary school was a milestone that required independence and responsibility and for many young people the 'final say' in clothing and personal care items.

This emphasis on personal consumption as the key sphere for the exercise of choice was both powerful and paradoxical. It led many parents to argue that sexualized goods were not 'worth the battle' – that is, they would not risk alienating their children or jeopardizing their relationship with them over issues such as clothes and hairstyles. These could be seen as not only as comparatively trivial ('there are worse things they could be doing'), but also as part of the 'natural' rebellion of adolescents against their parents (Bragg et al 2011, 284–285). It is clear that these parents are working out the best ways to engage with their children about sex. As with the other forms of consumption we have explored ongoing active negotiation between parents and children are everyday family practices. As with food, alcohol and the media, families negotiate what sexual information or commodities can be consumed, by whom and at what time. This negotiation over appropriate consumption at appropriate ages is undertaken in a complex environment where parents reflect on their own experiences and the choices made by other families as they strive to socialise their children into competent consumers, while keeping them happy and safe.

In this study, sexualised products were read in different ways according to the wearer and the context. An object or symbol coming into fashion could also alter the meaning of it for both the young people and their parents (Bragg et al 2011). The playboy bunny symbol appearing on fashion accessories was interpreted in complex and multiple ways. Most of the young people knew the bunny image had sexual references and was associated with Hugh Hefner and his exploits yet they also insisted that it had become popular because of fashion it was seen as 'a cute pink bunny' (Bragg et al 2011). The parents in this study engaged in sophisticated debates about the meaning of the playboy symbol and whether it could be read as a fashion brand dissociated from its pornographic history (Bragg et al. 2011). In stark contrast to the mother on the Collective Shout website described above, one woman in this study saw discussing Playboy with a 10-year-old as an infringement of childhood innocence.

> You don't want to force them to think about things that they're innocently thinking [is] a nice pink bunny . . . Just allow them to be children for that bit longer. You don't always want to be the one that's coming in spoiling it . . . They don't need to think about the moral issues of absolutely everything that they do, like what clothes to put on in the morning. (Bragg et al 2011, 287)

Most of the children and parents in Bragg and colleagues' (2011) study did not see sexualised products as a substantial problem and spoke about individual choice in these consumption decisions. Yet a range of constraints including desire to belong in peer groups (Pugh 2009) and autonomy claims by children limited the choices they could make about their children's engagement in consumer culture.

> Parents did not feel they should dictate how children spent money they had earned themselves; they did not want their children to be left out or bullied because they lacked what their friends had; they were susceptible to children's nagging, emotional blackmail, sheer determination and/or devious tactics in subverting their rules. (Bragg et al 2011, 288)

This suggests that negotiation and pressure on parents to buy sexualised goods shares substantial similarities with other consumer goods about which parents feel ambivalent or negative. Children's desire to belong in their peer group and local context fuels consumption and inhibits parental protest (Pugh 2009). Parental unease reflects concerns about the impact of sexualisation on young people, but also their understanding of the need to allow for and enable transitions including to greater sexual freedom for their children. If parents were certain that the purchase of such goods was 'bad' for their children, it seems unlikely that ambivalence would be so prevalent in family consuming discussions. Rather than seeing parental compromise in these decisions as ceding or giving up proper ground, we consider parents are working with competing pressures. Worries about sexualisation intersect with recognition of young people's sexual agency. Desires to constrain consumption sometimes collide with parental recognition that young people need to seek distance and independence through products and practices. Young people themselves actively seek opportunities to become sexually knowing and sophisticated. Buckingham and Bragg (2004) provide a lovely example of a mother reflexively examining a teen magazine with sexual information in it before allowing her 10-year-old daughter to purchase it.

> *Rachel:* Mine's more like a teenage magazine but my mum lets me read it . . . the first time I wanted to get it she read it all through in Asda [Supermarket] and so we were late coming back and dad started moaning cause he hadn't had his tea – but yeah she said it was OK cause it wasn't that bad and I'm fast at growing up. (Buckingham and Bragg 2004, 185)

We suggest then that in the management of 'sexy' clothing, as in other spheres, the negotiation of consumption can be seen as part of the making of family life and the nurture and development of dependent children.

When we turn however to sexual practices, the tensions and arguably parental worries are intensified. While some of the sexualisation panic deals with imagery and clothing, there are two specific areas that have mobilised public concerns about young people's sexual well-being: sexting and the ready availability of pornography. In the final sections of this chapter, we explore these contentious issues and what is known about how young people and parents are managing them in family life.

YOUNG PEOPLE AND 'SEXTING'

'Sexting' is the new term to describe the exchange of sexual images via text message. In Chapter 3 we discussed the negotiation of mobile phones as a potentially positive new mode for family connection and communication. But mobile phones can also be used for other types of connection, namely sexual connection, and the idea that young people are sending nude or sexually suggestive images of themselves to sexual partners has resulted in high public anxiety. There are fears and reports that teenage girls and young women are being pressured to send explicit images of themselves and these images are being further distributed by boyfriends to peers and the wider community (Powell 2010). However detailed knowledge about the social dynamics of sexting is yet to be developed.

Livingstone and Gorzig (2012) capture the dilemmas for parents in response to these new ICT possibilities, when they ask if sexting is just the new or latest moral panic produced by new media? Lynn's analysis of media reports in the US from 2008-2009 found that the problem of sexting was amplified by these reports and parents were presented as 'ignorant, technologically inept, and incapable of controlling their children's behaviors' (Lynn 2010, 1). The media articles tended to present parents as either 'exemplary tough lovers' or 'negligent enablers' and many of the articles suggested that parents should be authoritarian and restrict their teenagers cell phone use (Lynn 2010). To be sure, the development of cheap and accessible ICTs have enabled the 'quick-fire' exchanges of sexually intimate images that we never available to previous generations (Livingstone and Gorzig 2012). As we have discussed, mobile phone ownership has risen rapidly in recent decades and the majority of teens in the West now own a phone and in some contexts 'texting has become a centrepiece in teen social life' (Lenhart 2009, 2). Sexting may be for some young people a new mode of initiating and communicating about sex, but this is of course unsettling for adults because it makes sexual activity among young people more visible (Livingstone and Gorzig 2012). Sexting is an ambiguous social practice; it can be voluntary, humorous, trivial, private and pleasurable or it can be the converse involuntary, public, significant and damaging (Livingstone and Gorzig 2012). Sexting is perhaps primarily intended as a form of electronically mediated flirtation where young people exchange images between two romantic partners, or between people who are not yet in a relationship but one hopes to be (Lenhart 2009; Livingstone and Gorzig 2012). Yet the ease with which these images are distributed to unintended audiences and the damaging consequences of this pose a major problem (Lenhart 2009). There are reports of young people having their reputations damaged by vexatious or vengeful distribution of images following relationship breakdown and there are examples of the law intervening and teens being listed as sex-offenders because of sexting (Lenhart 2009).

Examining the way young people themselves make sense of sexting enables a more positive interpretation of the practice that is rarely presented in newspaper articles. Emma Bond (2010) found that young people in her UK study 'sext' naked images of themselves, as an expression of trust in relationships (Bond 2010). The young people in Bond's study spoke about access to sexual material as an everyday and fun experience. Bond likens this mobile phone use to previous generations' sexual exploration 'behind the bike shed'. A group of fourteen year old girls talked about sexual content generated by boys they knew—'Yeah like the boys flashing their meat and two veg' 'Yeah and they are like "Show us your blah blah blah". 'Yeah and they are like oh! Mine are better than his—do you know what I mean? And it's just like a competition' (Bond 2010, 596).

> The visual material of a sexual nature viewed and shared on the children's mobile phones was mostly discussed in the focus groups in a humorous vein by both the boys and the girls and appeared to play a role in their everyday lives in relieving boredom, generating humour and gaining popularity. (Bond 2010, 598)

Although some young people feel that sexting is a common experience and 'no big deal' the available evidence is that sexting is in fact a minority experience. In large scale surveys of young people aged 11–16 across Europe, and those aged 12–17 in the US only 15% have received texts of sexual images and only 3–4% report sending them (Lenhart 2009; Livingstone and Gorzig 2012). Yet the meanings and intentions young people attribute to sexting are diverse. Both girls and boys send sexual texts as the following quotes from the Pew Internet and American Life Project illustrate;

> I've sexted a few times . . . Just between my girlfriend and I. Just my girlfriend sending pictures of herself to me and me sending pictures of myself to her. (Lenhart 2009, 6)

> If a guy wants to hook up with you, he'll send a picture of his private parts or a naked picture of him[self] . . . It's mostly the guys I date or just a guy that . . . really want to hook up with you. I'm not really the type of person [who sends texts], but I have friends who have. (Lenhart 2009, 7)

One middle school boy wrote, 'I have not received or sent, but have asked. It's mostly people I know—I've only asked once' (Lenhart 2009, 7).

Other young people participating in the focus groups were wary about sending texts because of the negative outcomes—protecting reputations was important and boys did not want to be seen as a 'pervert' and girls did not want to be seen as a 'slut'. Others shared the concerns of adults about the legality of the images and the potential for wide distribution outside their control.

> I've never sent or received a picture involving nudity because I know that is illegal . . . Also, I think texting [sexually suggestive images] is too risky—a friend could take your phone and see it. That's not something you want to be in public. And at my school you can get in trouble for it. (Lenhart 2009, 9)

Despite the public panic about sexting available research suggests being harmed by sexting, or as it has been framed in survey research being 'upset' or 'bothered' about receiving images, is rare. From the European Kids Online survey those who were more likely to be upset by texts they had received were younger rather than older teens and girls rather than boys (Livingstone and Gorzig 2012). By contrast teens who scored highly on the psychological measure of 'sensation seeking' reported less harm from sexting (Livingstone and Gorzig 2012).

For young people then, sexting is ambiguous and experienced in diverse ways. For some, it can be deeply problematic particularly when it is involuntary and images are distributed to unintended audiences. For other young people it is part of school ground hilarity, akin to what used to go on behind the bike shed as Bond (2010) argues, or a new form of sexual flirtation or experimentation with intimate partners. The public panic, however, concentrates on the threat that sexting poses to the young and messages such as those offered by Livingstone and Gorzig (2012)—that 'we should not be overly concerned about the rise in online sexual messaging' because only are minority are sexting and only much smaller minority find it upsetting'—are not often a part of public discussions or commentary.

What role do parents play or should parents play in negotiating sexting with their children? Despite the increasing volume of popular books providing advice we have little information on how families manage this form of consumption. The quotes from the US study suggest diverse approaches; one younger high school boy reported that he doesn't sext because 'my mom goes through my phone' (Lenhart 2009, 10) while a young high school girl does not feel so constrained. 'Yes [sexting is pretty common] cuz some of my friends do it. [But it's] no big deal I would let my mom see if she wanted' (Lenhart 2009, 9). Yet the results from the large survey component found that whether or not parents looked at the contents of their children's mobile phones didn't affect how likely teenagers were to sext (Lenhart 2009). This is a new area of communication and a new everyday form of sexual intimacy; we don't seek to adjudicate on the harms and benefits for young people. But parental responses are likely to be fuelled by concern, hope and love.

The decision to review mobile phone content by some is clearly an effort to keep children safe. The decision to aim for trust and voluntary disclosure by other parents (and not to look at phones) reflects, we would argue, exactly the same hopes and aspirations expressed in a different strategy and approach. Worries about how much self exposure in sex is acceptable will be shaped by existing family practices: some parents are never naked before their children, others see the hiding of bodies as generating fear and shame for their children. Responses to sexting will be influenced by these experiences and preferences. In this area of consumption, as in many others, parents are seeking to keep children safe and help them learn to secure their own safety while pursuing love, sex and intimacy. In the next section we turn to the eye of the storm, the consumption of pornography.

YOUNG PEOPLE AND PORNOGRAPHY

The increasing sexual openness of society we discussed at the beginning of the chapter is illustrated by the growth of sexual material on family television sets and through other mainstream media. Parents sometimes observe these new developments with discomfort. As Penny a parent in Buckingham and Bragg's (2004) UK study noted 'Every newspaper you open now, every magazine, it's got a nude body on, or somebody's, pop star's, sex-life'; others spoke of material being 'rammed down kids throats' (2004, 212). Still other parents from this same study however took the opportunity presented by sexual material to 'raise debate and discussion with their children' and engage in 'pedagogical parenting' by teaching their children how to assess and read sexual material presented in the media (Buckingham and Bragg 2004, 195). Mothers in particular were keen to engage in 'ethical nurturing' by raising 'broader issues of ethics and personal conduct' when they viewed sexual material in soap operas or movies with their children (Buckingham and Bragg 2004, 199–200). These parental efforts are aimed at both monitoring and guiding children; when parents enter the challenging terrain of pornographic material, aspirations and practices are likely to be tested and tried.

States enforce censorship classifications for television and movie content; such classifications provide some guidance for parents even if their children lobby for watching 'older' or higher level classification material. Even here, the 'view with parental guidance' classification points to the complicated negotiation of familial and social norms. For the Internet, however, guidance and control are made significantly more difficult. The development of ICTs have enabled new forms of pornography production and exchange illustrated by the sharp rise in amateur pornography production and distribution and some amateur sex video sites rank in the top 50 global websites in terms of internet traffic (Powell 2010, 109). Accessible pornography is frequently viewed as one of the worst outcomes of the mediation of everyday life and pornography is portrayed as invading families via computer screens and destroying innocence.

As one young teenage boy described:

> It's incredibly easy to access. And I could pick up my phone right now and show everyone. I have internet on my phone, I have internet on my laptop, I have internet everywhere, I can get away with lots of things and my mum doesn't know how to access the internet, she can't look at my history. So easy just to get away with it (Boy 1). (Insight 2012)

Sorting out the fretting about pornography and actual harm posed by it is a complex task, both for experts and for parents. There is no doubt that the panic about pornography is intense, as evidenced by one content analysis of newspapers across Europe which found that media reports focus their attention on the risk of youth exposure to pornography rather than evidence of exposure or harm or any potential benefits of viewing sexual content online (Rovolis and Tsaliki 2012).

Yet in stark contrast to the moral panic about porn teenagers viewing sexual images online is potentially a minority experience. The large-scale EU *Kids Online* survey of 25,000 teens across Europe found that less than one quarter of teens had viewed sexual images. Older teens were most likely to have seen online content (14%) and accidental pop-ups (12%) and older teenage boys were the group most likely to have seen online sexual content (24% of those aged 13–16) (Rovolis and Tsaliki 2012). These findings contrast strongly with findings from smaller and possibly less representative samples. Australian research has found that exposure to porn was much more common 84% of males and 60% of females had inadvertently been exposed to pornographic images (Flood 2009; Powell 2010). This research found the deliberate consumption of pornography by young people was highly gendered (38% of males and 2% of females had sought to view porn). Males are more likely than females to view pornography for sexual excitement and masturbation, to report being sexually aroused by pornography and to have positive attitudes toward it (Flood 2009). Powell's detailed qualitative research on university students found similar gender patterns with young men being the main consumers of porn (Powell 2010).

The links between risks of viewing pornography, incidents of viewing porn and actual harm are tenuous and inconclusive (Rovolis and Tsaliki 2012). Michael Flood (2009) describes how the context of viewing and the character of exposure shape the way pornography is experienced and the impact it may have on young people in his review of the literature on pornography. Definitions of porn can vary widely as can reactions to sexual content (Rovolis and Tsaliki 2012). For ethical reasons it is difficult to gather detailed data on children's experiences of harm from exposure to pornography (Rovolis and Tsaliki 2012). Harm is necessarily defined in fairly neutral terms such as being 'bothered' by an image in the EU kids online survey or finding an image 'offensive or disgusting' in Flood's Australian study. In the Australian survey over half of the participants (aged 11–17) had experienced something on the internet they thought was 'offensive or disgusting' (Flood 2009). By contrast from the larger EU *Kids Online* survey only a third of young people who had seen sexual images online were 'bothered by them'—this is about 4% of the total sample of teens in the survey (Rovolis and Tsaliki 2012). As Rovolis and Tsaliki (2012) argue risk and even exposure doesn't necessarily result in harm. Of all teens who reported being bothered by images they had seen, the majority coped well and reported that they 'got over the experience immediately' (Rovolis and Tsaliki 2012). There were some differences in groups of young people reporting harm which mirrors the findings reported in the previous sections on sexting; younger children were more likely to be upset than older children, girls were more likely to be upset than boys and those with lower scores on the psychological self-efficacy scale were more likely to report being upset than others (Rovolis and Tsaliki 2012).

As noted earlier though, many young people want more sexual knowledge and boys in particular see it as 'a bit of an education' (Buckingham and Bragg 2004, 105). Yet as Michael Flood argues:

> Pornography is a poor sex educator. Most pornography is too explicit for younger children; most shows sex in unrealistic ways and neglects intimacy and romance; most pornography is sexist; and some is based on and eroticises violence. (Flood 2009, 395)

Pornography is more accessible for young people today than for earlier generations and there is some evidence that pornography has a negative impact on young people's relationships. Like the other realms of consumption we have discussed potential harms from exposure to pornography are real but the effects of consumption are complicated and vary according to social context. Sex educators increasingly voice concerns that young people have new and perhaps distorted expectations about sex because they are being influenced by the pornography they have seen, as Michael Flood says 'porn can shift our sense of what's normal' (Insight 2012). As young people's potential access to 'harder' and more 'extreme' pornography, including minority practices such as bestiality and scat play, increases, families are challenged to regulate and manage consumption (Insight 2012).

An excellent current affairs discussion program 'Generation XXX' was shown on Insight in Australia in early 2012 (Insight 2012). In this program diverse opinions were offered by a range of sex educators, academics, parents and young people themselves about the effects of pornography viewing on young people's sexual lives. The participants were remarkably open and one mother, Susan Kouloruris, demonstrated reflexive 'ethical nurturing' that contemporary mothers display (Buckingham and Bragg 2004) in response to her 15-year-old daughter's revelation that she had seen pornography at a young age.

Susan: But the issue I think is that me as a mum thinking that you had exposure to pornography at 13 before you even felt like you would have liked to participate in the sexual act makes my kind of a sad because where is your discovery of something that I discovered in the natural path of growing? It's almost it's just exposed to you and you've seen, is that where I should be? Yes, there should be emotion in it and when we started talking about, when we started talking about sex like as a mother daughter, I think if I had known that at 13 you were exposed to it my discussion with you would have been a lot more stronger about relationship, love and respect. And I think that, I think that somehow this pornography industry is stealing that away from you. (Insight 2012)

Yet research also demonstrates that young people are capable of viewing pornography and expressing complex and strong opinions about it. In Buckingham and Bragg's (2004) study the teenagers consistently stigmatised regular porn users as 'obsessed', 'sick', 'weird' or 'sad perverts' though many, particularly boys, were interested to see pornography (2004, 105). Many young people display a kind of media literacy where they are able to challenge media representations of sex and know that what they see on the media isn't necessarily true (Buckingham and Bragg 2004; Rovolis and Tsaliki 2012). As Olivia in Buckingham and Bragg's (2004) qualitative study in the UK said:

> Whereas with probably boys of our age and maybe a bit younger, say 15, 16, would sort of say if they watched a porn video, say 'my girlfriend's gotta be like that'. Or, 'I want my girlfriend to look like that'. But there's no hope in hell, 'cause not everyone's plastic. (Buckingham and Bragg 2004, 105)

Another of their participants described her advice to her younger brother and his friend when she walked in on them looking at porn.

> I just laughed a bit and then I went . . . I said 'Oh I'll leave you to it shall I? Don't want to get in the way of, like, your learning process!' I say to him, I say 'look, you know, it don't happen like that in real life'. (Buckingham and Bragg 2004, 105)

This comical exchange between older sister and younger brother illuminates the family context in which young people seek out and are exposed to pornography. As in our examination of media in family, access is through parent provided computers or mobile communication devices. The usual familial constraints around media use are intensified when 'forbidden' or embarrassing material is being accessed. For example, some children exposed to porn in an Australian study were more upset by the potential reactions of their parents if they found out rather than by the content itself (Flood 2009). This finding reinforces family roles in constructing and influencing sexual identities and experiences for young people. It suggests that children are always regulating their own consumption according to the limits parents have set, even when parents are not in effective control of teen desires, practices or media spaces. Other research found considerable resistance to parental regulation with teens secretly watching forbidden television shows or videos (Buckingham and Bragg 2004), but such conflict and resistance, we would argue, are a necessary part of familial consumption. The setting of limits, and the breaking of rules, reflects familial engagement and concern: they demonstrate parents' care and children's individuation in equal measure. All of the UK parents Buckingham and Bragg (2004) interviewed were concerned to regulate their children's consumption of sexual material though the strategies they used were diverse.

This reflects findings about parental practices in a range of consuming domains: diverse strategies are used to achieve what they see as the best possible outcomes for children and young people. The researchers identified more or less pedagogical styles of parenting though few of the parents relied on prohibition without discussion. 'Most were inclined to adopt a more democratic of "child-centred" approach, placing an emphasis on choice and self-reflection' (Buckingham and Bragg 2004, 234). This approach meant parents were required to continuously nurture and monitor their children and their consumption. This continuous engagement and negotiation also seemed to have paid off in terms of the accounts that children gave of their management of media. 'In many cases their parents had successfully helped them to develop strategies for coping with the media and for understanding them in particular ways' (Buckingham and Bragg 2004, 234).

CONCLUSION

Negotiating sexual relationships is a complex task for young people and parents in contemporary families. The sexual landscape has changed substantially in recent decades and there is more openness in society about sexuality, there is also more fluidity in family life. Our knowledge of how families negotiate the emerging sexuality of young people is uneven yet we can assume that many young people are 'seeing it' and 'doing it' in the family home. It is possible that many young people conduct their relationships autonomously from their parents –that engagement with sexual culture and sexual relationships are hidden from parents or perhaps wilfully ignored by parents. Yet we suggest that it is likely that sexual commodities are negotiated within the family context in similar ways to food, alcohol and other products. Parents fund mobile phones, Internet access and clothing and make-up purchases for their teens and try to influence their patterns of consumption and conduct of sexual relationships. They work reflexively with children's desires, and their own views about acceptable sexual images and practices, trying for compromise and consumption decisions that protect children but also enable them to grow into competent consumers.

The public anxiety about sexualisation is in some ways justified. The proliferation of sexual and pornographic images in popular culture offer deeply gendered, problematic and often limited representations of sexuality. Young people are sometimes targeted as key consumers for sexual products and information that is also marketed in earnest to adult audiences. In terms of sexual practices and relationships this generation of young people do have more freedom than previous generations but homophobia and sexism continue to have a negative impact on everyday practices and these are reinforced in the commercialisation of sex.

Yet the moral panic over sexualisation and the developing hegemony of the 'sexualisation discourse' does have a stifling effect on critical thinking about youth sexuality and the ways in which young people may accept or resist corporate marketing in their consumption (Egan and Hawkes 2008). In the sexualisation discourse parents are required to protect their 'innocent' children and strenuously reject 'sexualising products' even though these are not always clearly defined. There is a need for more research on the ways in which the consumption of sexual information and products are negotiated in families but the evidence that is available suggests that parents and young people are doing this in diverse ways. As with the other forms of consumption we have discussed in this book, the social environment for consumption of sexual commodities and information is complex and fraught. Yet parents and children negotiate consumption with care and face the inevitable conflicts over sex and intimacy. Young people's claims to separateness, maturity and belonging are wrangled alongside parental protection from the potentially negative effects of a more sexually open world. Parents are navigating new sexual norms alongside their children and negotiating the way forward with their children in complex ways driven by worry, love and care.

Conclusion

A New Purchase on Family Life

In *Consuming Families* we have examined the noisiest public anxieties about consumption in contemporary families. Consumption is the central battleground in public debates over morality, excess and responsibility and these contests have particular resonance in the characterisation of life in contemporary families in Western nations. Fears that excess goods and appetite, the paucity and speeding up of time, the decline of traditional family forms, and changing relational structures are threatening family life are common. Parents face blaming discourses about the spread of childhood obesity, teens binge drinking, and new media technologies damaging children, as they engage in the everyday tasks of love and care. Each of these areas of consumption presents real and difficult challenges for parents and children. The process of making good and appropriate consumption choices draws on knowledge, expertise, preference, social and economic resources and parental love and commitment. Daily negotiations and decisions are hard, often full of conflict, disappointment and compromise. Yet public anxiety about these issues is expressed in regulatory demands and responses that focus on prohibition and censure. Families are blamed for being asleep at the wheel, for not knowing what their children are up to, or not caring, for setting bad examples for their children. The common story is that the market has intruded too far into family life and the losses have been significant. Materialism and excess are now substituting for family intimacy and care.

Families have a complicated place in contemporary consumption debates. They are on one hand seen as the best protectors of children's well-being. Nourishment and support inside families is both a personal and social resource. States need families to step forward to manage the threats and negative consequences of consumption. But families are regularly castigated for failing to discipline and properly care for 'innocent' children. The consuming desires of individual family members, even parents, are perceived to overwhelm the bonds of responsibility, restraint and care. This willingness to attribute carelessness and/or narcissism, for us, does not accord with what we have observed in over a decade of family research and in the wonderful work of many family scholars across the Western world.

As we wrote this book the importance of relationality in consumption emerged more clearly. We have begun to work towards the idea of 'relational consumption' to describe how families do consumption everyday. Families consume relationally—in negotiation with each other and for each other. For us, the concept of relational consumption has three central components: it is about care, connection and belonging. It offers a way to thread together the diverse consuming pressures parents face as they care for their children in post-scarcity societies—it is care through provision as well as through constraint. It is care through experimentation and experience, through negotiation and compromise. Stories of family life usually reflect worry, effort, engagement and care even in and through conflict. Though outcomes are uncertain and ideal standards are rarely met, we see an enduring endeavour in contemporary families to live well and lovingly together. This book is animated by a desire to talk more about the reflexivity and effort, the resilience and responsiveness that can be seen in contemporary families, even in the most complicated and difficult areas of consumption. We have been keen to consider family consuming struggles as part of the making of families. We have positioned compromise and ambivalence as signs of parental care and engagement rather than as failure and fragility in family life.

The consumption that families do as they care for each other is subject to wider social forces operating in the state and the economy. There are a significant number of social and structural changes that are shaping contemporary family lives and family consuming decisions. Firstly, the relationship between the State and families has shifted. The State has retreated from the direct provision of care, as welfare and social services have been reduced or cut. Pressures on families to step into emerging care gaps, to 'take responsibility', have intensified. Secondly gender relations in response to economic change and feminism have shifted substantially too. As mothers have moved into the paid workforce family schedules now incorporate much more paid labour raising fears that more time is devoted to work than to caring at home. Underneath many of the public panics about consumption lurks the fear that mothers are no longer present or available to cook nutritious meals or effectively monitor their children's behaviour.

One of the key themes throughout the book has been managing the transition from child to adult in the West. With changes toward more open and permissive parenting styles, children have more recognised power in domestic negotiations as they learn to consume effectively. Young people have gained freedom to engage in 'adult' consumption practices at earlier ages. Yet at the same time young people's dependence on their parents has been extended into their twenties due to longer secondary and tertiary education and delayed entry into full time work. Paradoxically too as more women have entered the labour market expectations for parental supervision and cultivation have become more complex, meaning children are confined to home and dedicated parental attention is required. Many of the most difficult and contentious consumption challenges in family life centre on transitions to adulthood, in the domains of media, sex and alcohol. Some of the tensions between dependence and independence for children and teens are being played out through contests over consumption in families and in wider discussions about family care and responsibility.

In weighing these external pressures on family practices, we see a balance between the agentic and the reactive in how families chart their consuming courses. Families manage food pressures by trying for healthy eating, but recognise their children's preferences and incorporate treats. Parents worry about alienating media use but families play games and watch television together. Sitting side by side on separate screens is a form of intimacy albeit new and distinct from extant versions of family communication. Facilitating difficult consumption transitions in drinking or sexual freedom means parents walk a path between openness and restriction, between hope and fear. Young people negotiate rebellion and the relinquishment of dependence. These interactions are filled with trouble, with conflict but emerge most often in and through love and care.

In this book we have sought to look behind the consumption panics to what occurs in the daily lives of consuming families. Using our own research and the work of others, we have looked for the everyday negotiations that occur in families about what to eat, when and where teens can drink, what computer games can be played and how youthful sexual relationships can be managed. We have been inspired by the sense that consumption is properly embedded in everyday family life; indeed by the sense that consumption constitutes family. Most forms of consumption are everyday 'family practices', fuelled by the drive to nurture and sustain, beset by the inherent tensions in consuming desires and decisions, and framed by often proscriptive public discourses about what to do and what not to do. Parents worry about good food, about managing media, about sex and alcohol and try out a range of strategies to care for their children and support them to grow and develop. Far from showing recklessness or inattention, most families demonstrate a great deal of reflexivity in their daily struggles with good consumption decisions and competing types of information. Parents seek to achieve the best possible outcomes through control, through negotiation, through compromise and through conflict. In different spheres of consumption, they try different strategies. Food refusals mean mothers try anything and everything to nourish their children. Troubles over teen drinking move some families to collaborative alcohol consumption practices and others towards abstinence and prohibition. Ideas and information about sex provoke fights about clothing and some surprisingly open discussions between parents and children. In all of our searches, we have seen that families are 'doing' consumption with effort and attention.

An important thread running through the book has been the need to recognise the limits and constraints parents face in achieving good consumption outcomes for children. In many media articles about consumption problems of obesity or excessive television watching disadvantaged parents are blamed for not being able to effectively manage their children's consumption. The effect of social class on consumption is often framed through paradigms of blame and failure. The struggles faced by disadvantaged families in the context of reducing state support and the dominance of individual accounts of responsibility for health, well-being and success are not often the subject of public discussion. It is rare that the consuming decisions of parents facing multiple forms of disadvantage are valorised as love and care. Val Gillies reminds us that we need to think much more carefully about what certain purchases may mean in particular family contexts.

> Much desired items like brand name clothing or a favourite junk food for tea might make a difficult day at school more bearable for a child, while also communicating a strong message of love and care. (Gillies 2007 288)

If we are able to take a more generous view of what parents are seeking to do when they manage consumption in their family lives, we can see the threads of love and care in food, in goods, in family media use and in the difficult areas of sex and alcohol. We may be more alert to the difficult and inevitably compromised decisions parents make and why they make them.

We can observe, and we should expect, conflict over consumption as children refuse to eat, or defy their parents' rules, as teens retreat to their bedrooms and mobilise personal screens in a bid for privacy and independence. These conflicts are not family failures but are rather important family practices. Children and their parents express preferences, identities, belonging and distinction in consumption and in consuming conflicts. The balance of individual and collective aspirations has always been part of everyday family life and consuming practices play a key role in the management and negotiation of these tensions. But we also need to recognise that consumption is about pleasure and play in family life; that gifts, treats and rituals involving consumption are central to the production of daily life and love.

Our concept of 'relational consumption' offers, we hope, a promising new line of investigation in the field of consumption. By prioritising the dynamics of care, connection and belonging, new questions emerge that are not visible if consumption is viewed as only an individual or competitive. Family life is a struggle, and the consuming pressures that families, and family members face do create stresses and strains. But in the negotiation, the strife, the noise and the trouble, families provide for, share with and nurture each other. They laugh, play, eat and drink together. Family consumption is an expression and materialisation of love that holds together and sustains family life. Family consumption practices, for all of the challenges, the worry and the ambivalence, are the material expression of family connection and care.

Appendix

SHORT PROJECT TITLE: CONSUMING FAMILIES

Long Title: *Young people, families, consumption and health*
Project Team: Jo Lindsay, JaneMaree Maher, John Coveney
Project Funding: PSI, Monash University, \$6000. Flinders University \$1000

Project Description:

This is a pilot study that involved fifteen interviews conducted with families, children and young adults (either in-home or at a location of their choice) in Melbourne's inner and outer suburbs between November 14 and December 8, 2011. Specifically, interviews included five family interviews with 12–14-year-olds (including three from single parent families); five in-depth interviews children (12–14 years old) and Five in-depth interviews with (18–20 years old). In total data was collected about 9 families as multiple interviews (family and individual) were conducted for five of the families. Participants were recruited and interviewed by IPSOS a social research company following a sampling frame and interview schedule designed by the chief investigators (Lindsay, Maher and Coveney). Participants were paid a small amount to thank them for their time (\$50 for a family interview and \$20 for an individual interview).

The family interviews were designed to gather data on intergenerational negotiations about food. The interviews with 12–13–year–olds were designed to capture the experiences of children who had recently transitioned to high school, which is often a time of increased autonomy from families. The interviews with 18–20 year olds were designed to gain an insight into consumption at another key transition point when young adults leave school and enter the workplace or tertiary study. All of interviews provided rich data on the relationship between generations and how families are produced via the consumption of food.

SHORT PROJECT TITLE: FAMILY TIME

Long Title *New Configurations of Work and Family: Nurses and Builders Working and Caring*
Project Team JaneMaree Maher, Jo Lindsay, Anne Bardoel.
Project Funding: PSI/ACREW, Monash University, \$20, 000.

Project Description

In a 2007–2008 study, our research team interviewed twenty couples from Victoria, Australia where at least one partner was a nurse and there were young children under 12, using a criterion approach to sampling (Patton, 2002). We were interested in how these families negotiated work-care intersections in their daily lives, with particular reference to decisions about employment and commitments to children's care and activities. We chose semi-structured couple interviews so couples could describe together how they managed. Ethics approval was obtained and couples were recruited by advertising in a nursing magazine, placing posters in several large metropolitan hospitals and using electronic lists. In addition, some participants offered to circulate flyers to colleagues. In interviews, we focussed on the intersections of work and care in the nursing profession with attention to everyday schedules, care practices and work experiences. In all published material, pseudonyms have been used and identifying details changed.

Project Publications

Maher, J., Lindsay, J and A. Bardoel. (2010). "Freeing Time: The 'Family Time Economies' of Nurses." *Sociology* 44(2): 269–287.

Lindsay, J, J. Maher, and A. Bardoel. (2009). "Modified Maternalism: Nurses and Their Families Managing Work and Care in Australia." *Journal of Comparative Family Studies* 40(4): 659–675.

Maher, J., J. Lindsay, A. Bardoel, and J. Advocat. (2008). *Flexibility and More?: Nurses Working and Caring.* PSI/ACREW, Monash University. Available at: http://www.arts.monash.edu.au/womens-studies/staff/documents/nurses-report.pdf.

Maher, J. (2013). Nurse Mothers Valuing Care at Home and at Work: Beyond Notions of Care Scarcity? *Journal of Sociology.*

Maher, J. (Forthcoming). Women's Care/Career Changes as Connection and Resilience: Challenging Discourses of Breakdown and Conflict. *Gender, Work and Organisation.*

SHORT PROJECT TITLE: CHILDHOOD OBESITY

Long Title DP110101759 *Improving Australia's Response to Childhood Obesity: Prevention Education and Its Impact on Mothers and Families 2011–2012*

Project Team: Suzanne Fraser, Jan Wright (UNSW), JaneMaree Maher, Alan Petersen.

Project Funding: ARC $90000

Project Description

In the study, we interviewed 24 mothers (and staff—though I am not drawing on this data here) recruited through three different childcare sites about their knowledge of childhood obesity, their ideas about nutrition and their everyday food practices. The Monash University ethics committee approved the study and, in reporting pseudonyms are used, and identifying details have been changed.

The three childcare sites we used to recruit were located in different parts of Victoria: two were in metropolitan Melbourne, one was close to a largest regional city Geelong. These mothers all had toddler children who were in long daycare, although there were other children that ranged up to 16 years of age. Recruitment was through the centres and we offered a Coles voucher of $30 to mothers who participated. The socio-economic demographic characteristics of Site 1 and Site 2 were comparable in terms of average income brackets and housing prices. Both sites were in relatively wealthy areas where the median house prices were high (with Site 1 having a slightly higher median house price $775k in contrast to $645k). Site 3 was located in an area with a much lower median income and median house prices were approximately one third of the other two sites.

Project Publications

Maher, J., S. Fraser, and J. Lindsay. (2010). "Between Provisioning and Consuming?: Children, Mothers and 'Childhood Obesity.'" *Health Sociology Review* 19(3): 304–316.

Maher, J., S. Fraser, and J. Wright. (2010). "Framing the Mother: Childhood Obesity, Maternal Responsibility and Care." *Journal of Gender Studies* 19(3): 233–247.

Fraser, S., J. Maher, J. and J. Wright, J. (2010). "Between Bodies and Collectivities: Articulating the Action of Emotion in Obesity Epidemic Discourse." *Social Theory & Health* 8(2): 192–209.

Seear, K., S. Fraser, J. Wright, J.M. Maher, and A. PetersenA. (2010). *Peeling Away the Onion: Report on a National Consultation on Childhood Obesity Research, Policy and Practice in Australia*, Monograph. Clayton Vic: Centre for Women's Studies and Gender Research, School of Political and Social Inquiry, Faculty of Arts, Monash University.

SHORT PROJECT TITLE: ALCOHOL CONSUMPTION CONTEXTS

Long Title: Alcohol Consumption Contexts
Project Team: Jo Lindsay
Research Assistants: Malcolm McCall, Hannah Walker and Amanda Lanarus
Project Funding: VicHealth Research Grant 2002–2004 $70,000

Project Description

The purpose of this research was to examine public alcohol consumption contexts for young people in metropolitan Victoria. In particular, the research examined the ways social class and gender shaped these drinking contexts. The research gathered information on social practices and crowd behaviour in venues, and young people's perspectives on their alcohol consumption practices in different settings to identify high-risk contexts as a basis for effective health intervention.

University ethics clearance was gained and we undertook detailed observation sessions in ten licensed premises from the Melbourne metropolitan area and we conducted in-depth interviews with 35 patrons recruited from these venues. The observations were conducted in three-hour sessions over three nights per venue, with at least two observers taking notes on each night. Thirty-five patrons, 15 females and 20 males (aged 18 to 30), were recruited from these venues and they participated in interviews at a later date.

Project Publications

Lindsay, J. (2005). Drinking in Melbourne Pubs and Clubs: A Study of Alcohol Consumption Contexts, School of Political and Social Inquiry, Monash University.

Lindsay, J. (2006). "A Big Night Out: Drinking as an Enactment of Class and Gender." *Contemporary Drug Problems* (Sweden) 33/Spring: 29—61.

Lindsay J (2009) "Young Australians and the Staging of Intoxication and Self-Control." *Journal of Youth Studies* 12(4): 371—384.

SHORT PROJECT TITLE: DRINKING BIOGRAPHIES

Long Title: 'What a great night': The cultural drivers of drinking practices among 14–24-year-old Australians. Tender for the provision of qualitative and quantitative research into the cultural drivers of risk taking behaviour and their affects on 'low risk', 'risky' and 'high risk' use of alcohol among 14–24 year old Australian drinkers

Project Team: Jo Lindsay, Peter Kelly, Lyn Harrison, Chris Hickey

Research Assistants: Jenny Advocat and Sue Cormack

Project Funding: Drinkwise/ Australian Government Department of Health and Ageing Research Tender 2007–2008 $223,000

Project Description

This research project aimed to gather information about the cultural drivers of alcohol consumption by young people in Victoria, Australia. Firstly, the research examined the role of alcohol in the context of young people's lives from the perspective of young people themselves, finding rich insights into their experiences of alcohol consumption over their lives to date and the social and cultural drivers of alcohol use. This project also explored the role alcohol played in the ways young people established and practiced their identity, and the ways in which peer groups operated to normalise alcohol consumption within the context of community sporting club cultures, using Victorian community sporting clubs as a case study.

The project involved two complementary and largely qualitative studies: The drinking biographies study involved in-depth interviews and a quantitative questionnaire with 60 young people, aged 20–24 recruited from universities and entertainment precincts in Melbourne, Geelong and Warrnambool. The sporting clubs study involved in-depth interviews and focus groups with young people and key informants at 11 Victorian sporting clubs. Our research was conducted in inner and outer suburban settings and provincial and rural locations in Victoria to identify the most salient cultural drivers of youth alcohol consumption. University ethics clearance was gained prior to commencement of the project and pseudonyms are used in publications from the project.

Project Publications

Lindsay J., P. Kelly, L. Harrison, C. Hickey, J. Advocat, and S. Cormack. (2009). 'What a Great Night': The Cultural Drivers of Drinking Practices among 14–24-Year-Old Australians. PSI: Monash University.

Hickey C., P. Kelly, S. Cormack, L. Harrison, and J. Lindsay. (2009). "Sporting Clubs, Alcohol and Young People: Enduring Tensions and Emerging Possibilities." *Healthy Lifestyles Journal* 56(1): 17—21.

Lindsay J., L. Harrison, J. Advocat, P. Kelly, C. Hickey. (2009). "'It's My Time to Shine': Young Australians Reflect on Past, Present and Imagined Future Alcohol Consumption." *Youth Studies Australia* 28(4): 44—51.

Harrison L., P. Kelly, C. Hickey, J. Lindsay. (2011). "'I Don't Know Anyone that Has Two Drinks a Day': Young People, Alcohol and the Government of Pleasure." *Health, Risk and Society* 13(5): 469—486.

Kelly P., C. Hickey, S. Cormack, L. Harrison, J. Lindsay. (2011). "Charismatic Cops, Patriarchs and a Few Good Women: Leadership, Club Culture and Young Peoples' Drinking." *Sport, Education and Society* 16(4): 465—481.

Lindsay J. (2012). "The Gendered Trouble with Alcohol: Young People Managing Alcohol Related Violence." *International Journal of Drug Policy* 23: 236—241.

SHORT PROJECT TITLE: UNIVERSITY DRINKING

Long Title: Alcohol Use and Harm Minimisation Among Australian University Students

Project Team: Toni Schofield, Jo Lindsay, Fiona Giles, Julie Hepworth, John Germov, Rose Leontini, Tara McGee

Research Assistants: Rebecca Brown, Cathrin Bernhardt and Audra Glavas

PhD student: Brigid Henley

Project Funding: ARC Linkage Grant with Industry Partners—University Colleges Australia and the Victorian Health Department and New South Wales Health Department $370,000 2010–2012

Project Description

This ARC Linkage project is the largest ever Australian study of university students' alcohol use and the measures they take to limit harm. The aim is to develop a new theoretical approach to understanding harm minimisation and better strategies for achieving it. The project is driven by a multisector partnership of Campus-based university colleges, the State health authorities of NSW and Victoria, and an interdisciplinary research team from the University of Sydney (project leaders), Monash University, the University of Newcastle and the University of Queensland.

The project examines the alcohol use of both college and non-college university students from metropolitan and regional areas within NSW, Victoria and Queensland. On online survey with students from thirteen universities was undertaken to map practices in relation to alcohol (over 3,300 students participated). In addition, 19 focus groups and 100 interviews were undertaken with undergraduate exploring what drinking means to them, the social dynamics surrounding alcohol use and how students interpret harm minimisation.

Project Publications

In progress

Bibliography

Aarsand, Pal. 2007. "Computer and Video Games in Family Life: The Digital Divide As a Resource in Intergenerational Interactions." *Childhood* 14: 235–256.

Aarsand, Pal, and Karin Aronsson. 2009. "Gaming and Territorial Negotiations in Family Life." *Childhood* 16: 497–517.

Adema, Pauline. 2000 "Vicarious Consumption: Food, Television and the Ambiguity of Modernity." *The Journal of American Culture* 23: 113–123.

Advertising Standards Bureau. 2012. "Mossimo." Case no 0075/12 Canberra: Advertising Standards Board. Accessed August 19, 2012. http://122.99.94.111/cases/0075-12.pdf.

Ahlander, Nancy, and Kathleen Bahr. 1995. "Beyond Drudgery, Power, and Equity: Toward an Expanded Discourse on the Moral Dimensions of Housework in Families." *Journal of Marriage and Family* 57: 54–54.

AIHW. 2011. *Substance Use among Aboriginal and Torres Strait Islander People.* Canberra: Australian Institute of Health and Welfare.

Arnett, Jeffrey J. 2002. "The Sounds of Sex: Sex in Teens' Music and Music Videos." In *Sexual Teens, Sexual Media: Investigating Media's influence on Adolescent Sexuality.* edited by J.D. Brown, J.R. Steele, and K. Walsh-Childers. Mahwah, NJ: Lawrence Erlbaum Associates.

Arnold, Jeanne, and Ursula Lang. 2007. "Changing American Home Life: Trends in Domestic Leisure and Storage among Middle-Class Families." *Journal of Family and Economic Issues* 28: 23–48.

Australian Government. 2012. *Teenagers and Alcohol: A Guide for Parents.* Accessed September 13, 2012. http://www.alcohol.gov.au/internet/alcohol/publishing.nsf/content/brochure-teen-alcohol.

Babor, Thomas, Raul Caetano, Sally Casswell, Griffith Edwards, Norman Giesbrecht, Kathryn Graham, Joel W. Grube, Linda Hill, Harold Holder, Ross Homel, Michael Livingston, Esa österberg, Jürgen Rehm, Robin Room, and Ingeborg Rossow. 2010. *Alcohol: No Ordinary Commodity.* Oxford: Oxford University Press.

Backett-Milburn, Kathleen, Wendy Wills, Mei-Li Roberts, and Julia Lawton. 2010. "Food and Family Practices: Teenagers, Eating and Domestic Life in Differing Socio-Economic Circumstances." *Children's Geographies* 8: 303–314.

Bahr Bugge, Annechen, and Reidar Almås. 2006. "Domestic Dinner: Representations and Practices of a Proper Meal among Young Suburban Mothers." *Journal of Consumer Culture* 6: 203–228.

Bahr, Stephen, John Hoffmann, and Xiaoyan Yang. 2005. "Parental and Peer Influences on the Risk of Adolescent Drug Use." *Journal of Primary Prevention* 26: 529–551.

Bailey, Beth. 1988. *From Front Porch to Back Seat: Courtship in Twentieth-Century America.* Baltimore: Johns Hopkins University Press.

Baldassar, Loretta, Cora Baldock, and Raelene Wilding. 2007. *Families Caring across Borders: Migration, Ageing and Transnational Caregiving*. London: Palgrave.

Banwell, Cathy, Mary O'Brien, Margaret Hamilton, and Robyn Attewell. 1999. "Measuring Women's Alcohol Consumption in an Australian Inner-Urban Community Using the AUDIT." *Drug and Alcohol Review* 18: 379–388.

Barnes, Grace, Joseph Hoffman, John Welte, Michael Farrell, and Barbara Dintcheff. 2006. "Effects of Parental Monitoring and Peer Deviance on Substance Use and Delinquency." *Journal of Marriage and Family* 68: 1084–1104.

Bassett, Raewyn, Brenda Beagan, and Gwen Chapman. 2008. "Grocery Lists: Connecting Family, Household and Grocery Store." *British Food Journal* 110: 206–217.

Bauman, Zygmunt. 2007. *Consuming Life*. London: Polity Press.

Beagan, Brenda, Gwen Chapman, Andrea D'Sylva, and Raewyn Bassett. 2008. "'It's Just Easier for Me to Do It': Rationalizing the Family Division of Foodwork." *Sociology* 42(4): 653–671.

Beck-Gernsheim, Elisabeth. 2002a. "On the Way to a Post-Familial Family." In *Individualization: Institutionalized Individualism and its Social and Political Consequences*, edited by Ulrich Beck and Elisabeth Beck-Gernsheim, 85–100. London: Sage.

Beck-Gernsheim, Elisabeth. 2002b. *Reinventing the Family: In Search of New Lifestyles*, translated by Patrick Camiller. Malden, MA: Polity Press.

Beck-Gernsheim, Elisabeth. 2002c. "From Living for Others to A Life of One's Own." In *Individualization: Institutionalized Individualism and its Social and Political Consequences*, edited by Ulrich Beck and Elisabeth Beck-Gernsheim, 54–84. London: Sage.

Bell, Kirsten, Darlene McNaughton, and Amy Salmon. 2009. "Medicine, Morality and Mothering: Public Health Discourses on Foetal Alcohol Exposure, Smoking around Children and Childhood over Nutrition." *Critical Public Health* 19: 155–170.

Bianchi, Suzanne. 2000. "Maternal Employment and Time with Children: Dramatic Change or Surprising Continuity?" *Demography* 37: 401–414.

Bianchi, Suzanne, John Robinson, and Michael Milkie. 2006. *Changing Rhythms of American Family Life*. New York: Russell Sage Foundation.

Bittman, Michael. 2005. "Sunday Working and Family Time." *Labour & Industry* 1: 59–83.

Boero, Natalie. 2007. "All the News that's Fat to Print: The American Obesity Epidemic and the Media." *Qualitative Sociology* 30: 41–60.

Bond, Emma. 2010. "The Mobile Phone = Bike Shed? Children, Sex and Mobile Phones." *New Media and Society* 13: 587–604.

Bordo, Susan. 1993. *Unbearable Weight: Feminism, Western Culture and the Body*. Berkeley: : University of California Press.

Bourdieu, Pierre. 1986. *Distinction: A Social Critique of the Judgement of Taste*. Trans. R. Nice, London: Routledge.

Bove, Catriona. 2006. "Foodwork in Newly Married Couples: Making Family Meals." *Food, Culture and Society* 9: 69–89.

Bowlby, Sophie, Linda McKie, Sue Gregory, and Isabelle MacPherson. 2010. *Interdependency and Care over the Lifecourse*. London: Routledge.

Bragg, Sara, David Buckingham, Rachel Russell, and Rebekah Willett. 2011. "Too Much, Too Soon? Children, Sexualization, and Consumer Culture." *Sex Education* 11: 279–292.

Brain, Kevin, Howard Parker, and Tom Carnwath. 2000. "Drinking with Design: Young Drinkers As Psychoactive Consumers." *Drugs: Education, Prevention and Policy* 7: 5–20.

Brannen, Julia, and Anne Nilsen. 2005. "Individualisation, Choice and Structure: A Discussion of Current Trends in Sociological Analysis." *Sociological Review* 53: 412–428.

Brembeck, Helene. 2009. "Children's 'Becoming' in Frontiering Foodscapes." In *Children, Food and Identity in Everyday Life*, edited by Allison James, Anne Trine Kjørholt, and Vebjørg Tingstad, 130–148. Basingstoke: Palgrave Macmillan.

Brembeck, Helene. 2005. "Home to McDonald's: Upholding the Family Dinner with the Help of McDonald's." *Food, Culture & Society* 8: 215—226.

Brooks, Karen. 2008. *Consuming Innocence: Popular Culture and Our Children*. St Lucia: University of Queensland Press.

Bryce, Jo, and Jason Rutter. 2010. "Gender Dynamics and the Social and Spatial Organisation of Computer Gaming." *Leisure Studies* 22: 1–15.

Bryson, Valerie. 2007. *Gender and the Politics of Time: Feminist Theory and Contemporary Debate*. London: The Policy Press.

Buckingham, David. 2011. *The Material Child: Growing Up in Consumer Culture*. Cambridge: Polity.

Buckingham, David, and Sara. Bragg. 2004. *Young People, Sex and the Media: The Facts of Life?* Basingstoke: Palgrave Macmillan.

Budgeon, Shelley, and Sasha Roseneil. 2004. "Editors' Introduction: Beyond the Conventional Family." *Current Sociology* 52: 127–134.

Buffardi, Laura, and Kevin Campbell. 2008. "Narcissism and Social Networking Web Sites." *Personality and Social Psychology Bulletin* 34: 1303–1314.

Bumpus, Matthew, Ann Crouter, and Susan McHale. 1999. "Work Demands of Dual-Earner Couples: Implications for Parents' Knowledge about Children's Daily Lives in Middle Childhood." *Journal of Marriage & the Family* 61: 465–475.

Burridge, Joseph, and Margo Baker. 2009. "Food as a Medium for Emotional Management of the Family: Avoiding Complaint and Producing Love." In *Changing Families, Changing Food*, edited by Peter Jackson, 146–164. London: Palgrave Macmillan.

Burrows, Lisa. 2009. "Pedagogizing Families through Obesity Discourse." In *Biopolitics and the 'Obesity Epidemic: Governing Bodies*, edited by Jan Wright and Valerie Harwood, 127–140. London: Routledge.

Burrows, Lisa. 2008. " 'Fit, Fast, and Skinny:' New Zealand School Students 'Talk' about Health." *Journal of Physical Education New Zealand* 41: 26–36.

Burrows, Roger, Sarah Nettleton, and Robin Bunton. 1995. Sociology and Health Promotion: Health, Risk and Consumption under Late Modernism. In *The Sociology of Health Promotion: Critical Analyses of Consumption, Lifestyle and Risk*, edited by Roger Burrows, Sarah Nettleton, and Robin Bunton, 1–8. London: Routledge.

Caballero, Benjamin. 2005. "A Nutrition Paradox: Underweight and Obesity in Developing Countries." *New England Journal of Medicine* 352: 1514–1516.

Campbell, Hugh 2000. "The Glass Phallus: Public Masculinity and Drinking in Rural New Zealand." *Rural Sociology* 65(4): 562–581.

Campbell, Karen, David Crawford, and Kylie Hesketh. 2006. "Australian Parents' Views on Their 5–6-Year-Old Children's Food Choices." *Health Promotion International* 22: 11–18.

Campos, Paul, Abigail Saguy, Paul Ernsberger, Eric Oliver, and Glenn Gesser. 2005. "The Epidemiology of Overweight or Obesity: Public Health Crisis or Moral Panic?" *International Journal of Epidemiology* 35: 55–60.

Chambers, Deborah. 2012. *A Sociology of Family Life: Change and Diversity in Intimate Relationships*. Cambridge: Polity.

Chambers, Deborah. 2011. "'Wii Play As a Family': The Rise in Family-Centred Video Gaming." *Leisure Studies* 31: 69–82.

Chatterton, Paul, and Robert Hollands. 2001. *Changing our 'Toon': Youth, Nightlife and Urban Change in Newcastle.* Newcastle Upon Tyne: University of Newcastle.

Chayko, Mary. 2008. *Portable Communities: The Social Dynamics of Online and Mobile Connectedness.* Albany: SUNY Press.

Chitakunye, David, and Pauline Maclaran. 2008. "The Everyday Practices Surrounding Young People's Food Consumption." *Young Consumers* 9: 215–227.

Citybeach. 2012a 'Men's Tees" Accessed April 5, 2012. http://www.citybeach.com.au/en/mens/tees/211411_187-inc.-dff-tee.

Citybeach. 2012b "Men's Tees" Accessed April 5, 2012. http://www.citybeach.com.au/en/mens/tees/194881_two-in-the-shirt-work-hard-play-hard-tee.

Clarke, Peter, and Andrew McAuley. 2010. "Parental Evaluation of Popular Brand Names Given as Christmas Gifts and Sources of Information Used in These Decisions." *The Journal of Consumer Marketing* 27: 534–542.

Coleman, Lester, and Suzanne Carter 2005, "Underage 'Binge' Drinking: A Qualitative Study into Motivations and Outcomes" *Drugs: Education, Prevention and Policy* 12(2): 125–136.

Collective Shout. 2012a "About Collective Shout" Accessed September 12, 2012. http://collectiveshout.org/about/.

Collective Shout. 2012b "ASB Upholds Complaints against Mossimo Peepshow" Accessed April 5, 2012. http://collectiveshout.org/2012/03/asb-upholds-complaints-against-mossimo-peepshow/.

Collective Shout. 2012c "Porn Tees" Accessed April 5, 2012. http://porntees.blogspot.com.au/search/label/City%20Beach.

Collective Shout. 2012d "Diva Breaches Pledge to Remove Playboy Jewellery from Stores." Accessed April 5, 2012. http://collectiveshout.org/2012/03/diva-breaches-pledge-to-remove-playboy-jewellery-from-stores/.

Cook, Daniel. 2009a. "Semantic Provisioning of Children's Food: Commerce, Care and Maternal Practice." *Childhood* 16: 317–334.

Cook, Daniel. 2009b. "Children's Subjectivities and Commercial Meaning: The Delicate Battles Mothers Wage When Feeding Their Children." In *Children, Food and Identity in Everyday Life*, edited by Allison James, Anne Trine Kjørholt, and Vebjørg Tingstad, 112–129. Basingstoke: Palgrave Macmillan.

Cook, Daniel. 2008a. "The Dichotomous Child in and of Commercial Culture, *Childhood* 12(2): 155–159.

Cook, Daniel. 2008b. "The Missing Child in Consumption Theory." *Journal of Consumer Culture* 8: 219–243.

Cook, Daniel. 1995. "The Mother as Consumer: Insights from the Children's Wear Industry, 1917–1929." *The Sociological Quarterly* 36: 505–522.

Coory, Michael. 2000. "Trends in Birth Rates for Teenagers in Queensland, 1988 to 1997: An Analysis by Economic Disadvantage and Geographic Remoteness." *Australian and New Zealand Journal of Public Health* 24: 316–319.

Coveney, John. 2008a. "Children, Girth and Government." *Health Sociology Review* 17: 199–213.

Coveney, John. 2008b. "The Government of the Table: Nutrition Expertise and the Social Organization of Family Food Habits." In *A Sociology of Food and Nutrition: The Social Appetite*, 3rd ed., edited by John Germov and Lauren Williams. South Melbourne: Oxford University Press.

Coveney, John. 2006. *Food, Morals and Meaning: The Pleasure and Anxiety of Eating.* London: Routledge.

Cowan-Jenssen, Sue, and Lucy Goodison. 2009. "Narcissism: Fragile Bodies in a Fragile World." *Psychotherapy and Politics International* 7: 81–94.

Craig, Lyn. 2007. "How Employed Mothers in Australia Find Time for Both Market Work and Childcare." *Journal of Family and Economic Issues* 28: 69–87.

Craig, Lyn. 2006a. "Parental Education, Time in Paid Work and Time with Children: An Australian Time-Diary Analysis." *The British Journal of Sociology* 57: 553–575.

Craig, Lyn. 2006b. "Children and the Revolution: A Time-Diary Analysis of the Impact of Motherhood on Daily Workload." *Journal of Sociology* 42: 125–144.

Craig, Lyn, and Michael Bittman. 2008. "The Incremental Time Costs of Children: An analysis of children's impact on adult time use in Australia." *Feminist Economics* 14: 57–85.

Critcher, Chas. 2008. "Making Waves: Historic Aspects of Public Debates about Children and Mass Media." In *International Handbook of Children, Media and Culture*, edited by Kirsten Drotner and Sonia Livingstone, pp. 91–104. London: Sage.

Curtis, Penny, Allison James, and Katie Ellis. 2010. "Children's Snacking, Children's Food: Food Moralities and Family Life." *Children's Geographies* 8: 291–302.

Curtis, Penny, Allison James, and Katie Ellis. 2009. "'She's Got a Really Good Attitude to Healthy Food . . . Nanna's Drilled It into Her': Inter-generational Relations within Families." In *Changing Families, Changing Food*, edited by Peter Jackson, 77–92. London: Palgrave MacMillan.

De Crespigny, Charlotte, Niki Vincent, and Alex Ask. 1999. "Young Women's Social Drinking in Context–Pub Style: A Study of Decision Making and Social Drinking of Young Women in Urban South Australia." *Contemporary Drug Problems* 23: 31–46.

DeVault, Marjorie. 1999. "Comfort and Struggle: Emotion Work in Family Life." *Annals of the American Academy of Political and Social Science* 561: 52–63.

DeVault, Marjorie. 1991. *Feeding the Family: The Social Organization of Caring As Gendered Work*. Chicago: University of Chicago Press.

de Visser, Richard, and Johnathan Smith. 2007. "Alcohol Consumption and Masculine Identity among Young Men." *Psychology and Health* 22: 595–614.

DirectGov. 2012. "Encouraging Sensible Drinking." Accessed September 12, 2012. http://www.direct.gov.uk/en/Parents/Yourchildshealthandsafety/Youngpeopleandalcohol/DG_183763.

Dobson, Amy Shields. 2012. " 'Sexy' and 'Laddish' Girls: Unpacking Complicity between Two Cultural Imag(inations/)es of Young Femininity". *Feminist Media Studies*. doi: 10.1080/14680777.2012.713866.

Dobson, Amy. 2011. The Representation of Female Friendships on Young Women's MySpace Profiles: The All-Female World and the Feminine 'Other'. In *Youth Culture and Net Culture: Online Social Practices*, edited by Elsa Dunkels, GunMarie Franberg, and Camilla Hallgren, 126–152. Hershey PA: IGI Global.

Doring, Nicola. 2009. "The Internet's Impact on Sexuality: A Critical Review of 15 Years of Research." *Computers in Human Behavior* 25: 1089–1101.

Durham, M. Gigi. 2008. *The Lolita Effect: The Media Sexualisation of Young Girls and What We Can Do about It*. New York: The Overlook Press.

Edwards, Rosalind, Jane Ribbens McCarthy, and Val Gillies. In Press. "The Politics of Concepts: Family and Its (Putative?) Replacements." *British Journal of Sociology*. Accessed 8 November, 2012. http://eprints.soton.ac.uk/336914/

Egan, Danielle, and Gail Hawkes. 2008. "Endangered Girls and Incendiary Objects: Unpacking the Discourse on Sexualisation." *Sexuality and Culture* 12: 291–311.

Ekström, Karin. 2010. "Consumer Socialization in Families." In *Understanding Children As Consumers*, edited by David Marshall, 41–60. London: Sage.

Ellison, Nicole, Cliff Lampe, and Charles Steinfield. 2009. "Social Network Sites and Society: Current Trends and Future Possibilities." *Intersections* (Jan): 6–9.

Ellison, Nicole, Charles Steinfield, and Cliff Lampe. 2007. "The Benefits of Facebook 'Friends': Social Capital and College Students' Use of Online Social Network Sites." *Journal of Computer-Mediated Communication* 12: 1143–1168.

Eng Patricia, Ichiro Kawachi, Garrett Fitzmaurice and Eric Rimm 2005. "Effects of Marital Transitions on Changes in Dietary and other Health Behaviours in US Male Health Professionals" *Journal of Epidemiology & Community Health* 59: 56–62. doi:10.1136/jech.2004.020073.

Featherstone, Mike. 2010. "Body, Image and Affect in Consumer Culture." *Body & Society* 16: 193–221.

Ferris, Jacqueline. 1997. "Courtship, Drinking and Control: A Qualitative Analysis of Women's and Men's Experiences." *Contemporary Drug Problems* 24: 667–702.

Finch, Janet. 2007. "Displaying Families." *Sociology* 41: 165–181.

Flood, Michael. 2009. "The Harms of Pornography Exposure among Children and Young People." *Child Abuse Review* 18: 384–400.

Folbre, Nancy. 1995. " 'Holding Hands at Midnight': The Paradox of Caring Labour." *Feminist Economics* 110: 73–92.

Folbre, Nancy, and Julie Nelson. 2000. "For Love or Money–Or Both?" *The Journal of Economic Perspectives* 14: 123–140.

Francis, Babette. 2008. Mums the First Word Obesity. *Herald Sun* 1 June. Accessed September 24, 2008. http://www.news.com.au/heraldsun/story/0,,23837421-5000117,00.html.

Fullagar, Simone. 2009. "Governing Healthy Family Lifestyles through Discourses of Risk and Responsibility." In *Biopolitics and the Obesity Epidemic: Governing Bodies*, edited by Jan Wright and Valerie Harwood, 108–126. London: Routledge.

Funston, Andrew, and Katie Hughes. 2006. "Use and Value of ICTs for Separated Families." *Telecommunications Journal of Australia* 56: 76–85.

Furlong, Andy, and Fred Cartmel. 2007. *Young People and Social Change: New Perspectives*. 2nd Edn. Maidenhead: Open University Press.

Gabb, Jacqui. 2008. *Researching Intimacy in Families*. Basingstoke: Palgrave Macmillan.

Gallegos, Danielle, Suzanne Dziurawiec, Farida Fozdar, and Loraine Abernethie. 2011. "Adolescent Experiences of 'Family Meals' in Australia." *Journal of Sociology* 47: 243–260.

Gard, Michael, and Jan Wright. 2005. *The Obesity Epidemic: Science, Morality and Ideology*. London: Routledge.

Gard, Michael, and Jan Wright. 2001. "Managing Uncertainty: Obesity Discourses and Physical Education in a Risk Society." *Studies in Philosophy & Education* 20: 535–549.

Garey, Anita. 1995. "Constructing Motherhood on the Night Shift: 'Working Mothers' as 'Stay-at-Home Moms'." *Qualitative Sociology* 18: 415–437.

Gauthier, Anne, Timothy Smeeding, and Frank Furstenberg. 2004. "Are Parents Investing Less Time in Children? Trends in Selected Industrial Countries." *Population and Development Review* 30: 647–671.

Gibson, E., Jane Wardle, and Carolyn Watts. 1998. "Fruit and Vegetable Consumption, Nutritional Knowledge and Beliefs in Mothers and Children." *Appetite* 31: 205–228.

Gill, Rosalind. 2009. "Beyond the `Sexualization of Culture' Thesis: An Intersectional Analysis of `Sixpacks',`Midriffs' and `Hot Lesbians' in Advertising." *Sexualities* 12: 137–160.

Gillies, Val. 2011. "From Function to Competence: Engaging with the New Politics of Family." *Sociological Research Online* 16: 11 <http://www.socresonline.org.uk/16/4/11.html> 10.5153/sro.2393.

Gillies, Val. 2007. *Marginalised Mothers: Exploring Working Class Experiences of Parenting*. Routledge: Abingdon.

Gillies Val. 2006. "Working Class Mothers and School Life: Exploring the Role of Emotional Capital." *Gender and Education* 18: 281–293.

Gillies Val. 2005. "Raising the 'Meritocracy': Parenting and the Individualization of Social Class." *Sociology* 39: 835–853.

Gillis, John. 2003. "Childhood and Family Time: A Changing Historical Relationship". In *Children and the Changing Family; Between Transformation and Negotiation*, edited by An-Magrit Jensen and Lorna McKee, 149–164. London: Routledge Falmer.

Giroux, Henry. 1998. "Teenage Sexuality, Body Politics, and the Pedagogy of Display." In *Youth Culture: Identity in a Modern World*, edited by J.A. Epstein, 24–55. Oxford: Blackwell.

Giroux, Henry. 2000. *Stealing Innocence: Corporate Culture's War on Children*. New York: Palgrave.

Grace, Jocelyn, David Moore, and Jeremy Northcote. 2009. *Alcohol, Risk and Harm Reduction: Drinking amongst Young Adults in Recreational Settings in Perth*. Perth: National Drug Research Institute Curtin University of Technology. Accessed September 13, 2012. http://ndri.curtin.edu.au/local/docs/pdf/publications/T192.pdf.

Graham, Kathryn, Sharon Bernards, Myriam Munne, and Sharon Wilsnack. 2008. "Unhappy Hours: Alcohol and Partner Aggression in the Americas." Washington DC: Pan American Health Organisation.

Green, Trish, Jenny Owen, Penny Curtis, Graham Smith, Paul Ward, and Pamela Fisher. 2009. "Making Healthy Families? In *Changing Families, Changing Food*, edited by Peter Jackson, 205–225. London: Palgrave Macmillan.

Green, Nicola. 2002. "On the Move: Technology, Mobility and the Mediation of Social Time and Space." *The Information Society* 18: 281–292.

Greenfield, Thomas, and Robin Room. 1997. "Situational Norms for Drinking and Drunkeness: Trends in the US Adult Population." *Addiction* 92: 33–47.

Haddon, Leslie. 2007. "The Contribution of Domestication Research into Home Computing and Media Consumption." *The Information Society* 22: 195–203.

Halkoaho, Jenniina, and Pirjo Laaksonen. 2009. "Understanding what Christmas Gifts Mean to Children." *Young Consumers* 10: 248–255.

Hall, Sarah. 2011. "Exploring the 'Ethical Everyday': An Ethnography of the Ethics of Family Consumption." *Geoforum* 42: 627–637.

Hamilton, Clive, and Richard Deniss. 2005. *Affluenza: When Too Much is Never Enough*. Sydney: Allen & Unwin.

Hanson, Rochelle, Shannon Self-Brown, Adrienne Fricker-Elhai, Dean Kilpatrick, Benjamin Saunders, and Heidi Resnick. 2006. "Relations among Parental Substance Use, Violence Exposure and Mental Health: The National Survey of Adolescents." *Addictive Behaviors* 31: 1988–2001.

Harnett, Robert, Betsy Thom, Rachel Herring, and Moira Kelly. 2000. "Alcohol in Transition: Towards a Model of Young Men's Drinking Styles." *Journal of Youth Studies* 3: 61–77.

Harrison, Michelle, Amanda Lee, Michael Findlay, Ralph Nicholls, Dympna Leonard, and Caroline Martin. 2010. "The Increasing Cost of Healthy Food." *Australian and New Zealand Journal of Public Health* 34: 179–186.

Hartley, Robin. 1993. "Under the Same Roof: Young Adult Unmarried Sexual Relationships in Parents' Homes." *Family Matters* 34: 40–43.

Hawkes, Gail, and Danielle R. Egan. 2008. "Landscapes of Erotophobia: The Sexual(ized) Child in the Postmodern Anlophone West." *Sexuality and Culture* 12: 193–203.

Hays, Sharon. 1996. *The Cultural Contradictions of Motherhood*. New Haven: Yale University Press.

Hegarty, K., E. Hindmarsh, and M. Gilles. 2000. "Domestic Violence in Australia: Definition, Prevalence and Nature of Presentation in Clinical Practice." 2000 *Medical Journal of Australia* 173: 363–367.

Heinz, Walter R. 2009. "Youth Transitions in an Age of Uncertainty." In *Handbook of Youth and Young Adulthood: New Perspectives and Agendas*, edited by Andy Furlong. London: Routledge.

Henderson, Julie, John Coveney, Paul Ward, and A. Taylor. 2009. "Governing Childhood Obesity: Framing Regulation of Fast Food Advertising in the Australian Print Media." *Social Science & Medicine* 69: 1402–1408.

Henderson, Sheila, and Alan Petersen. 2002. "Introduction: Consumerism in Health Care." In *Consuming Health: The Commodification of Health Care*, edited by Sheila Henderson and Alan Petersen. London: Routledge.

Henderson, Sheila, Rebecca Taylor, and Rachel Thomson. 2002. "In Touch: Young People, Communication and Technologies." *Information, Communication & Society* 5: 494–512.

Henly, Brigid. 2011. 'At Risk' or 'Risk Seeking': Exploring the Risk/Gender Nexus in Relation to Young University Women's Alcohol Consumption. Paper Presented at the The Australian Sociological Association Annual Conference (Newcastle)–29 November 2011.

Henry, Robin. 2012. "Estranged Dad's Sneaky Gift: A SpyPad." *Sunday Times* (London) 13.

Herndon, April. 2005. "Collateral Damage from Friendly Fire? Race, Nation, Class and the 'War against Obesity." *Social Semiotics* 15: 127–141.

Hertz, Rosanna. 2006. "Talking about "Doing" Family." *Journal of Marriage and Family* 68: 796–799.

Hillier, Lynne, Deb Dempsey, Lyn Harrison, Lisa. Beale, Lesley. Matthews, and Doreen Rosenthal. 1998. *Writing Themselves In: A National Report on the Sexuality, Health and Well-Being of Same-Sex Attracted Young People*. Melbourne: Australian Research Centre in Sex, Health and Society.

Hochschild, Arlie. 2003. *The Commercialisation of Intimate Life: Notes from Home and Work*. Berkeley: University of California Press.

Hochschild, Arlie. 1997. *The Time Bind: When Work becomes Home and Home becomes Work*. New York: A Holt Paperback.

Hochschild, Arlie. 1995. "The Culture of Politics: Traditional, Postmodern, Cold-Modern and Warm-Modern Ideals of Care." *Social Politics* 23: 331–346.

Hoel, Sindre, Bjorn Magne. Eriksen, Hans-Yohan Breidablik, and Eivind Meland. 2004. "Adolescent Alcohol Use, Psychological Health, and Social Integration." *Scandinavian Journal of Public Health* 32: 361–367.

Holloway, Sarah, Gill Valentine, and Mark Jayne. 2009. "Masculinities, Femininities and the Geographies of Public and Private Drinking Landscapes." *Geoforum* 40: 821–831.

Holloway, Sarah, and Gill Valentine. 2003. *Cyberkids: Children in the Information Age*. Routledge Falmer: London.

Hook, Jennifer. 2006. "Care in Context: Men's Unpaid Work in 21 Countries, 1965–2003." *American Sociological Review* 71: 639–660.

Humphrey, Kim. 2009. *Excess: Anti-Consumerism in the West*. Cambridge: : Polity.

Insight. 2012 'Generation XXX' episode 8 May 2012. Facilitator Jenny Brockie. Accessed September 8, 2012. http://www.sbs.com.au/insight/episode/transcript/473/Generation-XXX.

Jabs, Jennifer, and Carol Devine. 2006. "Research Review—Time Scarcity and Food Choices: An Overview." *Appetite* 47: 196–204.

Jackson, Christine, Lisa Henriksen, and Denise Dickinson. 1999. "Alcohol-Specific Socialization, Parenting Behaviors and Alcohol Use by Children." *Journal of Studies on Alcohol* 60(3): 362–367.

Jackson, Peter. 2009. "Introduction: Food a Lens on Family Life." In *Changing Families, Changing Food*, edited by Peter Jackson, 1–16. London: Palgrave Macmillan.

Jackson, Peter, Sarah Olive, and Graham Smith. 2009. Myths of the Family Meal: Re-Reading Edwardian Life-Histories. In *Changing Families, Changing Food*, edited by Peter Jackson, 131–145. London: Palgrave Macmillan.

Jackson Peter. 1998. "Consumption and Identity: The Cultural Politics of Shopping." *European Planning Studies* 7: 25–39.

Jacobs, Jerry, and Kathleen Gerson. 2004. *The Time Divide: Work, Family, and Gender Inequality*. Cambridge: Harvard University Press.

Jagger, Gill, and Caroline Wright. 1999. "Introduction." In *Changing Family Values*, edited by Gill Jagger and Caroline Wright, 1–15. London: Routledge.

James, Allison, and Penny Curtis. 2010. "Family Displays and Personal Lives." *Sociology* 44: 1163–1180.

James, Allison, Anne Trine Kjørholt, and Vebjørg Tingstad. 2009a. "Introduction." In *Children, Food and Identity in Everyday Life*, edited by Allison James, Anne Trine Kjørholt, and Vebjørg Tingstad, 1–12. Basingstoke: Palgrave Macmillan.

James, Allison, Penny Curtis, and Katie Ellis. 2009b. "Negotiating Family, Negotiating Food: Children as Family Participants." In *Children, Food and Identity in Everyday Life*, edited by Allison James, Anne Trine Kjørholt, and Vebjørg Tingstad, 35–51. Basingstoke: Palgrave Macmillan.

Jarvinen, Margaretha, and Peter Gundelach. 2007. "Teenage Drinking, Symbolic Capital and Distinction." *Journal of Youth Studies* 10: 55–71.

Jarvinen, Margaretha, and Robin Room. 2007. "Youth Drinking Cultures: European Experiences." In *Youth Drinking Cultures: European Experiences*, edited by Margaretha Jarvinen and Robin Room, 1–16. Hampshire: Ashgate.

Jayne, Mark, Gill Valentine, and Myles Gould. 2011. "Family Life and Alcohol Consumption: The Transmission of 'Public' and 'Private' Drinking Cultures." *Drugs: Education, Prevention, and Policy* 19(3): 192–200.

Jonas, Helen, Annette Dobson, and Wendy Brown. 2000. "Patterns of Alcohol Consumption in Young Australian Women: Socio-Demographic Factors, Health-Related Behaviours and Physical Health." *Australian and New Zealand Journal of Public Health* 24: 185–191.

Kelly, Adrian, Martin O'Flaherty, John Toumbourou, Jason Connor, Sheryl Hemphill, and Richard Catalano. 2011. "Gender Differences in the Impact of Families on Alcohol Use: A Lagged Longitudinal Study of Early Adolescents." *Addiction* 106: 1427–1436.

Kelly, Adrian B., and Marusia Kowalyszyn. 2003. "The Association of Alcohol and Family Problems in a Remote Indigenous Australian Community." *Addictive Behaviors* 28: 761–767.

Kendrick, Rachel. 2008. "'We Can Change the Face of This Future': Television Transforming the Fat Child." *Australian Feminist Studies* 23: 389–400.

Kenway, Jane, and Elizabeth Bullen. 2001. *Consuming Children: Education-Entertainment Advertising*. Buckingham: Open University Press.

Kids Free 2B Kids. 2012. "About Us" Accessed September 12, 2012 http://www.kf2bk.com/about.htm.

Kline, Stephen. 2010a. *Globesity, Food Marketing and Family Lifestyles*. London: Palgrave Macmillan Ltd.

Kline, Stephen. 2010b. "Children as 'Competent' Consumers." In *Understanding Children as Consumers,* edited by David Marshall, 253–297. London: Sage.

Kline, Stephen. 1995. *Out of the Garden: Toys, TV, and Children's Culture in the Age of Marketing*. London: Verso.

Kloep, M., L. Hendry, J. Ingebrigtsen, A. Glendinning, and G. Espnes. 2001. "Young People in 'Drinking' Societies? Norwegian, Scottish and Swedish Adolescents' Perceptions of Alcohol Use." *Health Education Research* 16: 279–291.

Klostermann, Keith, and William Fals-Stewart. 2006. "Intimate Partner Violence and Alcohol Use: Exploring the Role of Drinking in Partner Violence and Its Implications for Intervention." *Aggression and Violent Behaviour* 11: 587–597.

Komter, Aafke, and Wilma Vollebergh. 1997. "Gift Giving and the Emotional Significance of Family and Friends." *Journal of Marriage and Family* 59: 747–754.

Kypri, Kypros, Dean Joanna., and Stojanovski Elizabeth. 2007. "Parent Attitudes on the Supply of Alcohol to Minors." *Drug and Alcohol Review* 26: 41–47.

Lareau, Annette. 2003. *Unequal Childhoods: Class, Race, and Family Life*. Berkeley: University of California Press.

Lasch, Christopher. 1995. *Haven in a Heartless World: The Family Besieged*. New York: Norton.

Lenhart, Amanda. 2009. *Teens and Sexting: How and Why Minor Teens Are Sending Sexually Suggestive Nude or Nearly Nude Images via Text Messaging*. Washington, DC: Pew Research Centre.

Levy, Ariel. 2005. *Female Chauvinist Pigs: Women and the Rise of Raunch Culture*. New York: Free Press.

Lewis, Jane. 2009. *Work-Family Balance, Gender and Policy*. Cheltenham: Edward Elgar.

Licoppe, Christian. 2004. "Connected Presence": The Emergence of a New Repertoire for Managing Social Relationships in a Changing Communication Technospace." *Environment and Planning D: Society and Space* 22: 135–156.

Lincoln, Sian. 2005. "Feeling the Noise: Teenagers, Bedrooms and Music." *Leisure Studies* 24: 399–414.

Lindsay, Jo. 2012. "The Gendered Trouble with Alcohol: Young People Managing Alcohol Related Violence." *International Journal of Drug Policy* 47: 491–524.

Lindsay Jo. 2006 "A Big Night Out: Drinking As an Enactment of Class and Gender' *Contemporary Drug Problems* 33: 29–61.

Lindsay, Jo. 2005a. "'Don't Panic!: Young People and the Social Organisation of Sex'." In *Perspectives in Human Sexuality*, edited by Gail Hawkes and John Scott, 85–94. South Melbourne: Oxford University Press.

Lindsay, Jo. 2005b. *Drinking in Melbourne Pubs and Clubs: A Study of Alcohol Consumption Contexts*. Clayton: School of Political and Social Inquiry, Monash University.

Lindsay, Jo. 2001. "Sex, Drugs and Drinking: Health Risks in the Social Lives of Young Workers." *Youth Studies* Australia 20: 11–19.

Lindsay, Jo, and Deb Dempsey. 2009. *Families, Relationships and Intimate Life*. Melbourne: Oxford University Press.

Lindsay, Jo, Lyn Harrison, Jenny Advocat, Peter Kelly, and Chris Hickey. 2009. "It's My Time to Shine: Young Australians Reflect on Past, Present and Imagined Future Alcohol Consumption." *Youth Studies Australia* 28: 44–51.

Lindsay, Jo, JaneMaree Maher and Anne Bardoel. 2009. "Modified Maternalism: Nurses and Their Families Managing Work and Care in Australia." *Journal of Comparative Family Studies* 40: 659–675.

Lindsay, Jo, JaneMaree Maher and John Coveney 2012 "Nagging and Resisting: Intergenerational Negotiations about Food." Paper presented at the Socio Politics of Food Workshop, Monash University, Melbourne, May 28, 2012.

Livingston, Michael. 2008. "Recent Trends in Risky Alcohol Consumption and Related Harm among Young People in Victoria, Australia." *Australian and New Zealand Journal of Public Health* 32: 266–271.

Livingston, Michael, and Robin Room. 2009. "Variations by Age and Sex in Alcohol-Related Problematic Behaviour per Drinking Volume and Heavier Drinking Occasion." *Drug and Alcohol Dependence* 101: 169–175.

Livingstone, Sonia. 2007. "Strategies of Parental Regulation in the Media-Rich Home." *Computers in Human Behavior* 23: 920–941.

Livingstone, Sonia. 2009. *Children and the Internet: Great Expectations, Challenging Realities.* Cambridge: Polity.

Livingstone, Sonia and A. Gorzig. 2012. "'Sexting': The Exchange of Sexual Messages Online among European Youth." In *Children, Risk and Safety on the Internet: Kids Online in Comparative Perspective.* Bristol: The Policy Press.

Livingstone, Sonia, L. Haddon, and A. Gorzig. 2012. *Children, Risk and Safety on the Internet: Kids Online in Comparative Perspective.* London: The Policy Press.

Lumby, Catherine, and Duncan Fine. 2006. *Why TV Is Good for Kids: Raising 21st Century Children.* Sydney: Macmillan.

Lury, Celia. 1996. *Consumer Culture.* Cambridge: Polity Press.

Lupton Deborah. 2004. "A Grim Health Future: Food Risks in the Sydney Press." *Health, Risk & Society* 6: 187–200.

Lynn, Randy. 2010. "Constructing Parenthood in Moral Panics of Youth, Digital Media, and 'Sexting'." The 105th Annual Meeting of the American Sociological Association 14 July, 2010. Atlanta Georgia.

Madianou, Mirca. 2012. "Migration and the Accentuated Ambivalence of Motherhood: The Role of ICTs in Filipino Transnational Families." *Global Networks* 12: 277–295.

Maggs, Jennifer, and John Schulenberg 2004. "Trajectories of Alcohol Use During the Transition to Adulthood" *Alcohol Research and Health* 28: 195–201.

Maher, JaneMaree, Suzanne Fraser, and Jo Lindsay. 2010a. "Between Provisioning and Consuming?: Children, Mothers and 'Childhood Obesity." *Health Sociology Review* 19: 304–316.

Maher, JaneMaree, Jo Lindsay, and Anne Bardoel. 2010b. "Freeing Time: The 'Family Time Economies' of Nurses." *Sociology* 44: 269–287.

Maher, JaneMaree, Suzanne Fraser, and Jan Wright. 2010c. "Framing the Mother: Childhood Obesity, Maternal Responsibility and Care." *Journal of Gender Studies* 19: 233–247.

Maher, JaneMaree. 2009. "Accumulated Time, Accumulating Value: Mothers beyond the Conflicting Temporalities of Caring and Work." *Time & Society* 18: 231–245.

Maher, JaneMaree, Jo Lindsay, and Suzanne Franzway. 2008. "Time, Caring Labour and Social Policy: Understanding the Family Time Economy in Contemporary Families." *Work, Employment & Society* 22: 547–588.

Marshall, David. 2010. "Introduction." In *Understanding Children as Consumers,* edited by David Marshall, 1–20. London: Sage.

Marshall, David. 2005. "Food as Ritual, Routine or Convention." *Consumption, Markets and Culture* 8: 69–85.

Marshall, David, and Stephanie O'Donohoe. 2010. "Children and Food." In *Understanding Children as Consumers,* edited by David Marshall, 167–183. London: Sage.

Martens, Lydia, Dale Southerton and Sue Scott, 2004. "Bringing Children (and Parents) into the Sociology of Consumption: Towards a Theoretical and Empirical Agenda." *Journal of Consumer Culture* 4: 155–182.

Masters, Chris. 2007. Working Mums Have Fat Kids. *Daily Telegraph*. 11 January. Accessed November 11, 2008 http://www.news.com.au/story/0,27574, 21041424–36398,00.html.

May, Sonya. 2008. "Living an Object Lesson for the Kids." *Sydney Morning Herald* 2 May. Accessed May 2, 2012. http://www.news.com.au/heraldsun/story/0,21985,23557821–662,00.html.

McDonnell, Kathleen. 2006. *Honey, We Lost the Kids: Re-Thinking Childhood in the Multi-Media Age*. North Melbourne: Pluto Press.

McDowell, Linda. 2008. "The New Economy, Class Condescension and Caring Labour: Changing Formations of Class and Gender." *NORA—Nordic Journal of Feminist and Gender Research* 16: 150–165.

McDowell, Linda. 2007. "The Spaces of the Home: Absence, Presence, New Connections and New Anxieties." *Home Cultures* 4: 129–146.

McKee, Lorna, Natalie Mauthner and Galilee, J. 2003, "Children's Perspectives on Middle-Class Work–Family Arrangements." In *Children and the Changing Family: Between Transformation and Negotiation*, edited by An-Magrit Jensen and Lorna McKee, 27–45. London: Routledge Falmer.

McKie, Linda, Sarah Cunningham-Burley and John McKendrick. 2005. "Families and Relationships: Boundaries and Bridges." In *Families and Relationships: Boundaries and Bridges*, edited by Linda McKie and Sarah Cunningham-Burley, 3–17. Bristol: Policy Press.

McKie, Linda, Sue Gregory and Sophia Bowlby. 2002. "Shadow Times: The Temporal and Spatial Frameworks and Experiences of Caring and Working." *Sociology* 36: 897–924.

McMorris, Barbara, and Christopher Uggen 2000 "Alcohol and Employment in the Transition to Adulthood" *Journal of Health and Social Behavior* 41: 276–294.

McNaughton, Darlene. 2011. "From the Womb to the Tomb: Obesity and Maternal Responsibility." *Critical Public Health* 21: 179–190.

McRobbie, Angela. 2009. *The Aftermath of Feminism: Gender, Culture and Social Change*. New York: Sage.

Measham, Fiona. 2006. "The New Policy Mix: Alcohol, Harm Minimisation, and Determined Drunkenness in Contemporary Society." *International Journal of Drug Policy* 17: 258–268.

Measham, Fiona. 2004. "The Decline of Ecstasy, the Rise of 'Binge' Drinking and the Persistence of Pleasure." *Probation Journal* 51: 309–326.

Measham, Fiona,.and Kevin Brain. 2005. "'Binge' Drinking, British Alcohol Policy and the New Culture of Intoxication." *Crime, Media, Culture* 1: 262–283.

Mendelson, Andrew, and Zizi Papacharissie. 2011. "Look at Us: Collective Narcissism in College Student Faceboook Photo Galleries." In *A Networked Self: Identity, Community, and Culture on Social Network Sites*, edited by Zizi Papacharissie. New York: Routledge.

Mendoza, Kelly. 2009. "Surveying Parental Mediation: Connections, Challenges and Questions for Media Literacy." *Journal of Media Literacy Education* 1: 28–41.

Mestdag, Inge, and Jessie Vandeweyer. 2005. "Where Has Family Time Gone? In Search of Joint Family Activities and the Role of the Family Meal in 1966 and 1999." *Journal of Family History* 30: 304–323.

Michael, Erin. 2011. "Provocative Images on Pencil Cases Cause a Furore in Schools" From: mX December 09, 2011 5:14PM." in *Herald Sun*. Melbourne. Accessed September 13, 2012. http://www.news.com.au/national-old/provocative-images-on-pencil-cases-cause-a-furore-in-schools/story-e6frfkvr-1226218501975.

Milburn, Kathleen. 1995. "Never Mind the Quantity, Investigate the Depth!" *British Food Journal* 97: 36–38.

Miller, Daniel. 2010. *Stuff*. Malden, MA: Polity.

Miller, Daniel. 2008a. *The Comfort of Things*. Malden, MA: Polity.
Miller, Daniel. 2008b. "Why Some Things Matters." In *Material Cultures: Why Some Things Matter*, edited by Daniel Miller, 3–21. London: UCL Press.
Miller, Daniel. 2004. "How Infants Grow Mothers." In *Consuming Motherhood*, edited by Janelle Taylor, Linda Layne, and Danielle Wozniak, 31–51. New Brunswick, NJ: Rutgers University Press.
Miller, Michael. 2012. *Facebook for Grown-Ups: Use Facebook to Connect with Old Friends, Family and Co-Workers*. Indianapolis: Pearson Education.
Miller, Peter, and Nikolas Rose. 1997. Mobilizing the Consumer: Assembling the Subject of Consumption. *Theory Culture Society* 14: 1–36.
Monaghan, Lee. 2005. "Discussion piece: A Critical Take on the Obesity Debate." *Social Theory & Health* 3: 302–314.
Moore, Susan, and Doreen Rosenthal 2006. *Sexuality in Adolescence: Current Trends*. Hove: Routledge.
Moore, Susan, Doreen Rosenthal, and Anne Mitchell. 1996. *Youth, AIDS and Sexually Transmitted Diseases*. London: Routledge.
Morgan, David. 2011a. *Rethinking Family Practices*. London: Palgrave McMillan
Morgan, David. 2011b. "Framing Relationships and Families." In *Researching Families and Relationships: Reflections on Process*, edited by Lynn Jamieson, Roona Simpson, and Ruth Lewis, 19–30. New York: Palgrave Macmillan.
Morgan, David. 1999. "Risk and Family Practices: Accounting for Change and Fluidity in Family Life." In *The New Family?*, edited by Elisabeth Silva and Carol Smart, 13–30. London: Sage
Murphy, Elisabeth. 2003. "Expertise and Forms of Knowledge in the Government of Families." *Sociological Review* 51: 433–462.
Murray, Samantha. 2008. "Normative Imperatives vs. Pathological Bodies: Constructing the 'Fat' Woman." *Australian Feminist Studies* 23: 213–224.
National Alcohol Strategy. 2001. *Alcohol in Australia: Issues and Strategies*. Canberra: Commonwealth Government of Australia.
Newman, Katherine. 2011. *The Accordion Family: Boomerang Kids, Anxious Parents, and the Private Toll of Global Competition*. Boston: Beacon Press.
Neysmith, Sheila, and Mary Reitsma-Street. 2005. "Provisioning": Conceptualizing the Work of Women for 21st Century Social Policy." *Women's Studies International Forum* 28: 381–391.
NHMRC. 2009. *Australian Guidelines to Reduce Health Risks from Drinking Alcohol*. National Health and Medical Research Council. Canberra: Commonwealth Government of Australia.
Niewenhuys, Olga. 2006. "Childhood Gifts." *Childhood* 13: 147–153.
Noll, Robert, Robert. Zucker, and Gregory Greenberg. 1990. "Identification of Alcohol by Smell among Preschoolers: Evidence for Early Socialization about Drugs Occurring in the Home." *Child Development* 61: 1520–1527.
Northcote, Jeremy. 2006. "Nightclubbing and the Search for Identity: Making the Transition from Childhood to Adulthood in an Urban Milieu." *Journal of Youth Studies* 9: 1–16.
O'Brien, Susie. 2008. "Family Meals a Recipe for Fit Kids." *Herald Sun*. 18 April. Accessed November 11, 2008. http://www.smh.com.au/news/opinion/living-an-object-lesson-for-the-kids/2008/05/01/1209235053940.html.
O'Connell, Rebecca. 2010. "(How) is Childminding Family Like? Family Day Care, Food and the Reproduction of Identity at the Public/Private Interface." *The Sociological Review* 58: 563–586.
O'Dea, Jennie. 2008. "Gender, Ethnicity, Culture and Social Class Influences on Childhood Obesity among Australian Schoolchildren: Implications for

Treatment, Prevention and Community Education." *Health and Social Care in the Community* 16: 282–290.

O'Dea, Jennie. 2005. "Prevention of Child Obesity: First, Do No Harm." *Health Education Research* 20: 259–265.

O'Dea, Jennie, and Paul Caputi. 2001. "Association between Socioeconomic Status, Weight, Age and Gender, and the Body Image and Weight Control Practices of 6- to 19-year-old Children and Adolescents." *Health Education Research* 16: 521–532.

OECD. 2002. *Babies And Booses: Reconciling Work And Family Life. Australia, Denmark and the Netherlands*. Geneva: OECD.

Olds, Timothy, G. Tomkinson, K. Ferrer, and C. Maher. 2010. "Trends in the Prevalence of Childhood Overweight and Obesity in Australia between 1985 and 2008." *International Journal of Obesity* 34: 57–66.

Orford, Jim, Richard Velleman, Alex Copello, Lorna Templeton, and Akanidomo Ibanga. 2010. "The Experiences of Affected Family Members: A Summary of Two Decades of Qualitative Research." *Drugs: Education, Prevention, and Policy* 17: 44–62.

Osborne, Joan. 2010. "Profile of 'Joan Osborne American Singer/Songwriter." *The Age Good Weekend Magazine*. 6 February. Fairfax Publishing: Melbourne.

Ostrow, Ruth. 2008. "Foreword: Mums who Kid Themselves." *Australian Weekend Magazine*. 26 April. Accessed July 24, 2008. http://www.theaustralian.news.com.au/story/0,25197,23596923–5012694,00.html.

Papadopoulos, Linda. 2010. *The Sexualisation of Young People: Review*. London: The Home Office.

Parker, Howard. 2005. "Normalisation as a Barometer: Recreational Drug Use and the Consumption of Leisure by Younger Britons." *Addiction Research and Theory* 13: 205–215.

Parks, Kathleen, Brenda Miller, Lorraine Collins, and Lisa Zetes-Zanatta. 1998. "Women's Description of Drinking in Bars: Reasons and Risks." *Sex Roles* 38(9): 701–717.

Parks, Kathleen, and Douglas Scheidt. 2000. "Male Bar Drinkers' Perspectives on Female Bar Drinkers." *Sex Roles* 43: 927–941.

Parsons, Andrew, and Paul Ballantine. 2008. "The Gifts We Buy for Children." *Young Consumers* 9: 308–315.

Patternson, Mark. 2006. *Consumption and Everyday Life*. London: Routledge.

Paul, Pamela. 2005. *Pornified: How Pornography is Transforming Our Lives, Our Relationships and Our Families*. New York: Times Books.

Peel, Mark. 2003. *The Lowest Rung: Voices of Australian Poverty*. Melbourne: Cambridge University Press.

Peterson, Alan, and Deborah Lupton. 1996. *The New Public Health: Health and Self in the Age of Risk*. Sydney: Allen & Unwin.

Phillips, Jan. 2008. "'Attention, Shoppers—Family Being Constructed on Aisle Six!': Grocery Shopping and the Accomplishment of Family." In *Lived Experiences of Public Consumption: Encounters with Value in Marketplaces on Five Continents*, edited by Daniel Cook. Houndmills: Palgrave Macmillan.

Pocock, Barbara. 2006. *The Labour Market Ate My Babies: Work, Children and a Sustainable Future*. Sydney: Federation Press.

Pocock, Barbara. 2003. *The Work/Life Collision: What Work Is Doing to Australians and What to Do*. Sydney: Federation Press.

Pocock, Barbara, and Jane Clarke. 2004. *Can't Buy Me Love?: Young Australians' Views on Parental Work, Time, Guilt and Their Own Consumption*. Canberra: Australia Institute.

Powell, Anastasia. 2010. *Sex, Power and Consent: Youth Culture and the Unwritten Rules*. Cambridge: Cambridge University Press.

Presser, Harriet. 2003. *Working In A 24/7 Economy: Challenges For American Families*. New York: Russell Sage.

Pugh, Allison. 2009. *Longing and Belonging: Parents, Children, and Consumer Culture*. Berkeley: University of California Press.

Raskin White, Helene, Barbara McMorris, Richard Catalano, Charles Fleming, Kevin Haggerty, and Robert Abbott. 2006. "Increases in Alcohol and Marijuana Use During the Transition Out of High School Into Emerging Adulthood: The Effects of Leaving Home, Going to College, and High School Protective Factors" 2006. *Journal of Studies in Alcohol*. 67: 810–822.

Rehm, Jurgen, Colin Mathers, Svetlana Popova, Montarat Thavorncharoensap, Yot Teerawattananon, and Jayadeep Patra. 2009. "Alcohol and Global Health 1: Global Burden of Disease and Injury and Economic Cost Attributable to Alcohol Use and Alcohol-Use Disorders." *The Lancet* 373(9682): 2223–2233.

Reichert, Tom, and Jaqueline Lambiase. 2006. *Sex in Consumer Culture: The Erotic Content of Media and Marketing*. Mahwah, NJ: Lawrence Erlbaum Associates.

Reiger, Kerreen. 1985. *The Disenchantment of Home: Modernizing the Australian Family 1880–1940*. Melbourne: Oxford University Press.

Reimer, Bo. 1995. "The Media in Public and Private Spheres." In *Youth Culture in Late Modernity*, edited by Fornas Johan and Goran Bolin. London: Sage.

Ribbens McCarthy, Jane. 2012. "The Powerful Relational Language of 'Family': Togetherness, Belonging and Personhood." *Sociological Review* 60: 68–90.

Ribbens McCarthy, Jane, Rosalind Edwards, and Val Gillies. 2003. Making Families: Moral Tales of Parenting and Step-Parenting. London: Sociology Press.

Ribbens McCarthy, Jane, Rosalind Edwards, and Val Gillies. 2000. "Moral Tales of the Child and the Adult: Narratives of Contemporary Family Lives under Changing Circumstances." *Sociology* 34: 785–803.

Rich, Emma, and John Evans. 2005. "'Fat Ethics': The Obesity Discourse and Body Politics." *Social Theory & Health* 3: 341–358.

Ringrose, Jessica. 2010. "Sluts, Whores, Fat Slags and Playboy Bunnies: Teen Girls' Negotiations of 'Sexy' on Social Networking Sites and at School." In *Girls and Education 3–16: Continuing Concerns, New Agendas*, edited by Carolyn Jackson, Carrie Paechter and Emma Renold, 170–182. Berkshire: Open University Press.

Rissel, Chris, Juliet Richters, Andrew Grulich, Richard de Visser, and Anthony Smith. 2003a. "Sex in Australia: First Experiences of Vaginal Intercourse and Oral Sex among a Representative Sample of Adults." *Australian and New Zealand Journal of Public Health* 27: 131–137.

Rissel, Chris, Juliet Richters, Andrew Grulich, Richard de Visser, and Anthony Smith. 2003b. "Sex in Australia: Attitudes towards Sex in a Representative Sample of Adults." *Australian and New Zealand Journal of Public Health* 27: 118–123.

Robinson, Laura. 2007. "The Cyberself: The Self-ing Project Goes Online, Symbolic Interaction in the Digital Age." *New Media & Society* 9: 93–110.

Roche, Anne, Petra Bywood, Joseph Borlagdan, Belinda Lunnay, Toby Freeman, Lisa Lawton, Amanda Tovell, and Roger Nicholas. 2008. *Young People and Alcohol: The Role of Cultural Influences*. Adelaide: Drinkwise Australia.

Room, Robin. 2010. The Long Reaction against the Wowser: The Prehistory of Alcohol Deregulation in Australia. *Health Sociology Review*: 19: 151–163.

Roper, Stuart, and Binita Shah. 2007. "Vulnerable Consumers: The Social Impact of Branding on Children." *Equal Opportunities International* 26: 712–728.

Roseneil, Sasha, and Shelley Budgeon. 2004. "Cultures of Intimacy and Care beyond 'the Family': Personal Life and Social Change in the Early 21st Century." *Current Sociology* 52: 135–159.

Rovolis, Antonis, and Liza Tsaliki. 2012. "Pornography." In *Children, Risk and Safety on the Internet: Kids Online in Comparative Perspective*, edited by Sonia Livingstone, Leslie Haddon, and Anke Gorzig: The Policy Press.

Rush, Emma, and Andrea La Nauze 2006. *Corporate Paedophilia: Sexualisation of Children in Australia*. Canberra: Australia Institute.

Russell, Mark. 2012. "How Teen Party Ended in Despair." *The Age*. Melbourne: Fairfax. Accessed May 15, 2012. http://www.theage.com.au/victoria/how-teen-party-ended-in-despair-20120416–1x3ue.html.

Rysst, Mari. 2010. "'I Am Only 10 Years Old'" Femininities, Clothing-Fashion Codes and the Intergenerational Gap of Interpretation of Young Girls' Clothes." *Childhood* 17: 76–93.

Saguy, Abigail, and Kevin Riley. 2005. "Weighing Both Sides: Morality, Mortality, and Framing Contests over Obesity." *Journal of Health Politics, Policy & Law* 30: 869–923.

Santelli, J., R. Lowry, N. Brener, and L. Robin. 2000. "The Association of Sexual Behaviours with Socioeconomic Status, Family Structure, and Race/Ethnicity among US Adolescents." *American Journal of Public Health* 90: 1582–1588.

Sayer, Liana. 2005. 'Gender, Time and Inequality: Trends in Women's and Men's Paid Work, Unpaid Work and Free Time." *Social Forces* 84: 285–303.

Schalet, Amy. 2010. "Sex, Love, and Autonomy in the Teenage Sleepover." *Contexts* 9: 16–21.

Schor, Juliet, 2004. *The Commercialized Child and the New Consumer Culture*. New York: Pocket Books.

Scott, Sue, Stevi Jackson, and Kathleen Backett-Milburn. 1998. "Swings and Roundabouts: Risk Anxiety and the Everyday Worlds of Children." *Sociology* 32: 689–705.

Shyam Sundar, S., A. Oeldorf-Hirsch, J. F. Nussbaum, and R. A. Behr. 2011. "Retirees on Facebook: Can Online Social Networking Enhance Their Health and Wellness?" *CHI* (May): 2287–2292.

Silva, Elisabeth. 2010. *Technology, Culture, Family: Influences on Home Life*. Basingstoke: Palgrave Macmillan.

Silva, Jennifer, and Allison Pugh. 2010. "Beyond the Depleting Model of Parenting: Narratives of Childrearing and Change." *Sociological Inquiry* 80: 605–627.

Silva, Elisabeth, and Carol Smart. 1999. "The 'New' Practices and Politics of Family Life." In *The New Family?*, edited by Elisabeth Silva and Carol Smart, 1–12. London: Sage.

Silverstone, Roger, and Eric Hirsch. 1994. "Introduction." In *Consuming Technologies: Media and Information in Domestic Spaces*, edited by Roger Silverstone and Eric Hirsch, 1–8. London: Routledge.

Skrbis, Zlatko. 2008. "Transnational Families: Theorising Migration, Emotions and Belonging." *Journal of Intercultural Studies* 29: 231–246.

Smart, Carol. 2007. *Personal Life: New Directions in Sociological Thinking*. Cambridge: Polity Press.

Smith, Anthony, Paul Agius, Anne Mitchell, Catherine Barrett, and Marian Pitts. 2009. "Secondary Students and Sexual Health 2008" in Monograph Series No. 70. Melbourne: Australian Research Centre in Sex, Health & Society, La Trobe University.

Smith, Anthony, Paul Agius, Sue Dyson, Anne Mitchell, and Marian Pitts. 2003a. *Secondary Students and Sexual Health 2002*. Melbourne: Australian Research Centre in Sex, Health and Society.

Smith, Anthony, Chris Rissel, Juliett Richters, Andrew Grulich, and Richard de Visser. 2003b. "Sex in Australia: Reproductive Experiences and Reproductive Health among a Representative Sample of Women." *Australian and New Zealand Journal of Public Health* 27: 204–209.

Smith, Clarissa, and Feona Attwood. 2011. "Lamenting Sexualization: Research, Rhetoric and the Story of Young People's 'Sexualization' in the UK Home Office Review." *Sex Education* 11: 327–337.

Southerton, Dale. 2006. "Analysing the Temporal Organization of Daily Life: Social Constraints, Practices and their Allocation." *Sociology* 40: 435–454.

Southerton, Dale. 2003. "'Squeezing Time': Allocating Practices, Coordinating Networks and Scheduling Society." *Time & Society* 12: 15–25.

Southerton, Dale. 2001. "Consuming Kitchens Taste, Context and Identity Formation." *Journal of Consumer Culture* 1: 179–203.

Stacey, Judith. 1998. *Brave New Families: Stories of Domestic Upheaval in Late Twentieth Century America*. Berkeley: University of California Press.

Stark, Julie. (2008) 'One in 10 Youngsters Start the Day with Junk Food' *The Age*. 14 January. Accessed July 30, 2008. http://www.theage.com.au/news/national/one-in-10-young-start-day-with-breakfast-of-junk-food/2008/01/13/1200159277521.html.

Story, Mary, Karen Kaphingst, Ramona Robinson-O'Brien, and Karen Glanz. 2008. "Creating Healthy Food and Eating Environments: Policy and Environmental Approaches." *Annual Review of Public Health* 29: 253–257.

Strazdins, Lyndall, Rosemary Korda, Lynette L-Y Lim, Dorothy H Broom, and Rennie M D'Souza. 2004. "Around-the-clock: Parent Work Schedules and Children's Well-being in a 24-h Economy." *Social Science & Medicine*. 59: 1517–1527.

Sulkunen, Pekka. 2009. *The Saturated Society: Governing Risk and Lifestyles in Consumer Culture*. London: Sage.

Sykes, R., R. Rowley, and J. Schafer. 1993. "The Influence of Time, Gender and Group Size on Heavy Drinking in Public Bars." *Journal of Studies on Alcohol* 49: 133–138.

Szmigin, Isabelle, Christine Griffin, Willm Mistral, Andrew Bengery-Howell, Louise Weale, and Chris Hackley. 2007. "Re-Framing 'Binge Drinking' as Calculated Hedonism: Empirical Evidence from the UK." *International Journal of Drug Policy*. doi:10.1016/j.drugpo.2007.08.009.

Taft, Angela. 2001. *Report of the Alcohol Misuse Research Project*. Melbourne: Centre for the Study of Mothers' and Children's Health.

Taylor, Janelle. 2004. "Introduction." In *Consuming Motherhood*, edited by Janelle Taylor, Linda Layne, and Danielle Wozniak, 1–15. New Brunswick, NJ: Rutgers University Press.

The VOICE Group (2010) Buying into Motherhood? Problematic Consumption and Ambivalence in Transitional Phases, *Consumption Markets & Culture* 13: 373–397.

Thomson, Rachel, Mary Jane Kehily, Lucy Hadfield, and Sue Sharpe. 2011. *Making Modern Mothers*. London: Policy Press.

Tinson, Julie and Clive Nancarrow. 2010. "Children and Shopping." In *Understanding Children as Consumers*, edited by David Marshall, 132–148. London: Sage.

Tolman, Deborah, and Sarah McClelland. 2011. "Normative Sexuality Development in Adolescence: A Decade in Review, 2000–2009." *Journal of Research on Adolescence* 21: 242–255.

Tronto, Joan. 2003. "Time's Place." *Feminist Theory* 4: 119–138.

Tubbs, Carolyn, Kevin Roy, and Linda Burton. 2005. "Family Ties: Constructing Family Time in Low-Income Families." *Family Process* 44: 77–91.

Tufekci, Zeynep. 2008. "Grooming, Gossip, Facebook and Myspace." *Information, Communication and Society* 11: 544–564.

Turkle, Sherry. 2008. "Always-On/Always-on-You: The Tethered Self." In *Handbook of Mobile Communication Studies*, edited by James Katz, 121–137. Cambridge, MA: MIT Press.

Twenge, Jean, and Kevin Campbell. 2009. *The Narcissism Epidemic: Living in the Age of Entitlement.* New York: Free Press.

Twenge, Jean, Sarah Konrath, Joshua Foster, Keith Campbell, and Brad Bushman. (2008). "Further Evidence of an Increase in Narcissism Among College Students." *Journal of Personality* 76: 919–927.

UQ News online. 2005. Family Meals Cut Teenage Fatness. *UQ News online*, 31 October. Accessed July 30, 2008. http://www.uq.edu.au/news/index.html?article=8233.

Uttal, Lynet. (2009). (Re)Visioning Family Ties to Communities and Contexts.In *Handbook of Feminist Family Studies*, edited by Sally A. Lloyd, April L. Few, and Katherine R. Allen, 134–147. Thousand Oaks: Sage.

Valentine, Gill. 2006. "Globalizing Intimacy: The Role of Information and Communication Technologies in Maintaining and Creating Relationships." *Women's Studies Quarterly* 34: 365–393.

Valentine, Gill. 1999. "Eating In: Home, Consumption and Identity." *Sociological Review.* 47: 491–524.

Valentine, Gill, Mark Jayne, and Myles Gould. 2012. "Do As I Say, Not As I Do: The Affective Space of Family Life and the Generational Transmission of Drinking Cultures." *Environment and Planning* 44: 776–792.

Valentine, Gill, Sarah Holloway, and Mark Jayne. 2010a. "Generational Patterns of Alcohol Consumption: Continuity and Change." *Health and Place* 16: 916–925.

Valentine, Gill, Mark Jayne, Myles Gould, and Julia Keenan. 2010b. *Family Life and Alcohol Consumption: A Study of the Transmission of Drinking Practices.* London: Joseph Rowntree Foundation.

van der Vorst, Hask, Rutger Engels, Wim Meeus, and Maja Dekovic. 2006. "The Impact of Alcohol-Specific Rules, Parental Norms about Early Drinking and Parental Alcohol Use on Adolescents' Drinking Behavior." *Journal of Child Psychology and Psychiatry* 47: 1299–1306.

Vincent, Carole, and Stephen Ball. 2007. "Making Up' the Middle-Class Child: Families, Activities and Class Dispositions." *Sociology* 41: 1061–1077.

Wajcman, Judy. 2008. "Life in the Fast Lane? Towards a Sociology of Technology and Time." *The British Journal of Sociology* 59(1): 59–77.

Wajcman, Judy, Michael Bittman, and Judith Brown. 2008. "Families without Borders: Mobile Phones, Connectedness and Work-Home Divisions." *Sociology* 42: 635–652.

Walsh-Childers, Kim, Alyse Gotthoffer, and Caroline Ringer Lepre. 2002. "From "Just the Facts" to "Downright Salacious": Teens' and Women's Magazine Coverage of Sex and Sexual Health." In *Sexual Teens, Sexual Media*, edited by Jane Brown, Jeannie Steele, and Kim Walsh-Childers. Mahwah, NJ: Lawrence Erlbaum Associates.

Warburton, Wayne, and Danya Braunstein. 2012. *Growing Up Fast and Furious.* Sydney: The Federation Press.

Ward, Bernadette, and Pam Snow. 2011. "Factors Affecting Parental Supply of Alcohol to Underage Adolescents." *Drug and Alcohol Review* 30: 338–343.

Ward, Bernadette, Pam Snow, and Rosalie Aroni. 2010. "Children's Alcohol Initiation: An Analytic Overview." *Drugs: Education, Prevention and Policy* 17: 270–277.

Warde, Alan. 1999. "Convenience Food: Space and Timing." *British Food Journal* 101: 518–527.

Warin, Megan, Karen Turner, Vivienne Moore, and Michael Davies. 2008a. "Bodies, Mothers and Identities: Rethinking Obesity and the BMI." *Sociology of Health and Illness* 30: 97–111.

Warin, Megan, Vivienne Moore, Karen Turner, and Michael Davies. 2008b. "Consuming Bodies: Mall Walking and the Possibilities of Consumption." *Health Sociology Review* 17: 187–198.

Weeks, Jeffrey. 2007. *The World We Have Won: The Remaking of Erotic and Intimate Life*. London: Routledge.

Weir, Allison. 2008. "Home and Identity: In Memory of Iris Marion Young." *Hypatia* 23: 4–21.

Wells, Samantha, Kathryn Graham, and John Purcell. 2009. "Policy Implications of the Widespread Practice of 'Pre-Drinking' or 'Pre-Gaming' before Going to Public Drinking Establishments—Are Current Prevention Strategies Backfiring?" *Addiction* 104: 4–9.

West, Anne, Jane Lewis, and Peter Currie. 2009. 'Students' Facebook 'Friends': Public and Private Spheres.' *Journal of Youth Studies* 12(6): 615–627.

White, Jack. 1996. "Making Time for Family: The Invention of Family Time(s) and the Reinvention of Family History." *Journal of Family History* 21: 4–22.

White, Martin. 2007. "Food Access and Obesity." *Obesity Reviews* 8 (Suppl. 1): 99–107.

White, Rob and Joanna Wyn. 2008. *Youth and Society: Exploring the Social Dynamics of Youth Experience*. Melbourne: Oxford University Press.

White, Victoria, and Jane Hayman. 2006. *Australian Secondary School Students' Use of Alcohol in 2005* Melbourne: The Cancer Council Victoria.

Whitty, Monica. 2008. "Revealing the 'Real' Me, Searching for the 'Actual' You: Presentations of Self on an Internet Dating Site." *Computers in Human Behaviour* 24: 1707–1723.

WHO. 2012. *Global Strategy on Diet, Physical Activity and Health*. Geneva: World Heath Organization. Accessed April 4, 2012. http://www.who.int/dietphysicalactivity/childhood_why/en/index.html.

Wilding, Raelene. 2006. "'Virtual' Intimacies? Families Communicating across Transnational Contexts." *Global Networks: A Journal of Transnational Affairs* 6: 125–142.

Wilk, Richard. 2010. "Power at the Table: Food Fights and Happy Meals." *Cultural Studies ↔ Critical Methodologies* 10: 428–436.

Williams, Stephen, and Lynda Williams. 2005. "Space Invaders: The Negotiation of Teenage Boundaries through the Mobile Phone." *The Sociological Review*. 53: 314–331.

Wills, Wendy, Kathleen Backett-Milburn, Mei-Li Roberts and Julia Lawton. 2011. "The Framing of Social Class Distinctions through Family Food and Eating Practices." *The Sociological Review* 59: 725–740.

Wills, Wendy, Kathleen Backett-Milburn, Sue Gregory, and Julia Lawton. 2008. "If the Food Looks Dodgy I Dinnae Eat It': Teenagers' Accounts of Food and Eating Practices in Socio-Economically Disadvantaged Families." *Sociological Research Online* 13: 15. Accessed May 19, 2012. http://www.socresonline.org.uk/13/1/15.html.

Wilson, Sarah, Sarah Cunningham-Burley, Angus Bancroft, and Kathleen Backett-Milburn. 2012. "The Consequences of Love: Young People and Family Practices in Difficult Circumstances." *Sociological Review* 60: 110–128.

Wright, Jan. 2009. "Biopower, Biopedagogies and the Obesity Epidemic." In *Biopolitics and the 'Obesity Epidemic': Governing Bodies*, edited by Jan Wright and Valerie Harwood, 1–16. London: Routledge.

Yancey, Annette, Joanne Leslie, and Emily Abel. 2006. "Obesity at the Crossroads: Feminist and Public Health Perspectives." *Signs* 31: 425–443.
Yoon, Kyongwon. 2006. "The Making of Neo-Confucian Cyberkids: Representations of Young Mobile Phone Users in South Korea." *New Media & Society* 8: 753–771.
Zelizer, Viviana. 2005. *The Purchase of Intimacy*. Princeton: Princeton University Press.
Zelizer, Viviana. 2002. "Kids and Commerce." *Childhood* 9: 375–396.
Zelizer, Viviana. 1985. *Pricing the Priceless Child: The Changing Social Value of Children*. New York: Basic Books.
Zukin, Sharon, and John Maguire. 2004. "Consumers and Consumption." *Annual Review of Sociology* 30: 173–197.

Index

For Product Safety Concerns and Information please contact our
EU representative GPSR@taylorandfrancis.com Taylor & Francis
Verlag GmbH, Kaufingerstraße 24, 80331 München, Germany